Ancient Epic

For Scott,

May your mind continue
to be forever touched by the
"tears and dying things"
underlying the great celebrations
of literature, (Aeneid I. 461-2)

Best regards,

Katherine K.

BLACKWELL INTRODUCTIONS TO THE CLASSICAL WORLD

This series will provide concise introductions to classical culture in the broadest sense. Written by the most distinguished scholars in the field, these books survey key authors, periods and topics for students and scholars alike.

Published

Greek Tragedy
Nancy Sorkin Rabinowitz

Roman Satire
Daniel Hooley

Ancient History
Charles W. Hedrick, Jr.

Homer, second edition
Barry B. Powell

Classical Literature
Richard Rutherford

Ancient Rhetoric and Oratory
Thomas Habinek

Ancient Epic
Katherine Callen King

Catullus
Julia Haig Gaisser

Virgil
R. Alden Smith

Ovid
Katharina Volk

Roman Historiography
Andreas Mehl, translated by Hans-Friedrich Mueller

Ancient Epic

Katherine Callen King

WILEY-BLACKWELL

A John Wiley & Sons, Ltd., Publication

This paperback edition first published 2012
© 2012 Katherine Callen King

Edition history: Blackwell Publishing Ltd (hardback, 2009)

Blackwell Publishing was acquired by John Wiley & Sons in February 2007. Blackwell's publishing program has been merged with Wiley's global Scientific, Technical, and Medical business to form Wiley-Blackwell.

Registered Office
John Wiley & Sons Ltd, The Atrium, Southern Gate, Chichester, West Sussex, PO19 8SQ, United Kingdom

Editorial Offices
350 Main Street, Malden, MA 02148-5020, USA
9600 Garsington Road, Oxford, OX4 2DQ, UK
The Atrium, Southern Gate, Chichester, West Sussex, PO19 8SQ, UK

For details of our global editorial offices, for customer services, and for information about how to apply for permission to reuse the copyright material in this book please see our website at www.wiley.com/wiley-blackwell.

The right of Katherine Callen King to be identified as the author of this work has been asserted in accordance with the UK Copyright, Designs and Patents Act 1988.

Wiley also publishes its books in a variety of electronic formats. Some content that appears in print may not be available in electronic books.

Designations used by companies to distinguish their products are often claimed as trademarks. All brand names and product names used in this book are trade names, service marks, trademarks or registered trademarks of their respective owners. The publisher is not associated with any product or vendor mentioned in this book. This publication is designed to provide accurate and authoritative information in regard to the subject matter covered. It is sold on the understanding that the publisher is not engaged in rendering professional services. If professional advice or other expert assistance is required, the services of a competent professional should be sought.

Library of Congress Cataloging-in-Publication Data

King, Katherine Callen.
    Ancient epic / Katherine Callen King.
       p.   cm. – (Blackwell introductions to the classical world)
    Includes bibliographical references and index.
    ISBN 978-1-4051-5947-0 (hardcover : alk. paper)
    ISBN 978-1-118-25534-6 (pbk. : alk. paper)
    1. Epic poetry–History and criticism.   2. Poetry, Ancient–History and criticism.   3. Heroes in literature.   I. Title.
    PN1307.K56 2009
    809.1′32 – dc22

                                                              2008036233

A catalogue record for this book is available from the British Library.

Set in 10.5 on 13pt Galliard by Toppan Best-set Premedia Limited
Printed in Malaysia by Ho Printing (M) Sdn Bhd

1   2012

To Esther and Wallis Pereira for their unfailing support, to the many graduate and undergraduate students from whom I have learned so much, and to research assistant extraordinaire, Catharine Platt McGraw

Contents

Chronologies

[most dates are approximate]

GILGAMESH

2700 BCE	Gilgamesh King in Uruk
2100–2000	Summerian Gilgamesh epics composed in writing
1800	Earliest tablets of Summerian epics *(Gilgamesh & Agga*; *Gilgamesh & Huwawa*; *Gilgamesh & Bull of Heaven*; *Death of Gilgamesh or Gilgamesh in the Netherworld)*
1700s	Akkadian epic composed = Old Babylonian Version
1500–1100	Middle Babylonian Versions (Hurrian and Hittite translations)
1200	Sin-leqe-unninni creates Standard Version
700	Oldest extant tablets of Standard Version

GREEK AND ROMAN EPIC

1400–1200	Bronze Age Greece
1184	Traditional date of Trojan War
750	Writing reintroduced to Greece
	Traditional date for founding of Rome by Romulus
725–625	*Iliad* and *Odyssey* composed
600–500	Epic Cycle poems composed
400	Antimakhos of Kolophon composes the lost *Thebaid* and *Lyde*
335–23	Aristotle writes and lectures at the Lyceum in Athens
331	Alexander the Great founds Alexandria on the coast of Egypt

323	Alexander the Great dies
305–283	Founding of the Museum and Library at Alexandria under kingship of Ptolemy I (Soter). Alexandria is now the royal capital of Egypt.
284–270	Zenodotos, first Director of the Library at Alexandria, categorizes epic and edits the texts of the *Iliad* and *Odyssey*
285–?	Kallimakhos catalogues the collection and writes poetry at the Library of Alexandria
282–246	Reign of Ptolemy II (Philadelphos) at Alexandria
270–245	Apollonios of Rhodes composes the *Argonautika* while working as Director of the Library of Alexandria
264–241	First Punic War
235–204	Naevius composes *Poem of the Punic War* in Saturnian verse
218–202	Second Punic War
169	Ennius completes the *Annales*, composed in dactylic hexameter
149–6	Third Punic War, destruction of Carthage
132–121	The Gracchi brothers trouble the Roman Senate and are assassinated
107–100	Marius elected Consul six times
83–1	Sulla's dictatorship
70	Virgil is born
63	Octavian (later Caesar Augustus) is born
51	Cicero writes "The Dream of Scipio"
49	Julius Caesar crosses the Rubicon and marches on Rome
44	Julius Caesar elected dictator and assassinated
43	Ovid is born
38–35	Virgil completes the *Eclogues*
31	Octavian defeats Marc Antony and Cleopatra at Actium
29	Virgil completes the *Georgics*, begins the Aeneid
27	Octavian becomes Augustus
23	Ovid publishes the *Amores*, the first of many elegiac works
19	Virgil dies leaving manuscript of the *Aeneid*
8 CE	Ovid's *Metamorphoses* published when he is exiled
17 CE	Ovid dies

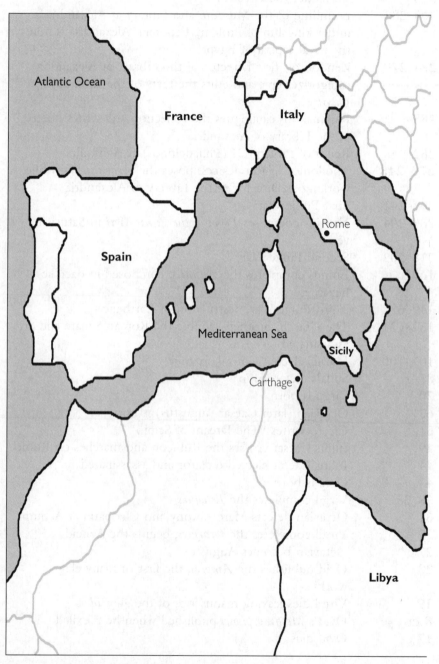

Map prepared by Cat Buckles

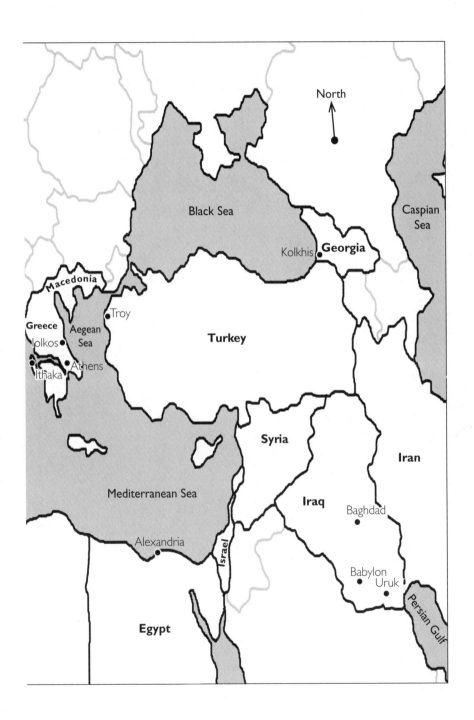

Introduction

Why do students compelled to read ancient epics in college classrooms invariably discover that they have learned something valuable? What could a story composed thousands of years ago have to say to us today?

An active-duty Air Force captain who has served four tours in Iraq explains why he intends to tattoo "the wrath of Achilles" in Greek on his right Achilles tendon:

> *I want to mark the anger on my body for a lot of reasons . . . I try to imagine what that Myrmidon [Achilles] must have thought, and his frustration [at] serving for a king who did not want to listen to his best fighters to learn how to fight a war.* (Email dated April 20, 2008, to the author)

Iraq Veteran Michael Zacchea, who has been slowly integrating himself back into peacetime society, says,

> *[Odysseus] resolved his issues by killing all the suitors . . . really the message is that I have to make my peace with people who, you know, did not go to Iraq or insulated [themselves] from the reality of Iraq.* (Interview September 28, 2007 with David Brancchacio for PBS news show, *NOW*)

Achilles' angry idealism and Odysseus' difficult return from war clearly still speak to modern readers in urgent and personal ways.

Searing scenes invite questions about modern life, as when Aeneas' effort to live only for an imperialist future leads him to hug his son goodbye encased in full armor (*Aeneid* 12. 432–442). In 1974, John Arthur Hanson, professor of classics and a keen observer of the ideological clash between the generation of the fifties and that of the sixties, saw a parallel between this scene and the "Puritan ethic" backbone of

American capitalism, and he subsequently transformed it into "Mr Brass Bids Farewell to his Son Julius:"

> *But after he had buttoned up his heavy Harris tweed overcoat,*
> *and clutched his briefcase,*
> *He surrounded his son with his scratchy sleeves*
> *and made a pass at kissing him – but his hatbrim got in the way.*
> *"Boy," he said, "from me you have to learn guts,*
> *and where hard work gets you.*
> *Ask some other guy about luck.*
> *It's because of my own efforts that you've got a roof over your head,*
> *and you're going to come into a big pile.*
> *You just remember that, when you get some real balls on you.*
> *You don't need to look outside the family,*
> *just be like your old man and your uncle Hector."*
> *Then he made a break for the carport.*

Other epic protagonists generate similarly intense recognition. Gilgamesh's struggles against the forces of nature resonate both with those who worry about the environment and anyone who has lost a loved one to death. Who could fail to be awed by Medea's obsession for Jason or to sympathize with Arachne's artistic rebellion?

The epic poems in which these memorable protagonists appear – the *Epic of Gilgamesh, Iliad, Odyssey, Aeneid, Argonautika,* and *Metamorphoses* – remain a fount of inspiration for poets, dramatists, and musicians, partly because they tell good stories in an aesthetically beautiful way, but mostly because they wrestle with issues important to generation after generation of readers. They speak to hearts and minds concerned about human potentiality and limitation, about the consequences of passion (righteous anger, sexual love, intense grief, or desire for honor), and about the competing claims of civilization, the environment, and the need to reconcile self-interest with the common good. Their explorations of armed violence – what it achieves, what it costs, and what it serves – have much to impart to everyone who thinks about what heroism might mean today.

Chief among epic themes that are still of deep concern to modern societies are the basic implications of being human: intelligence gives us a godlike potential to master our environment, but we are limited by the deadly consequences of our not actually being gods. Human passions – anger, grief, pride, love – often interfere with intelligence, and while gods can make mistakes without serious consequences to themselves because they will always have a tomorrow, human mistakes can end life or make it permanently unbearable. Worst of all, human beings inevitably grow old and die. What meaning, then, attaches to our existence? Is there anything we can do to make ourselves outlive our ephemeral bodies? The latter is the question most consistently pondered by epic poems.

Another fact of life recognized by all six epic poets is that most people want power but almost all who get it abuse it. Long before Lord Acton talked about absolute power corrupting absolutely, Babylonian, Greek, and Roman poets explored the catastrophic effects of a powerful person's refusal to acknowledge the claims of others, depicting it as stemming from a failure to acknowledge limits. This is what the Greeks called *hubris*, an extreme type of arrogance. In the epics, abuses of power range from general exploitation of a populace to violence against individuals and even the gods. In the case of violated gods, sometimes their retaliation is limited to the offender; often, however, they send wars, plagues, famines, and other disasters to coerce recompense and teach lessons. How a hero reacts to his own or to another's power is an important, if not central, interest in all six epics. All are concerned with ways to control the arrogance of power, but some focus more on internal restraints, that is, moral codes and self-control, and others on external ones like social codes and counteractive physical force.

Both the efficacy and effect of violence are concerns for many poets. Physical force is used sometimes to counter abuses of power, sometimes to support or commit them. Often it has unintended consequences. Although all epic heroes must be capable of committing great bodily injury to enemies, none of these six epics celebrates violence. Instead, they are careful to balance their heroes' violence with the more cooperative virtues of compassion and intelligence, and they invite their audiences to view many of their heroes' violent deeds with ambiguity even when they are committed in the service of "good" causes.

What exactly is an epic? "Epic" comes from the Greek *epos*, which means "word," and, by extension, a "story told in words." Only certain kinds of stories told in certain kinds of words, however, qualified as epic for the ancient Greeks and Romans. First and foremost, epic stories had to be told in verse, not prose, and they had to be told in a specific kind of verse: the six-beat hexameter line that was considered to be the most stately and dignified of all classical meters. Less discriminating Greeks apparently considered all works written in this meter (scientific treatises, genealogies, martial exhortations, hymns to a god, stories about the gods interacting with each other) to be epics, but Aristotle, fourth-century BCE

Athenian scientist and literary critic, is more exacting: epic poetry must tell a long but focused story with the same kinds of reversals, disasters, and recognitions that we find in tragedy; its language must be highly adorned with metaphors and exotic words; and the poet must not speak in his own voice, but must keep himself in the background (*Poetics* 1447b, 1459–1460). Lastly, the subject of epic must be the deeds of heroes, a criterion so important that Aristotle uses the word "heroic" interchangeably with "hexameter" to designate the meter proper to the genre.

Heroes were a special class of men, superior beings whose deeds earned them a status between a human and god. Most of them had a divine parent or grandparent, and they could do things that no modern man could do. The age in which they lived and fought and died was named the Age of Heroes, a legendary period that preceded the modern age of ordinary people by hundreds of years. Some of them, like Herakles, performed deeds in individual story cycles, but most participated in at least one of the three major story cycles that became cultural touchstones throughout Greece: the Voyage of the Argonauts, the Theban Troubles, and the Trojan War. In archaic and classical Greece, the spirits of long-dead heroes were regularly invoked by priests who hoped they would protect the localities in which they were buried, and their stories were continually evoked by poets and rhetoricians who made them speak anew to modern cultures. In other words, ancient heroes continued to affect religious, political, and cultural life long after their magnificent muscles were thought to have ceased wielding swords and spears.

Since the Babylonian, Greek, and Roman communities were male dominated, epic action revolves around male heroes. Orbiting around the heroes are women and deities, enabling, hindering, motivating. There is a clear differentiation between male and female roles and a tendency to associate the male with cultural progress and the female with repetitious natural cycles. The female is usually more concerned with preserving or perpetuating biological life, the male with preserving his name or enhancing social position. Both sexes can be equally concerned with revenge. Only in the later epics is emotionality per se labeled a female characteristic; in *Gilgamesh*, the *Iliad*, and the *Odyssey*, men as well as women love, weep in grief, and suffer moments of despair. The poets of *Gilgamesh* and the *Iliad* are even willing to depict their heroes in an agony of fear, clearly not feeling that this detracts from their heroism. In the *Aeneid*, on the other hand, fear and open lamentation are closely associated with females, as are all strong passions except love of father and country. Achilles' desire for heroic revenge, which is honorable in the *Iliad*, in the *Aeneid* is portrayed as primitive and as the province of the goddess Juno.

Larger-than-life representatives from the Age of Heroes, who illuminate human action through their closeness to the divine, help to create the seriousness that characterizes epic genre. Heaps of dead enemies and conquered monsters are not an end in themselves; only when a hero's action engages the whole poetic universe, the gods as well as his human community, can it rise to epic status. Presenting it in verse and enriching it with metaphorical language may be important, but they are not enough: epic action must profoundly affect or illustrate important community values.

Some of these values are political. The *Epic of Gilgamesh*, for example, explores kingly responsibility via its hero's monster slaying, city building, and quest for knowledge. The *Iliad* and the *Odyssey* use Achilles' prowess and Odysseus' multifaceted intellect to explore what kind of man deserves to be at the top of a given political system, who deserves to be the Greek army's commander in chief or the king of Ithaka. The *Aeneid* uses Aeneas' piety to examine not only what kind of man, but also what nation deserves to rule.

Closely related to these political aspects of epic are social and theological, or cultural, ones. Gilgamesh probes the human condition in a universe of both irascible and beneficent gods who must all be respected despite their being sometimes at odds. Achilles' choices restore the community's heroic ethic while validating a tragic vision of life in which the gods' favor ensures glorious death. Odysseus' success, on the other hand, confirms the idea of hereditary kingship called into question by the *Iliad*, while it validates a "comic" vision of life in which the gods' favor secures prosperous survival. The hero's desire for self-fulfillment is paramount in all three. Aeneas' achievement, on the other hand, promotes a hierarchical ranking of nations at the same time as it elevates self-sacrifice to supreme worth: in the *Aeneid*, Jupiter's favor ensures national survival, and validates – or seems to validate – a superior national character.

The poets of both the *Argonautika* and the *Metamorphoses* challenge epic norms by marginalizing the heroes and the heroism of their predecessors and by calling attention to the artifice of their creations. Nonetheless, both offer value systems that could be described as important to their communities. The *Argonautika* promotes communal cooperation rather than individual heroics, while the *Metamorphoses*, more negatively, encourages wariness against clinging to or heroizing any story, identity, or power.

Overview of the Six Epics

Just as modern poets are inspired by Greek and Roman epic, Greek poets were inspired by the ancient poetry of western Asia, the area that today includes Iraq, Turkey, Syria, Lebanon, Israel, and Palestine. The epic poetry that came from southern Mesopotamian civilizations (first Sumer, later Babylonia) was especially influential. After many years of neglect, mainstream English speakers are now beginning to recognize the Babylonian *Epic of Gilgamesh* as a masterpiece and its hero, grief-stricken Gilgamesh, as a forerunner of Homer's Achilles.

Composed in three stages (roughly 2100, 1700, and 1200 BCE), this magnificent poem originated in ancient Sumer as five short epics that focused on King Gilgamesh's extraordinary feats against warriors, monsters, and the obliterating forces of nature. All his deeds were performed in the context of defending and improving his city. These five Sumerian poems evolved first into a long Old Babylonian epic concerned with Gilgamesh's struggle against human mortality. A final poet created the still longer Babylonian Standard Version, which focuses firmly on the value of cultural immortality as counterweight to biological death. In this final version, Gilgamesh lives on for future generations both in the walled city he built and in the adventures he experienced and "recorded." The *Epic of Gilgamesh* celebrates the hero's extraordinary learning as much as it does his conquering of monsters, his story as much as his city.

The *Iliad* and *Odyssey* were most likely composed on the west coast of Asia Minor around 700 BCE. Their poet(s), whom we, like the Greeks, will call Homer, emphasized the idea of cultural immortality in epic song as much as did the poet of *Gilgamesh*. In the *Iliad*, however, the emphasis is on its potential to compensate for heroic death in battle. City-building, which plays a central role in *Gilgamesh*, does not become supremely important again until Virgil's *Aeneid*, for the heroes of the *Iliad* and the *Odyssey* pride themselves rather on being city-sackers. However, if we define "city" more loosely to include community and its shared values of governance, as opposed to the lawlessness found in nature, we find that "city" values do play a role in the Homeric epics, especially the *Odyssey*, where the hero's goal includes not only reuniting with his wife and son, but also reestablishing the proper political functioning of his kingdom. The *Iliad*'s tragic vision is very much concerned with community, in this case a community of warriors, but more in the sense of showing how vulnerable a human community is when its leader forces its greatest hero to choose between his responsibility to members of the community and his responsibility to its broken ideals, that is, between the ethical self and the unethical community.

The *Iliad* and *Odyssey* became the touchstone for all classical literature created in Athens, Alexandria, and Rome, and they are essential for understanding all other classical genres as well as subsequent manifestations of epic poetry. These two universally known monumental poems shaped Greek and Roman concepts of narrative structure, tragedy, comedy, war, marriage, relationships between human and divine beings, and achieving immortality through fame. Aristotle modeled his definition of epic on the *Iliad* and *Odyssey*, and all epic poets and readers seem to have regarded the Homeric poems as the standard of epic excellence. Hellenistic and Roman authors could work either with or against the Homeric poems; they could not ignore them.

Apollonios' *Argonautika*, written in Greek Alexandria around 260 BCE, is interesting both for how it brilliantly reworks Homer and for its extensive influence on Virgil's *Aeneid*. This Hellenistic poet celebrates a different kind of literary heroism, one that is collective rather than singular, and one that seems unconcerned with mortality. The Argonauts want fame, but not in the context of compensation for death. Although much of the epic seems like a pure adventure story, a kind of epic seriousness is achieved by the foundational rituals with which the Argonauts transform the landscape and bring a touch of civilization to the "barbarian," that is, non-Greek, world. Apollonios also interjects into epic a new passion imported from Greek tragedy, obsessive erotic love, and along with it a tragic heroine, Medea, who is more memorable than most of the male heroes.

Virgil's *Aeneid* incorporates and reworks not only Homeric epic and Apollonius' inventions, but the best of Greek and Roman lyric, narrative, and philosophic poetry. The *Aeneid* deploys a singular heroic protagonist like those of the Homeric poems, but subordinates the Homeric ego to a collective purpose. Perhaps because its author had witnessed both civil war and the ascendancy of an emperor, the *Aeneid* insists that the truly epic struggle is not for the happiness or immortality of a singular self, but for the perhaps unachievable ideal of dispassionate leadership. The result is an overtly nationalist but profoundly ethical masterpiece whose vast influence on subsequent art and literature makes it, like the *Iliad* and *Odyssey*, essential reading for any student of western culture.

Ovid's *Metamorphoses* differs in many essential ways from the above five epics, not least in that it has no protagonist. No questing, angry, or foundational king focuses its verses. The "hero" of Ovid's *Metamorphoses* is "shapes changing" in an apparently endless progression from the origin of the world to his present-day Rome. Ovid's poem plays with his predecessors' ideas of heroism, identity, and immortality while challenging epic norms of unity, heroic singularity, and martial prowess. Because of these challenges, and because of its apparent lack of seriousness, some scholars refuse it the name of epic. Nonetheless, the *Metamorphoses* is often studied together with Homeric and Virgilian epic, largely because Ovid chose to make it epic in form and also because there is no better way of appreciating this tragicomic masterpiece.

Divine Contexts

Since epic ponders universal questions only within specific cultural settings, it is important to become acquainted with the major gods and goddesses whose myths shaped the poets' religious and cultural worlds. The gods in Mesopotamia and those around the Aegean Sea lived in similar hierarchies and share many features, but their relationship to each other and to their human worshipers was significantly different. What follows is a brief account of the Greek and Babylonian Divine Succession Myths, which names all the gods important to the epics, and a summary of their major differences. At the end of the book there is appended a list of major gods that may be used for reference as you read about the epics themselves. Although I focus on "national" to the exclusion of local gods, it is important to know that every river was a god and that every beautiful woodland, meadow, or cove was alive not just with trees and plants, but with numerous protective nymphs and fauns.

The Mesopotamian Divine Succession Myth

Sumerian myth tells of a struggle among primal Mesopotamian gods, but the issue is status or class rather than absolute rule. One group of gods, the **Anunna**, forced another group of gods, the **Igiggi**, to do all the work of growing and cooking food and building and maintaining palaces to dwell in. When the Igiggi gods rebelled, a war did not ensue. Instead, the Anunna gods created human beings to do the work for all the gods, who can now live in relative harmony.[1]

Anu (Heaven), the supreme god, together with **Enlil** (Storm God) and **Ea** (God of Underearth Waters) ruled the other gods. The goddess **Ereshkigal** ruled in the Netherworld. **Ishtar** (Goddess of Sex and War), sister of Ereshkigal, ensured fertile cycles of birth and death, and was nearly as powerful as the three dominant male gods. In some myths she is the daughter of Anu, in others of **Sin**, the Moon God. Her brother **Shamash** (Sun God), ruled the skies during the day, bringing injustice to light, while his father the Moon God ruled the sky at night and spoke darkly to humans through oracles.

The Greek Divine Succession Myth[2]

Gaia (Earth) came into being from chaos, and she bore **Uranos** (Sky) and **Pontos** (Deep Sea). Both became her husbands.

Gaia and Uranos are the progenitors of generations of Uranian gods, gods who in the third generation took Olympos as their center of power. Uranos impregnated Gaia, but would not let his children be born because he was jealous of Gaia's attention. Gaia became angry and formed an alliance with one of the unborn sons held within her womb. She created a sickle out of a stone and gave it to **Kronos** with instructions to castrate his father the next time he came to lie with her. After Kronos castrated him, Uranos drifted off to become elemental sky, no longer involved in divine affairs. Blood from Uranos' severed genitals dripped on the earth, where it gave birth to the **Furies**, who avenge crimes against kin. Where the genitals fell into the sea, sperm mingled with sea foam to beget **Aphrodite**.

Once Uranos was emasculated, all of Gaia's children came forth. This generation of gods are called **Titans**. In addition to Kronos, the most important of them are: **Mnemosyne** – "Memory," mother (with Zeus) of the nine Muses; **Okeanos**, "Ocean," and Tethys, who together gave birth to all rivers, lakes, springs, and wells, and also to **Metis**, mother of Athena; **Rheia**, Kronos's sister-wife; **Themis**, goddess of Natural Law, whose name means roughly "What has been established;" Hyperion, "He who moves on high," who fathered **Helios**, the Sun, and Selene, the Moon; Iapetos, who is important mostly as the father of **Prometheus**, whose name means "Foresight;" and Phoebe, "Radiant," whose daughter is **Leto**, mother of Apollo and Artemis.

Kronos was naturally the Titans' ruler. He took as wife his sister **Rheia**, and begot six children, whom he feared because of a prophecy that one of his offspring would dethrone him. At the moment of birth he swallowed each of them, thus angering mother Rheia and causing her, like Gaia before her, to turn to a son for vengeance. When baby **Zeus** was born, Rhea wrapped a stone in swaddling clothes and gave it to Kronos to swallow. She reared Zeus in secret, and she and Gaia helped him release his two brothers and three sisters and then overcome Kronos. Kronos, and the Titans who sided with him, were thrown into Tartaros, which lies as far below the surface of the earth as Olympos lies above it. Zeus, **Poseidon**, and **Hades** drew lots to determine their realm in which each would be supreme – sky, sea, and underworld – but they share the earth (see *Il.* 15. 187–193). Hades took up residence in the underworld, but Zeus, Poseidon, and their sisters **Hera**, **Demeter**, and Hestia took possession of Olympos.

The other god of the oldest generation, **Pontos**, is the progenitor of generations separate from but not warring with the Olympian gods. Pontos fathered **Nereus**, a sea god who fathered **Thetis**, mother of **Achilles**, and forty-nine other daughters, all of whom have names and personalities but who are collectively called **Nereids**, "Daughters of Nereus."

The same thing that happened to Kronos and Uranos would have happened to Zeus had he not learned a prophecy and acted in time. Zeus was having sexual relations with his cousin **Metis**, daughter of Okeanos, when he learned from his grandmother that after bearing the daughter with whom she was now pregnant, Metis was destined to bear a son who would surpass his father. Zeus did not wait to swallow the threatening child at birth, as his own father had done, but immediately swallowed the pregnant mother instead. This secured him a triple advantage: not only would the son who might challenge him never be conceived, but immortal Metis (Shrewd Counsel) now lived inside his own body, and her daughter **Athena**, subsequently born from his head, would regard him as her sole parent and give him total allegiance.

Zeus's marriage to Hera produced two sons: **Ares**, god of war, and **Hephaistos**, god of fire and the forge.[3] Zeus' marriage did not preclude him from having offspring with many goddesses. With Titan Leto, he fathered twins **Apollo** and **Artemis**, divinities of the sun and moon, respectively. With the nymph Maia, he fathered **Hermes**, god of messengers, hidden treasure, and thievery. With Semele, a minor goddess who comes into recorded mythology as a mortal woman, he fathered **Dionysos**, god of wine and nature. The *Iliad* also makes Zeus the father of **Aphrodite** via the womb of a goddess named Dione, whose name means roughly "Mrs. Zeus." These eight children of Zeus live with him, Hera, Poseidon, and Demeter above Mount Olympos.

Later, both Zeus and Poseidon courted Thetis, daughter of Nereus and granddaughter of Pontos. Then **Themis** (or Prometheus) revealed a prophecy that Thetis would bear a son more powerful than his father. Both gods not only withdrew their suit, but also forced Thetis to marry a mortal so that her offspring could never challenge them. Thus the Olympian regime with Zeus at its head was permanently stabilized. And thus **Achilles** was born half-mortal, to the endless sorrow of his mother.

Cosmic Implications

The Greeks' violent Succession Myth shows a progression from more elemental gods (Earth, Heaven, Sea) to more anthropomorphic gods who rule various elements (Zeus who rules the heavens, Poseidon who rules the sea). More importantly, it reveals two immense tensions within Greek culture: intense competition between fathers and sons and a related competition between husbands and wives. The wife's prime goal is to keep her young children alive, even if it means "killing" the father, while the husband's is to preserve his own power even if it means killing his children (immortality through one's children is not an issue with gods). From this divine behavior, we can extract what the Greeks would have assumed to be "natural" female and male behavior: that is, women are focused on biological survival and men on power. Homeric epic confirms this inference, but on the human plane, father–son competition for power shifts to brother–brother or simply male-on-male competition. The quarrel between Achilles and the older, sceptered king Agamemnon over who is "best of the Akhaians" is an example of the latter.

Perhaps the most important element in the Succession Myth is the extreme violence by which power is transferred and "progress" is made. Females, too, fully participate in violence, but with this difference: they use cunning to aid a male to commit the physical violence that will effect the transfer of power. The exclusively violent transfers of power seem to indicate that all living beings, including intelligent ones, are programmed to respect physical more than verbal prowess. In the human realm as portrayed in epic, in fact, negotiations mostly fail, and order is established and maintained only by physical force. As Odysseus says in *Iliad* 14, 85–87: "Zeus has made war our lot, from youth to old age, until each of us dies."

One thing that is striking to one steeped in Greek mythology is that in the early Babylonian pantheon the generations coexist in power. Anu is parallel to the Greek Uranos, whose name also means heaven, or sky, but he has not been castrated or otherwise ousted from his seat of power. He may be more remote than the other gods, but he is still supreme. Enlil corresponds to Zeus, God of the Lightning Bolt, but he has not overthrown his father nor is he the father of all the Olympian gods who are not his siblings. Both generations of Mesopotamian gods make appearances in epics about Gilgamesh, but only the youngest generation of Greek gods, the ones who make their home on Olympos, are important in Greek and Roman epic. The absence of zero-sum familial competition in the Mesopotamian cosmogony mirrors the relative lack of civil strife in the *Epic of Gilgamesh.*

Succession myths aside, there is often dissension among the gods, dissension that makes it difficult for human beings to achieve success without paying great prices. Tragic epic universes portray heroes caught in this dissension. For example, in the *Epic of Gilgamesh*, Shamash and Ea privilege human intelligence and culture, while Ishtar and Enlil promote natural processes and a natural justice that treats human beings as no more important than other elements of the world; Gilgamesh cannot obey the Sun God without violating prerogatives of the Storm God. In the *Iliad*, opposing groups of gods headed by Zeus and Hera protract the war that makes immortal glory possible; this protraction increases the agonizing loss of life and helps bring into sharp focus the impossible choices human beings must make. The *Aeneid* privileges the fiercely competitive Greek pantheon over native Italian gods; drawing on succession myths that pitted divine fathers against mothers, it magnifies the Iliadic quarrel between Jupiter (Zeus) and Juno (Hera) into a cosmic opposition between masculine forces of rationality and culture and female forces of irrationality and raw nature, using these forces simultaneously to validate the hero's achievement and to question the possibility of human progress.

Comic epic universes, that is, those with happy endings, play down cosmic dissension, at least at the highest levels. Zeus and Athena in the *Odyssey* and Zeus and Hera in the *Argonautika* are in total harmony; the heroes' major obstacles in both epics are human wickedness, monsters, and the elements. Poseidon's one appearance on Olympos marks the *Odyssey*'s only true tragedy; throughout Odysseus's trials he is an elemental rather than an Olympian god. Olympian harmony allows the *Odyssey*'s poet to work with clear categories of good and evil, justice and injustice, categories that are somewhat muddied in tragic universes.

In the highly self-conscious *Argonautika* and *Metamorphoses*, Greek and Roman gods inhabit a purely literary cosmos. They have devolved to divine machinery in an essentially secular world. Not until poets like Dante, Tasso, Spencer, and Milton deploy their heroes in Christian universes do gods again power European epic with the cosmic reverberations it had in its origins.

Notes

1   Later Babylonian myth did recount a divine succession story that is in some ways similar to the Greek, but the decisive battle is not between father and son divinities, but between an older widowed goddess and the young male god who had "killed" her husband. There is no hint, however, that its two major actors, Tiamat and her nemesis Marduk, son of Ea, were known to the poet of *Gilgamesh*.

2   The Succession Myth is found in Hesiod's *Theogony*, which was composed roughly at the same time as the *Iliad*, and in Apollodorus's *Library* 1.1–2, which was compiled during the Roman empire.

3   Such is the parentage given Hephaistos by the *Iliad*. Later myths make Hera the sole parent of Hephaistos.

I

The *Epic of Gilgamesh*

On the banks of the Euphrates River, not far from what is today known as the Persian Gulf, there once stood the great Sumerian city of Uruk. Its monumental defensive walls and magnificent temple of Inanna, Queen of Heaven, attested to the superlative kingship of its legendary king, Gilgamesh, whom later Sumerians believed to have reigned in 2750 BCE. Over 600 years later, during the reign of an ambitious king who identified closely with his "brother and friend" Gilgamesh, five verse narratives about Gilgamesh's adventures, which no doubt drew on a long oral tradition, were composed, recorded on stone tablets, and deposited in royal libraries, or Tablet Houses.[1] These poems, which apparently ranged in length from 115 lines to over 300, soon became widely known and were translated from the Sumerian into Akkadian, which was now becoming the dominant language throughout Mesopotamia.

We have in the original Sumerian, which was a dead language by 1800 BCE, substantial portions of these epic poems. They establish Gilgamesh as no ordinary king. He has a divine mother, Ninsun, and a royal father, Lugalbanda. His protector gods are Enki, the wise god of the deep waters, and Utu, the sun god. All five epics include his beloved servant and steadfast comrade, Enkidu, but only one, *The Death of Gilgamesh*, mentions beloved but nameless wives and children. The stories tell of victory in a defensive war (*Gilgamesh and Akka*); of a deadly quarrel with Inanna, Queen of Heaven, that is resolved by Gilgamesh's killing the Bull of Heaven and making flasks for her of its horns (*Gilgamesh and the Bull of Heaven*); of Gilgamesh's leading a perilous expedition across seven mountain ranges to cut wood in the Cedar Forest, a task which eventually entails Gilgamesh tricking into submission and Enkidu brutally slaying its monstrous but divinely placed guardian (*Gilgamesh and Huwawa*). What is most interesting about *Gilgamesh and Huwawa* in terms of later epic is Gilgamesh's motive for undertaking the dangerous venture: the need for fame to counteract the inexorable coming of death. Because of this motivation, one ancient copyist made *Gilgamesh and Huwawa* the sequel to another of the epics, *Gilgamesh, Enkidu and the Netherworld*, in which Enkidu brings back a grim report from the Netherworld after getting trapped there for seven days. Other copyists did not make this link, which leaves open the possibility that Enkidu's return to upper-world, which Gilgamesh procures through the help of Enki and Utu, is only a temporary reprieve.

The last of the five, *The Death of Gilgamesh*, conveniently sums up the dying hero's achievements, which include, first, unspecified combats, deeds of strength, words of wisdom, climbing mountains and traveling all roads, and then, more specifically, journeying to the Cedar Forest, killing its guardian Huwawa, founding many temples of the gods, reaching the impossibly distant home of the immortal survivor of the Flood, and subsequently reestablishing forgotten rituals for worshiping the gods. The gods decree that despite this accumulation of superlative achievements and despite his being part god, Gilgamesh must still undergo death, the fate of all human beings. Although they do reward him with a prestigious judgeship and make him a lesser god in the Netherworld, there are indications that he is not as fully consoled as both the gods and his counselors think he ought to be.[2] He does, however, rally enough to make sure that his tomb is prepared correctly, which allows the poem to end with funerary ritual and offer a concrete means (statuary) for ensuring that a man's name, at least, will survive his death.

These Sumerian stories are the literary antecedent to the epic that was created in Akkadian, or Old Babylonian, around 1700 BCE and was reworked around 1200 BCE by a scholar-scribe named Sin-leqe-unninni. His Middle Babylonian version, which we call either the Standard Version or the Eleven Tablet Version, was preserved in a Babylonian copy made around 700 BCE. Between the different copies, we now have about 60 percent of the epic's approximately 3,000 lines.[3]

The Old Babylonian epic was known as *Surpassing all other kings* from its first line, which in the Standard Version comes after the twenty-eight-line preamble, or proem, added by Sin-leqe-unninni. The Standard Version was known as *He who saw into the depths*, a title again taken from its first line. Although both epics include basically the same adventures, Sin-leqe-unninni appears to have contracted and expanded some scenes in addition to adding the prologue. All translators fill in lines lost from the tablets of the Standard Version by turning to fragments from the

Old Babylonian, some more than others. Some popular translations also use the Old Babylonian fragments to expand what Sin-leqe-unninni contracted. More rarely, a translator will turn to the five Sumerian epics to fill in blanks or add material, a technique that, while aiming at completeness, can undermine the tragic arc of Sin-leqe-unninni's masterpiece. I will base my discussion here on A. R. George's translation of the Standard Version, which comes as close as is possible today to revealing the story that its ancient audience knew.

The Babylonian poets kept key elements from the popular Sumerian stories. Gilgamesh is still protected by the god of deep waters (Ea) and the sun god (Shamash), and he has a difficult but enduring relationship with the Queen of Heaven (Ishtar), whose temple is at the center of his city. The roles of these Babylonian counterparts to the Sumerian Enki, Utu, and Inanna, however, are deepened and altered in ways that create new tensions. The expedition to the Cedar Forest, the slaying of Huwawa (Babylonian Humbaba), the killing of the Bull from Heaven, and Enkidu's vision of the underworld are all reworked to form a tight sequence of action rather than a simple series of adventures. Gilgamesh's journey to the ends of the earth to talk with the immortalized Flood hero, to which we have only an allusion in the extant Sumerian stories, is elaborated to include a detailed story of the great Flood itself and two tests which Gilgamesh fails. The knowledge Gilgamesh brings back from this journey, especially in Sin-leqe-unninni's version, centers not so much on restoring lost rituals as on understanding – and coming to terms with – the unbridgeable difference between man and god.

Significantly, the Babylonian epics omit two of the Sumerian stories entirely: that of Gilgamesh's military victory over an attacking army and that of Gilgamesh's death, promised deification, and funerary ritual. Although they take Gilgamesh's prowess in battle for granted, neither the Old nor the Standard Babylonian *Epic of Gilgamesh* is interested in warfare. The introductory lines of the Old Babylonian version briefly exalt a brave hero who protects his warriors and can smash through walls, but the poem then devotes twice as many lines to praising his cultural achievements: digging wells, opening mountain passes, his immense journey to the distant home of Flood survivor Utanapishtim, and his subsequent restoration of cult centers and their rituals (SV I.31–44). Although violence pervades the epic, Gilgamesh uses it to conquer "monsters," not cities, and he never kills another human being. As for death and funerary ritual, they are displaced onto Enkidu, and the promised deification is ignored so that the poem's stark focus on mortality will not be diluted.

The proem created by Sin-leqe-unninni gives his epic an intellectual aura that it did not have in the Old Babylonian version. The first six lines, beginning with "He who saw into the depths," that is, he who saw into the underground realm of the god Ea, mark the story as primarily one of mental achievement and align its hero, Gilgamesh, with the god of life-giving waters and wisdom, rather than, for example, with the sun god who will help him kill monsters. His immense physical achievement, the journey to Utanapishtim, is described in intellectual terms: he "saw" what had been secret, "uncovered" what was hidden, and brought back a "story" of what happened before the Flood. Not only did he bring Utanapishtim's story back, he composed his own story, inscribing all his adventures on a tablet of stone (SV I.7–10). As readers discover later at the end of the proem (lines 25–28), the book they are holding in their hands purports to contain the actual words of Gilgamesh himself, an autobiography written in the third person.

There is no real division between brain and brawn here, however. Gilgamesh did not become wise through his ability to read a book, but through the physical stamina and strength that enabled him to complete a heroic journey to the ends of the earth. Immediately after mentioning the story that came out of this journey, Sin-leqe-unninni moves on to a material accomplishment that was made possible by Gilgamesh's skill: he built the great wall of Uruk and, inside it, a magnificent temple of Ishtar, feats that no one has ever been able to equal. Taking readers on an imaginary tour of the wall, the poet dwells on the solidity of its fired-brick foundations, the large city, date grove and clay pit it encloses, and Ishtar's huge temple. The wall's foundations, he exclaims, must have been laid by the Seven Sages, mythic figures who were believed to have taught newly created humankind the arts of civilization.

Let us stop for a moment and think about the word "civilized." It comes from the Latin word for city, *civitas*. Let us think also about city walls. What is their function? In Greek and Roman culture, they signify mainly defense against attacking enemies, and that would certainly have been their main function in ancient Sumer. It is not, however, their main function in this text. In addition to human enemies, a city wall keeps out the wild creatures of nature, just as the sheepfold, which is an important metaphor for the city in Sin-leqe-unninni's version of the epic, keeps wolves and lions away from domesticated animals. City walls separate controlled and civilized society, which includes religion, agriculture, and artifacts, from the uncontrolled world of nature, which contains, as we will see later, beasts, tempests, and the terrifying unknown. Symbolically speaking, the city wall demarcates the human from the bestial. It also encloses gods alongside humans, claiming them for civilization. However, as Gilgamesh will learn to his sorrow, the divine belongs to both sides of the wall.

To Sin-leqe-unninni, these two cultural achievements, the story and the walled city, are what make Gilgamesh "surpass all other kings," as the opening words of the Old Babylonian poem assert. Gilgamesh is the supreme king because he not only protects his city, but enhances its culture. All the deeds that his story recounts are done on behalf of the city in the sense that they open up the wilderness to exploration and exploitation and bring under control the heretofore uncontrollable. Even his quest to Utanapishtim, which achieves no material gain, produces essential knowledge – of history, of unknown realms, of the nature of the gods – and adds an important story to his people's culture.

What Gilgamesh learns from his epic journey has to do with his nature as man and his role as king. Gilgamesh is two-thirds god and one-third human. He inherits extraordinary size, beauty, strength, and energy from his mother Ninsun ("Lady Wild Cow"), a minor goddess, and he inherits social position and mortality from his human father. The unlimited potential of the one clashes with the limitations inherent in the other, putting him and his people through much turmoil throughout the epic.

As the story begins, Gilgamesh's superhuman energy is getting in the way of his being a good king. His energy expresses itself *physically* in appropriating the energy of the young men, probably for building proj- ects or athletic competitions,[4] and *sexually* in exercising the god king's right to sleep with all virgin brides before the bridegroom. His people, exhausted and annoyed, call on the gods for help, and the gods respond by creating for him an equal upon whom he can expend his energy. This is Enkidu, and he is not only his equal in strength but also his exact opposite. If Gilgamesh is two-thirds god, Enkidu seems more than half animal with his hairy body, diet of grass and water, and alliance with wild gazelles whom he protects against human hunters. The rest of Tablets I and II describe the process whereby Enkidu becomes fully human and how, when two heroes come together, their friendship begins to humanize Gilgamesh.

The process of humanizing Enkidu begins with heterosexual sex. At the request of a hunter, Gilgamesh sends a temple courtesan to entice Enkidu to bond with his own kind in the most basic biological way. Enkidu lies with the woman Shamhat for seven days, at the end of which time he tries to rejoin his gazelle friends. They bolt away, and he, physically weakened, cannot follow. At the same time, Enkidu becomes capable of new understanding, which makes him receptive to Shamhat's invitation to come with her to Uruk the Sheepfold and to Gilgamesh. Significantly, his first response to Shamhat's description of Gilgamesh as the strongest man in Uruk is to vaunt that he will challenge him and change the order of things, much as one alpha male might challenge another in the wild. Shamhat responds that Enkidu's destined relationship with Gilgamesh, who is stronger and loved by the gods, is that of counselor and friend. She then begins the process of civilizing Enkidu by first giving him clothing and then taking him to a shepherd's encampment where she teaches him to eat bread and ale, that is, cooked and therefore specifically human food. The cloth garment, like the bread and the ale, is a product of human technology, as is the barber's tool that grooms him and the weapon Enkidu later takes up to protect the shepherds' domesticated animals from wild lions and wolves. No longer merely biologically human, Enkidu is now a civilized man, fit to enter the city.

Enkidu is motivated to leave the shepherds' camp for the city specifically to stop Gilgamesh's exercising his divine right to sleep with a new bride. Just as sex with one woman transformed Enkidu from animal to human, so being restricted from sex with *all* women is the first step in Gilgamesh's becoming more human than god. It is a step toward communality: that is, recognition of the claims of other males as a limitation on "might makes right," the law of raw nature.

The wrestling bout, then, is what marks the shift of each into humanity. For Enkidu it marks full humanity – he is now established in the city, the locus of civilized life. Gilgamesh, on the other hand, has met his near equal in strength, who has restricted his divine sexual license, and who will now be his friend, something he has never had. Friendship, in fact, seems to be the mark of the fullest humanity (as opposed to divinity and bestiality) in the *Epic of Gilgamesh*. Note that this friendship is male–male and specifically supplants the male–female bonding that marks basic humanity. While Enkidu was being prepared for city life, Gilgamesh had dreamed of picking up a meteor and an axe and loving each "like a woman." His mother interpreted these dreams as foreshadowing the coming of a comrade whom Gilgamesh would love "like a woman." What are the implications of this transference of male devotion from female to male? From a relationship with a woman comes renewed life of the body, of the biological species, which puts the heterosexual relationship into the category of biology, of nature. No offspring can result from a relationship between two men. What does result, at least in this epic, is a restrained, more civilized behavior, which puts the masculine homosocial relationship firmly into the higher realm of culture.

The wrestling bout and the resultant friendship, which mark the end of what I will call the first movement of the epic, are only the beginning of Gilgamesh's becoming fully human. In the next movement, which covers the last third of Tablet II through Tablet VI, the poet depicts Gilgamesh and Enkidu asserting themselves against the forces of nature in order to overcome their own human nature, that is, in order to overcome death by achieving fame. Their partnership enables them to succeed in two great adventures, but the aftermath of these successes teaches the friends just how inexorable human nature is.

The first adventure is the expedition to the far-off Cedar Forest to conquer its protective demon Humbaba and cut down the trees for timber; the second is slaying the Bull of Heaven sent by an offended Ishtar. Both episodes are modified from their Sumerian sources to fit their new intellectual framework. The modifications to the Humbaba episode, which are far more extensive, intensify the focus on friendship and heighten the heroism of Gilgamesh's attempt to transcend human limitation.

In the Sumerian *Gilgamesh and Huwawa*, when Gilgamesh conceives the idea to win fame by an expedition to cut cedars on Mount Lebanon, Enkidu does not try to dissuade him, but merely advises him to inform the Sun God and get his help. In *The Epic of Gilgamesh* sustained opposition to the expedition highlights both the extraordinary danger involved and, to borrow a later Greek concept, the possible hubris of Gilgamesh's refusal to believe that there is any challenge he cannot conquer. Enlil has made Humbaba terrifying in order to protect the cedars from men; entering the forest will mean certain death, insist both Enkidu and Uruk's elders. Gilgamesh, fearless and driven by the desire to create a name that will live after his body dies, ridicules their concerns. Although he recognizes human death, at this point he is clearly unable to identify with human fear.

After he overrides their opposition, the elders commit Gilgamesh to Enkidu, enjoining him to protect his friend and bring him back safely. Their words about Enkidu's importance to Gilgamesh (III.4–12), which are absent from *Gilgamesh and Huwawa*, are reinforced in the subsequent scene with Ninsun, which is also absent from the earlier poem. In *The Epic of Gilgamesh*, Gilgamesh comes to Ninsun hand in hand with Enkidu to ask for her blessing (III.19–116). After successfully imploring

Shamash to aid her son, she binds Enkidu to Gilgamesh by adopting him as Gilgamesh's brother (III.121–128). There follows a fragmentary departure scene, in which the elders repeat their earlier words committing Gilgamesh to Enkidu's care, and, after a final attempt to get Gilgamesh to turn back, Enkidu finally embraces his role as partner in the expedition. The resulting focus on the two men as essential to each other is sustained by yet another change from *Gilgamesh and Huwawa*. In the Sumerian poem, Gilgamesh conscripts fifty young men to help bring back the timber he will cut, and the poet refers to these young men several times throughout the adventure. Although in the *Epic of Gilgamesh* the end of the departure scene is missing, an Old Babylonian tablet indicates that Gilgamesh makes the people happy by saying that none of them should go with him, and the two set off totally alone (Yale 279–283). Thus the poetic focus is locked on the importance of their relationship rather than on Gilgamesh's heroic leadership.[5]

The *Epic of Gilgamesh* makes it clear that a single hero could not accomplish this quest. It requires two who will help each other at times of need. Enkidu, who is closer to nature, acts as guide. He also acts as encouraging interpreter of nightmares. When they enter the forest each has moments of panic, and it takes the other to encourage and goad to action. Their nonprocreative bonding produces, instead of new bodies, "progress," – that is, wood for building and a glorious story to add to the culture.

Let us return to the scene with Ninsun, which, as mentioned above, was absent from the Sumerian poem. This scene, which was apparently added in the final shaping of the epic, not only cements the brotherhood of Gilgamesh and Enkidu, but also invokes Gilgamesh's human mortality in the most moving way possible: through the eyes of a grieving mother. The immortal mother plaintively asks Shamash, "Will Gilgamesh not share the sky with you and the Moon God, will he not grow wise with Ea, will he not rule in Uruk with Ishtar, will he not live in the high court of the Netherworld?" (III.100–106).[6] Ninsun, fearful that her son will be killed by Humbaba, is asking for a long life for her son that will be crowned by deification in the Netherworld, a reward granted by the gods in the Sumerian *The Death of Gilgamesh* in acknowledgment of his having brought back the cedar, his building projects, and his bringing back rites from the Flood survivor. It could also be interpreted as Ninsun's vain wish that her son might be as immortal as his mother, a wish explicitly considered by the gods and denied in *The Death of Gilgamesh* (Mê-Turan, 78–79). In either interpretation, the poignant fear of the immortal mother for her mortal son heightens the reader's sense of risk and brings Gilgamesh's mortality to the fore in a way that neither Enkidu nor the elders can.

The scene with Ninsun also contributes to a theme specific to the Babylonian versions of the epic: the tension between nature and culture. Ninsun lays at Shamash's door Gilgamesh's desire to confront Humbaba, and rid the world of the "evil thing you hate" (III.45–54). If Humbaba is the agent of Enlil, the great god who rules the earth and its inhabitants, how can he be evil? Why would the Sun God hate Humbaba and want him removed from the Cedar Forest? This is an important question because Shamash is also the god of Justice. The answer lies in how Justice is conceived.

Shamash's light penetrates everywhere on earth so that no one and no deed can escape his notice. Justice is what brings the facts to light. For the same reason, the Greeks considered their sun god, Apollo, to be the god of truth. A virgin forest, however, lets in almost no light, and Humbaba's purpose is to keep it that way, untouched and uncontrolled. Furthermore, Justice and Law, which Shamash represents, pertain to human interaction, but Humbaba keeps human beings out of the forest. Shamash reveals his lack of power in the depths of the forest later when he urges Gilgamesh to attack Humbaba before he makes it deep into the forest where his seven auras are (IV.199–203). "Evil" therefore appears to be a cultural valuation based solely on human aspirations and Shamash's apparent desire to have no area closed to him. To Shamash, whatever keeps humans from using natural resources and transforming natural areas into social places where humans can interact under his watchful eye is evil.

This valuation is not, however, uncontested. After Gilgamesh has overpowered Humbaba with the help of thirteen powerful winds sent by Shamash, the poet gives him a pivotal choice. When Humbaba offers to serve him if he will spare his life, Gilgamesh must choose either to collaborate with the forest's guardian in securing supplies of wood or, as Enkidu advises, to win the eternal fame of totally eradicating his power. Despite Shamash's obvious desire for the latter, this is not a choice that has an unequivocally right answer. As Enkidu warns, if Gilgamesh doesn't kill quickly, supremely powerful Enlil and other important gods will find out, become angry, and stop them (V.185–189 = 241–245). Enlil clearly does not consider Humbaba evil, and, as we find out later, neither does Anu, father of the Babylonian pantheon and coresident with Ishtar in the temple of Uruk. Though Shamash will continue to defend Gilgamesh and Enkidu, the other gods will exact a high price for their action in the forest.

After Gilgamesh cuts off Humbaba's head, the two heroes immediately begin cutting down trees, and Enkidu boasts that he will turn a particularly lofty cedar into a huge door for Enlil's temple in the city of Nippur. This magnificent product of nature transformed into art may be meant as atonement for killing Enlil's appointed guardian, but if so it does not work.

Much later, when Enkidu curses this door on his deathbed, the poet invites his readers to think about the killing of Humbaba in terms of a conflict in which neither side will be victorious without serious cost. He offers a double vision: both the rewards of conquering nature and also the costs.

Gilgamesh continues his violent response to the challenges of nature in the next episode, in which he rejects the goddess of procreation and kills the Bull of Heaven she sends in retaliation. Ishtar, Queen of Heaven, is the goddess of life and death, of natural cycles. One of the ancient ways for a community to gain control over nature was for the king to celebrate a Sacred Marriage with Ishtar in her holy temple. Ishtar, filled with the king's seed, would ensure overflowing fields and barns. As many myths about Ishtar and her consorts indicate, however, there was danger involved for the king, who, if asked, would have to surrender his life force completely to the goddess, losing his identity as individual actor in the human world, and undergoing the equivalent of death. When Ishtar propositions Gilgamesh in this way, Gilgamesh resists sacrificing himself. As he will soon prove, he has other ways of overcoming the uncertainties of nature.

Gilgamesh not only refuses Ishtar, he insults her egregiously. His long list of insults, which include comparing her to a malfunctioning door, an ill-fitting shoe, and limestone that weakens a wall (VI.33–43), represent the goddess as spoiling human artifacts that are specifically constructed to give humans more control over nature. His last charge, that of fickleness, is perhaps most telling: Ishtar, goddess of natural cycles, represents change from happiness to unhappiness and, more generally, impermanence. Impermanence is Gilgamesh's prime enemy throughout the epic.

Gilgamesh's refusal prompts a murderous revenge in the form of the Bull of Heaven. Anu's insistence that Ishtar prepare her people with seven-year's worth of grain before he will give her the Bull, taken together with its effect on the land (VI.104–111, 117–122), indicates that the

Bull embodies a seven-year drought. Gilgamesh's joining forces with Enkidu's to battle the Bull from Heaven represents an attempt to conquer the problems of nature with masculine strength and intelligence, that is, through the homosocial bond rather than the heterosexual act. Once the two men succeed, they go off hand in hand to celebrate Gilgamesh's status as "the best, most glorious of men" (VI.167–175).

Gilgamesh and Enkidu divide up the slain Bull in a culturally significant way. There are three parts: heart, haunch, horns. The Bull's heart is offered to the male sun god Shamash (VI.148–150). Enkidu insults Ishtar (who has cursed Gilgamesh) by flinging the haunch at her. Some scholars say that since the haunch is the god's portion of the sacrifice, the act represents simple hubris. Other scholars view the haunch as a euphemism for genitals, which makes the insult worse because Enkidu flings organs of generation into the goddess of generation's face. In any case, while Ishtar and her female votaries mourn over the haunch, which represents a fleshly, ephemeral part of the Bull, Gilgamesh decorates the durable horns with precious stone, making them into oil flasks for his protector god Lugalbanda, and displays them as an artifact in the house.

The poet has made several significant changes from the Sumerian *Gilgamesh and the Bull of Heaven*. In the earlier poem, Gilgamesh's mother warns that accepting gifts from Ishtar will weaken his warrior strength; Gilgamesh's rejection of Ishtar includes no insults, just a statement that he would prefer to fill her sheepfolds and bull pens by hunting; his mother and sisters aid Gilgamesh through ritual prayer; and in the disposition of the slain Bull, the parts are less starkly symbolic: Gilgamesh himself cuts and throws the Bull's haunch at Inanna, casts the corpse and innards into street, gives the meat to orphans, takes the skin to a tanner, and has the horns made into oil flasks for *Inanna*, not Lugalbanda. The last line of the poem concludes with praise of the goddess after first celebrating slaying the Bull. Although the Sumerian poem's message is essentially the same – Gilgamesh is capable of using nature for the benefit of his people without sacrificing himself to the goddess – his arrogance is much less than it is in the revised Babylonian story. The later version makes starker the opposition between male-identified culture and female-identified nature and, by depicting Gilgamesh as utterly scornful of the latter, heightens the reader's sense of hubris and motivates the retribution to come.

Victory over the Bull is the last happy moment the two friends have. The third movement of the poem, in which nature asserts its ultimate power, begins on the very night after Gilgamesh and Enkidu celebrate their triumph. Tablet VII opens with Enkidu relating to Gilgamesh a dream vision, in which he hears Anu decree that either Gilgamesh or Enkidu must die because they killed Humbaba and the Bull of Heaven. Enlil chooses Enkidu, which is logical since he is fully human while Gilgamesh is part divine. Shamash clashes with Enlil, insisting that Enkidu is innocent of wrongdoing, but since Anu and Enlil are more powerful, Enkidu is doomed.[7]

As he lies dying, Enkidu curses the huge cedar door he had built for Enlil's temple. He curses the hunter who first brought him to the attention of Gilgamesh. Last and at greatest length he curses Shamhat, the woman who made him a civilized human being. At this point, however, Shamash intervenes and reminds him of the benefits he acquired through her: haute cuisine, haute couture, a beloved friend who will mourn him, and elaborate funeral ritual. Enkidu, persuaded that these cultural benefits are worth the cost, grows calm and blesses her. Soon, however, he is disturbed by a dream of the Netherworld, a place of darkness and dust whose inhabitants eat clay and wear feathers. Unfortunately forty lines of this vision have been lost, but we have enough to know that there is nothing desirable there.

Enkidu takes twelve days to die, and Gilgamesh the monster slayer can do nothing to save him.

Gilgamesh's first response to Enkidu's death is to tell his story in a long lament, thus creating a memorial in words. Second he creates a magnificent statue, that is, a permanent image. Third he puts on a state funeral with splendid gifts for Enkidu to take to the underworld gods. We are missing the last thirty lines of this funeral, but we know from what he later says that he is reluctant to end it: he sits by his friend's corpse for six days and only buries him after a maggot drops from his nostril (X.58–60, 135–137, 235–237). The sight of the disintegrating body being eaten by worms brings home to Gilgamesh the full horror of death and impels him to begin his greatest quest: a journey beyond the confines of the human world to wrest the secret of physical immortality from Flood survivor Utanapishtim ("He Who Saw Life"). This quest for physical immortality, punctuated by the constant refrain: "My friend has died. Will I not die also and be like that?" (IX.3, X.69–71, 146–148, 246–248) will take up the rest of the epic.

The irrevocable loss of a loved one, one loved as dearly as himself, is what teaches Gilgamesh the reality and the *fear* of death. This fear sends him away from the city and its lifestyle, turning him into, as it were, an animal: he "wanders the wilderness" wearing lion pelts instead of woven clothing, with hair long and matted, sleeping in the open, and exposing his skin to sunburn and frost (X.44–45, XI.251–254). Shamash tries to return him to the city, saying that he will never find what he seeks, but to no avail. Gilgamesh persists, at one point outracing the Sun God through the Twin Peaks where he rises and sets, that is, to and past the limit of Shamash's influence on the living world.

Gilgamesh's journey qualifies as a descent to the underworld, which is a common motif in quest epics and a mark of the greatest of heroes. First he must pass the Scorpion Guardians to make an unprecedented and terrifying twenty-four-hour journey through the utter darkness of the Twin Peaks, (IX.80–170). When he emerges, Gilgamesh is in an earthly paradise whose jewel flowers signify imperishable but dead beauty (IX.171–190). Last, he must cross the Waters of Death, over which no mortal has ever been able to go (X.79–80).

Gilgamesh is pointed the way to the Waters of Death by Shiduri, the tavern keeper. In the Standard Version of the epic Shiduri's role is kept to a bare minimum, but in the Old Babylonian epic she speaks to Gilgamesh at length, advising him to stop his hopeless quest and live out his ephemeral human life enjoying the daily pleasures of dining, dancing, dressing, and making love. Many translators of *The Epic of Gilgamesh* include Shiduri's *carpe diem* advice in their versions of Tablet X, and thus it may be profitable to compare it to the message Utanapishtim later conveys to Gilgamesh and also to Shamhat's previous education of Enkidu. Utanapishtim will tell Gilgamesh many of the same things Shiduri does: the gods set a limit on human life, but there is no point in anticipating it; one should dress well and eat well. Utanapishtim, however, paints a picture of human life that is essentially tragic and he stresses not pleasure, but responsibility: Gilgamesh, he says, is a king and should act like one (X.267–322). As we see with both Shamhat and Shiduri, a woman is important to a man's achieving basic humanity, but it takes a male counselor to move to move him to a higher socioreligious plane.[8]

Shiduri helps Gilgamesh cross the Waters of Death to Utanapishtim by telling him about the boatman Urshanabi, who is currently on this side of the Waters. Two things are important about Gilgamesh's interaction with Urshanabi. First, he approaches the boatman hostilely, and when Urshanabi and his companions, the mysterious Stone Ones, defend themselves, he smashes the Stone Ones to bits. Second, because the Stone Ones turn out to be what make crossing possible – being stone, they are impervious to the Waters of Death – technology must substitute for their natural ability: under Urshanabi's direction, Gilgamesh makes and uses 120 poles to punt boat across, and then creates a sail out of the lion's skin he was wearing to carry them the rest of the way. Gilgamesh has brought it about unwittingly this time, but once again he is associated with a cultural process that ensues when a natural process has been forcefully destroyed.

Gilgamesh asks Utanapishtim for the secret of eternal life, but Utanapishtim's only response is that there is *nothing* eternal in human affairs and that Gilgamesh should go back to Uruk and be a good king. Utanapishtim's wisdom induces Gilgamesh to abandon the violence he had been prepared to use to wrest his secret from him (XI.5–6). Instead of fighting him, Gilgamesh asks for and gets the story of how Utanapishtim became immortal. There follows the famous story of the Flood (XI.11–206).

Utanapishtim's version of the Flood is most interesting in what it reveals about the gods, who, at the instigation of Enlil, decide to send it for no explicit reason. One Old Babylonian version tells that the cause is a bothersome racket caused by overpopulation, but in any case, the cause is not human wickedness as it is in the Hebrew and, later, Latin versions.[9] Utanapishtim is saved because he is a protégé of Ea, who wants to preserve the human species and the animal and plant life it depends on. The flood is so terrible that all the gods except Enlil are horrified and weep at the destruction. When it is over, Enlil is furious to find that anyone has escaped, but Ea chides him, saying that he could have found another less destructive way to reduce the population, and in the end Enlil blesses Utanapishtim and his wife, changes them into gods, and sets them to dwell far away at the source of flowing waters. Since Enlil, the most powerful god in the Babylonian pantheon, acts irrationally, inconsistently, and without forethought both here and throughout the epic, the opposition and then the reconciliation between him and Ea invite the moral interpretation that Wisdom should always temper Power. Furthermore, since in this story Ea represents specifically human-oriented intelligence, their interaction becomes exemplary of the interplay between nature and culture that we have been tracing. Humans as individuals and as a species can ameliorate by shaping, but can never fully control, the overwhelming forces of nature.

At the end of Utanapishtim's story, it is clear that his and his wife's achievement of eternal life is unique. To prove his point that Gilgamesh is mortal like all other human beings, Utanapishtim sets Gilgamesh a test: to stay awake for six days and seven nights. Gilgamesh, of course, falls asleep, and to mark the time he is asleep, Utanapishtim has his wife bake a loaf of bread and set it by Gilgamesh's head every day. By the time he awakes, there are seven loaves in various stages of freshness and decay (XI.207–241). We may compare this use of bread near the end of the epic to how it was used at the beginning with Enkidu. There it was a mark of human technology, of civilization; here what is stressed about this archetypal human food is that it is perishable.

Gilgamesh laments the loss of his hopes, seeing nothing but death all around him. Utanapishtim says nothing to him, but turns to Urshanabi, whom he now banishes and puts in charge of getting Gilgamesh home in a civilized manner (XI.247–261). Banishing the boatman cuts Utanapishtim off completely from the human world and means that no other hero will be able to repeat Gilgamesh's journey. Gilgamesh's journey is unique, and his story will be unique. This moment marks the beginning of the last, short movement of the epic.

Gilgamesh's return to civilization begins when he obeys Utanapishtim's order to bathe, put on clean royal clothes, and cover his head with a cloth. That is, he discards signs of mourning and accepts the reality of life. He goes back home as if new born – and as a king again. No longer solitary, he has Urshanabi as companion all the way back. Urshanabi isn't given anything to say, but he is present to allow Gilgamesh to communicate in his own voice, first to express glee when in one last heroic feat he acquires the plant of rejuvenation, then to weep and berate himself when through carelessness he loses it to a snake, and finally, to describe with pride the city walls that mark his successful return to Uruk and the human world.[10]

The last words of the hero and of the epic circle back to the admiration of Uruk expressed in Sin-leqe-unninni's proem. As Gilgamesh approaches his city, the man who has been totally focused on death and disintegration seems newly aware of his own human achievement. Here may be some compensation for the sorrow, fear, and disillusionment that Gilgamesh has learned are inseparable from the human condition. Gilgamesh's mood at the end of the epic has been variously interpreted as obedient to the gods' will, defiantly self-reliant, accepting his kingly responsibility, profoundly happy in his newfound wisdom, and resigned to his mortal status. All interpretations are available, but all must be nuanced by what was foretold at the beginning, that Gilgamesh would return weary but at "peace" (I.9). As he points out the wonders of his city to Urshanabi and his readers, it is easy to imagine the next day when, enfolded by the enduring wall of Uruk, Gilgamesh will begin to compose the still more enduring story we have just read.

Further Reading

Translations

There now exist many excellent translations of the *Epic of Gilgamesh*. Assyrian scholars Andrew George (Penguin, 1999, 2003) and Benjamin R. Foster (Norton, 2001) have each produced recent ones that append useful translations of fragments from the Summerian epic cycle and from the Old Babylonian version of the epic. Both translations are careful to indicate gaps in the text and places where conjecture takes the place of actual translation; George's introduction and his appendix on the difficulties of translating from the cuneiform are superb. These two translations, which include material not available to earlier translators, now supersede all other scholarly translations, including excellent ones by Maureen Gallery Kovacs (Stanford University Press, 1989) and John Gardner and John Maier (Random House, 1984); both clearly indicate when they interpolate material from the Old Babylonian version, and they provide running commentary and useful notes. Stephen Mitchell (Free Press, 1984) and David Ferry (Noonday Press, 1993) offer engaging poetic translations; Mitchell's contains a long interpretive essay and extensive notes that offer literary and historical background and carefully explain translations of particular passages. Danny P. Jackson's rhymed verse (Bolchazy-Carducci, 1982) is interestingly illustrated by Thom Kapheim. For those who prefer a prose translation, N.K. Sandars' *The Epic of Gilgamesh* (Penguin, 1960) is still in print; readers should be aware that Sandars freely combines the Standard and the Old Babylonian versions. Herbert Mason's *Gilgamesh* (Mentor, 1972) is a very free adaptation rather than a translation.

For literal translations of the Sumerian epics on the Internet, go to The Electronic Text Corpus of Sumerian Literature at http://etcsl.orinst.ox.ac.uk/catalogue/catalogue1.htm.

Important Mesopotamian stories relevant to *the Epic of Gilgamesh* have been conveniently collected and translated by Stephanie Dalley in *Myths from Mesopotamia: Creation, the Flood, Gilgamesh, and Others* (Oxford, 1998) and by Benjamin R. Foster in *From Distant Days. Myths, Tales, and Poetry of Ancient Mesopotamia* (Bethesda, MD: CDL Press, 1995). In order to read *Atramhasis*, or *The Flood*, in its oldest Babylonian version without later supplements from later versions, see Foster's translations in *Before the Muses, An Anthology of Akkadian Literature* vol. 1 (Bethesda, MD, 1993).

Analysis

The introduction and appendix to Andrew George's translation in *The Epic of Gilgamesh. The Babylonian Epic Poem and Other Texts in Akkadian and Sumerian* (Penguin Books, 1999), provide analysis as well as excellent historical, textual, and cultural background to the poem.

Two major articles by Tzvi Abusch are worth tracking down. "Ishtar's Proposal and Gilgamesh's Refusal: An Interpretation of the "The Gilgamesh Epic," Tablet 6, Lines 1–19." History of Religions 26, 2 (November 1986), 143–187, analyzes Ishtar's proposal of marriage as a deceptive offer for Gilgamesh to become her consort in the Netherworld, where he would become a source of life for others but lose his own human identity. The Bull represents "the old order" and seasonal cycles which now must "give way to assertions of will" (178). The second article, "The Development and Meaning of the Epic of Gilgamesh: An Interpretive Essay," *Journal of the American Oriental Society* 121, 4 (2001), 614–622, analyzes changes in meaning from the Old Babylonian (1700 BCE) to the eleven tablet Standard Version (1500–1000 BCE) to what he believes is a meaningful Twelve-Tablet version. The kernel of all three is the conflict between Gilgamesh's heroic identity and his social, political and religious identities as human being, king, and god; the main change is the emphasis on man in the first, king in the second, and god in the third. Most scholars do not accept his argument that the Twelfth Tablet is more than an appendix, but Abusch makes the strongest case possible.

Still worth reading is Thorkild Jacobsen's *The Treasures of Darkness: A History of Mesopotamian Religion* (New Haven, CT: Yale University Press, 1976). This volume contains a chapter on Gilgamesh ("'And Death the Journey's End': The Gilgamesh Epic," pp. 195–215) that is noteworthy for its analysis of Gilgamesh as holding on to boyhood through his attachment to Enkidu. See also his "The Gilgamesh Epic: Romantic and Tragic vision," in T. Abusch, J. Huehnergard and P. Steinkeller, eds., *Lingering Over Words, Studies in Ancient Near Eastern Literature in Honor of William L. Moran* (Atlanta: Scholars Press, 1990) 231–249. Brilliant for its day, Jacobsen's analysis is now superseded by those who have more text to interpret.

George F. Held offers a different take on the effects of Gilgamesh's friendship with Enkidu, arguing that they are analogous to the effects of love on the philosopher in Plato's *Symposium* in "Parallels between the

Gilgamesh Epic and Plato's *Symposium*," *Journal of Near Eastern Studies* 42 (1983) 133–141. Reprinted in W. R. Dynes and S. Donaldson, eds. *Homosexuality in the Ancient World* (New York and London: Garland Publishing, 1992) 199–241.

David Damrosch's *The Buried Book: The Loss and Rediscovery of the Great Epic of Gilgamesh* (Henry Holt & Co, 2007) gives a cultural and archeological history of the epic and offers a stimulating interpretation of the text(s).

Mesopotamian Literature and Culture

A Companion to Ancient Epic, John Miles Foley, ed. (Malden and Oxford: Blackwell Publishing, 2005), contains two essays of particular interest by Jack M. Sasson ("Comparative Observations on the Near Eastern Epic Traditions," pp. 215–232), and Scott B. Noegel ("Mesopotamian Epic," pp. 233–245).

Jack M. Sasson has edited the multivolume *Civilizations of the Ancient Near East* (Peabody MA, 2001), which includes essays on the art, economics, history, literature, and religion of Sumer, Akkad, and Babylon.

Modern Adaptations:

Joan London has written an award-winning novel whose Australian heroine is inspired by stories of Gilgamesh: *Gilgamesh, A Novel* (London, 2001; New York, 2003). Philip Roth uses the epic hero (one of his protagonists is a baseball player named Gil Gamesh) to satirize McCarthyite cold-war America in the 1950's–60's in *The Great American Novel* (New York, 1973).

Pulitzer prize-winning Yusef Komunyakaa has collaborated with Chad Garcia to turn the *Epic of Gilgamesh* into the lyric *Gilgamesh: A Verse Play* (Middletown CT, 2006).

Notes

1   The ambitious king was Shulgi, a ruler who celebrated intellectual achievement as much as martial achievement. The quotation comes from "A praise song for Shulgi" by Shulgi C, 105–106, which can be found in The Electronic Text Corpus of Sumerian Literature, http://etcsl.orinst. ox.ac.uk/section2/tr24203.htm.

2   The main indication that he is not consoled is that the Counselors of Uruk continue to ask "what is the cause of your tears?" after he tells them his dream (quoted from Andrew George's *The Epic of Gilgamesh. The Babylonian Epic Poem and Other Texts in Akkadian and Sumerian* [London and New York, 1999], 205, N.vi.6.) All translations are by George.

3   Twenty percent of the lines are entirely missing, and many of the lines that we do have are fragmentary. A twelfth tablet found with the eleven discovered at Nineveh contains a translation into Akkadian of the second half of one of the Sumerian epics, *Gilgamesh, Enkidu and the Netherworld*. Most scholars believe that this tablet was stored with the other eleven because it contained a related story, but that it is not part of the unified *Epic of Gilgamesh*.

4   The Sumerian poem *Gilgamesh, Enkidu and the Netherworld* contains a scene in which Gilgamesh insists that the young men play an exhausting game with him for days on end. Their mothers and sisters, who have to bring them bread and water constantly, cry out for help to the gods, who respond by causing the gaming tools to fall into the Netherworld.

5   Textual citations refer to George's translation; line numbers will be slightly different in other translations. Roman numerals I–XI refer to the tablets found at Nineveh; "Yale" refers to the Old Babylonian Tablet III in the Yale collection, which George labels Y; Mê- Turan refers to manuscripts found at Tell Haddad, which George labels M.

6   Paraphrase of III.100–106. The Old Babylonian version represents Gilgamesh as praying to Shamash at the point where the Standard Version makes him go with Enkidu to get Ninsun's blessing (Yale tablet 214–221, George, pp.112–113).

7   After the first line of Tablet VII, 35 lines are lost. Their content is reconstructed from a fragmentary Hittite prose paraphrase of the Old Babylonian epic.

8   Shiduri's advice is found in Sippur Tablet III.2–15. George feels that the author of the Standard Version shortened Shiduri's part in order to "keep the wisdom for the climax" (xliii).

   The lines which deliver Utanapishtim's advice about the responsibilities of kingship are fragmentary, but the gist is apparent. One of them indicates that the reason Gilgamesh is presently behaving like a fool is that he has no counselors (X.276–277).

9   Some scholars have recently suggested that the "racket" that disturbs the gods' sleep is metaphoric for wickedness (Lawrence T. Geraty, "Theology of the Flood," GRI Faith and Science Conference, August 18, 2003, p. 5. http://www.grisda.org/2003-FSC-open/Geraty-TheologyOfFlood.doc).

10 The snake's theft of the plant of rejuvenation, which denies humankind its restorative benefits, has a parallel in Greek and other mythologies. Such stories illustrate the fact that old age as well as mortality are part of the human condition. See M. L. West's *East Face of Helicon* (Oxford, 1999) p. 118 for the Greek parallel.

2

The Context of Homeric Epic

The *Iliad* and *Odyssey*, like the *Epic of Gilgamesh*, were created from already existing stories. We cannot know what the "original" stories about Achilles and Odysseus might have been, because Greek tradition was totally oral, and the heroes are minor kings for whom we have no proof of historical existence. We do, however, have evidence from the wider epic tradition to help us imagine how the epics came into being. Our imagination is aided by bards within the epics, including both heroes' attempts to "compose" their own stories. These attempts make them strikingly similar to Gilgamesh. The key difference is that Gilgamesh writes his story down when it is over, while Achilles and Odysseus sing and speak theirs as they are still unfolding.

Poet-singers, or bards, created and recreated epic stories to entertain audiences in wealthy households and at public ceremonies in Archaic Greece. Choosing from a vast repertoire of stories passed down by poets from the Bronze Age to the present, poets sang of extraordinary deeds done in the distant past by gods and heroes, ancestors of the ordinary men and women who listened to their stories. As they sang, the bards put their own touches on the stories, expanding certain episodes, contracting others, and inventing new ones to please local interests.

The archaic epic universe comprised roughly six major groups of stories, sometimes called story cycles because they "circled" around particular heroes and/or events like the spokes of a wheel. One set of stories focused on the gods, giving their genealogies, struggles for power among themselves, and how they established their worship among humankind; a surviving example of this theme is Hesiod's *Theogony* (*Divine Genealogy*). The other five cycles constituted what we call heroic epic: the superhuman deeds of Heracles, son of Zeus, who alone of mortals earned a place among the gods in Olympos; the deeds of Theseus, national hero of the Athenians; the violent goings on (incest, infanticide, suicide, civil war) in Thebes, native city of Oedipus; the voyage of Jason and the Argonauts to Asia, undertaken to bring the Golden Fleece back to a Greek king; and the siege and destruction of Troy, a wealthy city in Asia Minor, which eventually produced the *Iliad* and *Odyssey*.

Whether the Trojan War was much more real than Jason's golden sheepskin is still not known, but both the Argonaut and Trojan War stories reflect a real contest for power between kingdoms in Greece and Asia Minor in the Late Bronze Age (1500–1100 BCE.). Egyptian records and recently deciphered Hittite documents show that during this time Greeks became a power in the Aegean, trading extensively with their neighbors and establishing at least one colony on the coast of Asia Minor. As their aspirations grew, these Danaja and Achijawa, as the inhabitants of Greece are called in the ancient Egyptian and Hittite documents, began to raid the coastal cities of their Egyptian and Asian neighbors, causing the Hittite king to become quite hostile by 1220 BCE. Through raiding and/or trading, the Greeks would have come to know the city of Wilusa, a large trading center with a walled citadel and walled lower town in a strategic location between the Aegean and the Black Sea. The destruction of this city in an earthquake in 1250 BCE would have been shocking and fascinating news, as would the rebuilding of the city and its later destruction by fire around 1180 BCE. Whether or not the Greeks had anything to do with the second catastrophe, stories about the fall of Wilusa, or "Ilios" in Greek, made their way into Greek culture. So, undoubtedly, stories about the Greek raids traveled across the sea, for Bronze Age Greek society was a warrior society, whose kings would have enjoyed songs about the deeds of warrior forebears.

Words and phrases came into the epic stories at various times, preserving items like the "towering" shield of Aias, which apparently went out of use after 1400 BCE, the massive spears wielded by Achilles and Hektor, which were supplanted by smaller weapons after 1300 BCE, and the two-storied grandeur of Odysseus' palace, which is not found in the more modest palaces built after Mycenaean society collapsed around 1200–1170 BCE. Artistic themes from trading partners entered the culture and the epic tradition very early. For example, the motif of a besieged and conquered city, common in Egypt and Asia, appears in Greek art around 1500 BCE. At the same time, lions were adopted from Egyptian and Asian rulers as a symbol of royal power in battle, inspiring the magnificent lion gates of the palace of Mycenae as well as the lion-like heroes of epic song.

A period of great violence engulfed the Mediterranean region near the end of the thirteenth century. The Hittite empire fell. Mycenaean prosperity collapsed and its palaces were destroyed. The scribes in the palaces also disappeared, taking with them the knowledge of writing. Pirates and raiders roamed the seas. Migration from mainland Greece to islands off the coast of Asia Minor continued off and on through the tenth century. Phoenicia rose to power as a great merchant culture centered in the north African city of Carthage, and Phoenician sailors and craftspeople could be found everywhere by 800 BCE. By 750 BCE, cities throughout Greece were once again prosperous and trading, and writing had been relearned from the Phoenicians. Stories from throughout these tumultuous centuries would have found their way into the oral epic tradition, enriching it with new ideas, characters, and situations from all the regions where Greek culture had established itself. Stories that originated in the Mycenaean age were prized, but they could be told in a myriad of ways to please a modern audience.

The Homeric world, therefore, reflects many histories of many regions and many periods, all preserved in the oral-formulaic art language of professional bards. Even though most scholars believe that Homer composed, or at least polished, the *Iliad* and the *Odyssey* with the help of writing, the oral tradition in which he was clearly trained accounts for many stylistic features that may seem strange to modern readers. It was a language that evolved with the dactylic hexameter verse in which epic stories were sung, a language that spoke in phrases and scenes as well as individual words.

Hexameter means "six measures," which in English is most often translated as six feet. In the case of dactylic hexameter, six "fingers" would be more appropriate, because the dactylic measure is named for the three joints – one long, two short– that are found in the human finger. It is not a meter that works well in English, which uses stressed syllables rather than long and short ones, but English hexameter verses do exist. My favorite example is the opening line of Henry Wadsworth Longfellow's *Evangeline*,

"**This** is the **for**est prim**e**val, the **tow**ering **pines** and the **hem**locks,"
— ∪ ∪ / — ∪ ∪ /—∪∪/—∪∪/— ∪ ∪ /　　— —

a perfect specimen with five dactyls and a closing two-syllable measure called a spondee. (For the second long syllable of the spondee, think of your two top-finger segments as if they were in a splint: together they are roughly the length of the base segment as measured from fist joint to knuckle joint.) Spondees always conclude the hexameter verse, and depending on the effect the poet wants to produce and the vocabulary available, they can replace any other dactyl as well. For example, Longfellow's pines and hemlocks

> "**Stand** like **har**pers **hoar**, with **beards** that **rest** on their **bo**soms," (*Evangeline* 3).
> — — /   — — / — — /   — — /   — ∪ ∪ /   — —

This is a much slower verse with five spondees and only one dactyl. The single dactyl occurs in the fifth "finger," a location that normally resists spondees in classic hexameter verse. Phrases that consist of a noun plus characteristic adjective, or epithet, are the most striking examples of the oral-formulaic language that developed to fit this meter. Noun-epithet phrases like "wine-dark sea," "rosy-fingered Dawn" and "well-armed Akhaians" (to cite some of the more famous ones) provide ready-made phrases to fill half a hexameter verse in Greek. When a person is named, his or her name plus an epithet regularly fills the second half of the verse, one combination filling three and a half feet (for example, "the fleet-footed godlike Achilles," "the king of men Agamemnon," "much-suffering godlike Odysseus," "the goddess grey-eyed Athena"); another filling two and a half feet ("swift-footed Achilles," "strong Agamemnon," "resourceful Odysseus"), and yet another filling only the last two feet ("godlike Achilles," "crafty Odysseus"). Therefore, whether Odysseus is designated as "resourceful" or "much-suffering" in a particular passage, or whether the Akhaians are "well-armed or "flowing-haired," or Achilles is "swift-footed" or "godlike" may often be more a matter of meter than significance.

Some epithets, like "godlike" (*dîos*, literally "of Zeus" and often translated as "brilliant"), are used with many heroes, the only qualifications being important status and a metrically compatible name. Other epithets evoke qualities associated only or mainly with one hero, like the fleetness of Achilles, craftiness of Odysseus, and political power of Agamemnon. Achilles has three epithets unique to him denoting swiftness (*pódas ôkus, podarkês, podôkeos*); which allows this quality to be evoked in many metrical situations. Odysseus has four unique to him: three denoting craftiness (*polútropos, polumếchanos,* and *polúmetis*[1]) and one denoting his equally notable capacity to endure hardship (*polútlas*). Such unique noun-epithet phrases evoke a hero's full mythic identity when they are used. Indeed, *polútropos,* "resourceful" is apparently so identified with Odysseus that it can evoke him when coupled with "man" (*ándra*) instead of his name in the first line of the *Odyssey*.[2]

Meter also accounts for the three names used interchangeably for Greeks as a people. In the early stories, the Greek heroes would have been called Danaans or Akhaians – the Greek forms of Danaja and Achijawa – and also Argives, a name derived from the region of Argos, where Mycenae, the greatest Bronze Age Greek city, was located. As stories and songs accumulated over the centuries, these names remained in the epic poetry, each synonymous with Hellenes, the name the Greeks called themselves in classical times. Even after "Hellenes" supplanted them in common usage, all three names remained in the formal epic art language, providing three metrically different words to fill different parts of the hexameter line.

In addition to repeated noun-epithets, many scenes are repeated verbatim or nearly verbatim. Examples are messages that recount an event the audience has just "witnessed," introductions to speeches, scenes of a person being welcomed into a dwelling and offered hospitality, and scenes of sacrifice when an animal is killed and its meat prepared for eating. Such scenes not only aid the poet in his extemporaneous composing, but also give the audience its moral bearings in the traditional epic world that is being recreated for them. Some scenes, like those of putting on armor (for example, *Il.* 3.330–339, 11.16–45, and 19.364–391), follow strict patterns that both assist the singer and allow an audience steeped in the tradition to understand immediately how a particular detail marks a particular warrior as different from others. Some repeated phrases act as a kind of punctuation, guiding the audience's expectations. For example, as John Miles Foley has shown, the oft-repeated clause "Then when they had put away their desire for food and drink" (as at *Il.* 1.469) marks the end of a ritual of hospitality and the beginning of a (usually successful) attempt to resolve a problem.

Many stories about the Greek invasion and destruction of Troy were passed down in this oral-formulaic art language through generations of Greeks who were illiterate. Each version was new at the same time that it carried forward old truth. Let us listen to what the *Iliad* says about how the poet composes:

> Tell me now, Muses who dwell on Olympos –
> for you are divine, are everywhere and know everything,
> while we hear only a story (*kléos*) and know nothing, –
> who were the Danaan leaders and chiefs?
> I could not name nor describe the multitudes

not even if I had ten tongues, ten mouths,
an unbreakable voice and heart of bronze,
if the Olympian Muses, daughters of aegis-bearing Zeus,
should not tell me the number who came before Ilion.
                                             (*Il.* 2.484–492)

The immortal Muses witnessed what happened long ago at Troy, while people living today, including the poet, have heard only *kléos*, that is, fame preserved in epic verse, about what happened there. Muses represent divine inspiration, but the more prosaic among us today may think of the Muse as representing not only the master poet's genius, but also the medium he had mastered: the epic art language or tradition which had passed down stories of heroic forebears to succeeding generations of oral poets.

Between 700 and 400 BCE, many epics were composed in this art language and also written down. Although no other epic has survived, quotations, references, and summaries indicate that the poet of the *Iliad* and the *Odyssey* had a wealth of plots to choose from. In order to achieve the focus that made his poems so special to the Greeks and to all inheritors of their literature, Homer had to be highly selective. However, he would have presupposed his audiences' knowledge of all the other stories. Homer's Greek audiences would have known the entire group of stories associated with the Trojan War and would thus have appreciated even more than we do his consummate artistry. It is important therefore that modern audiences know the Trojan War Cycle from start to finish, both for appreciating the art of the *Iliad* and *Odyssey* and for understanding how later poets like Virgil and Ovid manipulate the tradition in their own Trojan War poems.

The Trojan War Epic Cycle

The story begins with the discovery by Zeus and Poseidon that Thetis, whom they were both courting, would bear a son greater than his father. Mindful of how Zeus had overthrown his father Kronos and how Kronos had overthrown his father Uranos, they decided that their lust for the lovely sea goddess was less important than maintaining the status quo in Olympos. They forthwith made arrangements with her father, the sea god Nereus, to have her marry a mortal so that their power would never be threatened. Some stories told how Peleus, the hero Zeus picked out for her, wrestled Thetis into submission, holding fast as she changed shape from beast to fire to water.

All the gods, both major and minor, were invited to the wedding of the goddess Thetis and the mortal hero Peleus. All were invited, that is, except Strife, who naturally came anyway. Striding in while the Olympians were seated at the wedding couple's banquet table, Strife threw onto the table a golden apple inscribed, "For the Fairest." Hera, Athena, and Aphrodite immediately claimed it as theirs and turned to Zeus to decide. Zeus, who possibly wanted to start a war as a means of population control and who certainly did not want to judge between his wife and daughters, deflected the decision onto a Trojan prince, who was at that moment shepherding sheep on a mountain slope.

The young judge was Paris Alexander, son of Priam King of Troy. Just before his birth, his mother Hekabe had dreamed that she gave birth to a firebrand. The dream was interpreted correctly as meaning the infant would grow up to destroy Troy, so the child was taken from his mother and left to die in the wilds. However, a shepherd found him and reared him as his son. Hence his availability to judge the goddesses' beauty on the slopes of Mount Ida.

The three goddesses approached Paris and showed him their beauteous selves. In addition, each also promised him a reward if he should choose her. Hera promised to make him the most powerful ruler on earth; Athena promised to make him wise and victorious in war; Aphrodite promised to make him husband of the most beautiful woman on earth. Paris, a man whose talents and inclinations lay more in the sensuous arts (see *Il.* 3.52–66), awarded the apple to Aphrodite. This episode, which is called the **Judgment of Paris**, accounts for Hera's and Athena's enduring hatred for Troy.

There was a problem with Aphrodite's promise: the most beautiful woman in the world already had a husband, a husband with a large army. She was Helen, offspring of Zeus's extramarital affair with Leda, wife of Tyndareus, king of Sparta. Helen's older sister Klytemnestra had married Agamemnon, the wealthy King of Mycenae, and Helen soon after had married his brother Menelaos, who thereby succeeded Helen's father as King of Sparta.

Because of Helen's unearthly beauty, and perhaps also because of the kingdom that was her dowry, she had been courted by every prince of Greece. Over fifty of them gathered at her father's court when she came of age, and he, fearing that the suitors would turn violent when he picked one of them to be her husband, made them all swear an oath to defend the chosen one's right to her. One tradition says that the idea for the oath had come from Odysseus, who though nominally Helen's suitor, actually had his eye on her cousin Penelope. The princes all swore, never thinking that their oath would later involve them in a foreign war.

Some years later Aphrodite, for whom marriage is never a constraint, fulfilled her promise to the young judge. Paris, who had by this time been reunited with his royal parents, managed to get himself sent to Sparta as an envoy from Troy. Menelaos, good host that he was, welcomed him, and then, a trusting sort, he left his beautiful wife and the handsome young prince together while he attended to business elsewhere. By the time he returned, Paris and Helen had fallen in love and eloped to Troy. This episode is often termed the **Rape of Helen**.

They took with them much treasure, which Helen may have regarded as her rightful dowry. In patriarchal Greece, however, women were not allowed to choose their own husbands and bestow their dowries to their liking, so the Greeks regarded Paris' act of carrying off Helen and her wealth as a grave breach of hospitality. In addition, all poets agree, it was a terrible blow to Menelaos' heart. Menelaos enlisted Agamemnon's help, and together they organized Helen's former suitors to get Helen back from Troy. After they had gathered all the oath-bound kings, they also enlisted Achilles, semidivine son of Thetis and Peleus, who had been only a child at the time of Helen's wedding.

Many adventures befell the Greeks on their way to Troy, adventures that Homer generally declines to evoke: for example, Odysseus' feigning insanity so as not to have to leave his wife and baby son; Agamemnon's sacrifice of his daughter Iphigeneia to Artemis in order to get the winds to blow the fleet to Troy; the sacking of Teuthrania, which was mistakenly thought to be Troy; Achilles' magically curing a wound he gave Telephos, king of Teuthrania, in exchange for Telephos guiding them to Troy. Other adventures that Homer does allude to are: the abandonment of Philoktetes, wielder of Herakles' bow, because of a disgusting incurable wound; and Achilles' sojourn on Skyros, where he begot his son Neoptolemos.

When the Greeks attempted to land at Troy, Hektor, eldest son of Priam, nearly repelled them by killing Protesilaos, the first hero ashore. Achilles saved the day by killing Kyknos, son of Poseidon, which made the Trojans flee back to the city. The Greek leaders tried diplomacy before besieging the city: Odysseus and Menelaos went to Priam's court and asked for Helen to be returned. Despite Odysseus' eloquence (see *Il.* 3.221–223), Priam yielded to Paris' wishes and refused, thus implicating Troy in Paris' moral error and ensuring its ultimate downfall.

During the first nine years of the siege, Achilles ambushed and killed Troilos, son of Priam, at Apollo's shrine outside the city, captured Aeneas' cattle, got Thetis to set up a meeting so that he could see Helen's beauty firsthand, restrained the Greek army from sailing home, and sacked twenty-one cities. From the spoils of one of these cities, Achilles received Briseis as his prize of honor; from the spoils of another, Agamemnon received Khryseis. Also during this time, Odysseus contrived the death of Palamedes, the man who had tricked him into revealing his sanity when Agamemnon's recruiters had come to Ithaka.

In the tenth year of the war, Achilles quarreled with Agamemnon and temporarily withdrew from the fighting. When he returned to the fighting, he killed Hektor, thereby eliminating Troy's greatest fighter. Next he killed Penthesileia, the fierce Amazon queen who arrived to help the Trojans. Soon afterwards he killed Thersites, a Greek rabble-rouser who taunted him for allegedly falling in love with Penthesileia. Then came a new Trojan ally, Ethiopian Memnon, who like Achilles was the son of a goddess (Dawn) and wore divine armor. After Memnon killed Nestor's young son Antilokhos, Achilles' friend, Achilles killed him. Memnon's mother, Dawn, then asked Zeus for immortality for her son and was granted it.

All the great Trojan champions were now dead, and it was Achilles' turn. As he pursued the Trojans to the gate of Troy, Apollo and Paris shot him with a fatal arrow. Odysseus fought off the Trojans while Ajax carried his body to the Greek ships. During his magnificent funeral, Nereids and Muses sang a lament, and then Thetis whisked Achilles' body off the pyre to immortality in the White Islands.

Notice that both goddess mothers secured immortality for their sons, just as Ninsun did in the original Sumerian Gilgamesh epics. These goddess mothers are not unique in Greek epic tradition. We know of another story that Athena granted immortality to Diomedes, and another that Zeus granted alternating immortality to Kastor and Polydeukes, Helen's brothers. Artemis also granted immortality to Iphigeneia when she was sacrificed by Agamemnon. In addition, Hesiod says that while some of the godlike heroes who participated in the Theban and Trojan Wars were overwhelmed by death, "Zeus gave others life apart from humankind . . . at the ends of earth/by deep-whirling Ocean, where they dwell without care/in the islands of the blessed, blissful heroes . . ." (*Works and Days* 167–172). Obviously immortality was not an uncommon fate for the half-divine heroes who fought and died in the epic tradition that preceded the Homeric poems. In the *Iliad* and *Odyssey*, however, immortality is not on the horizon for any hero except

Menelaos, who will get it only because he is the husband of Zeus's daughter (*Od.* 4.561–569).

Achilles' funeral games included the discus throw, chariot race, foot-race, and archery. The most important contest, however, was not athletic. Two contestants vied to be voted most valuable warrior and win the prize of Achilles' armour. Ajax, Achilles' cousin, argued it should be his because he was the strongest warrior now left to the Greeks and because he had carried Achilles' body out of the fighting. Odysseus argued it should be his because he had fought off the Trojans while Ajax was carrying the body and also because he was the smartest warrior. Odysseus won with the help of Athena, whereupon Ajax became so distraught that he went temporarily insane, attacked livestock, thinking the animals were the Greek leaders, and then committed suicide. This famous episode is called the **Judgment of Arms**.

With Achilles and Aias dead, Odysseus' strategic skills were fore-grounded: he traveled to Skyros and used Achilles' armor to entice Neoptolemos, Achilles' son, to join the Greek army; he retrieved Philok-tetes from his desert island when an oracle said the Greeks could not take Troy without him; he snuck into Troy disguised as a beggar and got information from Helen; and he snuck in again with Diomedes to steal the Palladium, a statue of Athena that would protect Troy as long as it stayed in its temple. Most importantly, with the help of Athena, Odysseus conceived the trick of the **Trojan Horse**: a huge wooden horse whose hollow belly was filled with Greek heroes. The Greek fleet sailed away to a nearby island, leaving one foot soldier behind to convince the Trojans that the Greeks had left for good. Despite Kassandra's warnings, the Trojans were fooled into believing that the horse was sacred to Athena and should be brought into the city. But while they were celebrating the end of the war, the Greek soldiers emerged, opened the gates to the army that had come back in the night, and proceeded to slaughter the drunk and sleeping Trojan men.

Many acts of hubris occurred during the final conquest and destruction of Troy. Neoptolemos killed Priam as he clung to the altar of Zeus. The Greek known as Locrian Ajax dragged Kassandra from Athena's altar and raped her. All the women and children were enslaved, all except the son of Hektor and Andromakhe, who was hurled from the battlements, and Polyxena, youngest daughter of Priam, who was sacrificed on Achilles' tomb. The city, including its temples, was burned to the ground. These extreme acts incurred the wrath of the gods, which pursued the perpetrators on their homeward journeys.

Paris had been killed by Philoktetes shortly after he returned to the Greek army, and Helen had then married Paris' brother Deiphobos. Suspicious, she visited the Trojan Horse with her new husband, calling out in the voice of each man's wife to see if she could evoke a response from within it. She failed only because of Odysseus' astuteness. Menelaos killed Deiphobos during the final night of slaughter, but when he turned to kill Helen, she bared her beautiful breasts and he dropped the sword. She accompanied Menelaos home where she became, once again, Queen of Sparta.

The stories in the Trojan War cycle did not end with the destruction of Troy. There was a whole category of Trojan War epic called the *nóstoi*, or "homeward journeys," which related the trials and tribulations of many heroes as they returned to their kingdoms. One of many violent storms raised by the gods' anger killed Locrian Aias in punishment for his hubris. Another storm destroyed most of Menelaos' fleet and drove him off course to Egypt, where he and Helen lingered for seven years. Agamemnon made it to Mycenae relatively quickly, but he was forthwith killed by his wife Klytemnestra and her lover Aigisthos; later his son Orestes avenged him. The *Odyssey*, which is Odysseus's own homecoming story, can evoke these other well-known *nóstoi* for comparison and contrast to its own hero's adventures. Indeed, it early on cues its audience to think in these terms by making Ithaka's own bard sing the "Sorrowful Homecoming of the Akhaians" in the palace from which Odysseus is still absent (*Od.* 1.36–37).

Not evoked in the *Odyssey* are stories in the *nóstoi* that included his fathering six postwar sons by four females: the goddesses Circe and Kalypso, a Thesprotian princess whom he "marries" for a while, and his wife Penelope. Odysseus' fruitfulness is in keeping with the general tendency in the non-Homeric epics to furnish widespread local audiences with links to heroic ancestors.[3] It is also in keeping with an apparent lack of interest in deep character development. In the non-Homeric epic world, Odysseus, the smartest warrior at Troy, was apparently simply a trickster figure, lacking the ethical compass that keeps him always focused on getting the war won in the *Iliad* and on getting home to Ithaka and his family in the *Odyssey*. Similarly, Achilles in the Epic Cycle appears to have been a superhuman warrior without any hint of the tragic choices he must make in the *Iliad*. The cyclic poems appear to have contained a romantic, magical, more-is-better world not dissimilar from the Sumerian epic that first immortalized Gilgamesh.

Ancient sources indicate that once the *Iliad* and *Odyssey* became recognized as masterpieces, other Trojan War epics were cropped or altered so as to lead either into or away from the episodes that Homer had chosen to develop. The eleven scrolls of the *Cypria*, which are probably named after an author from Cyprus, told of the genesis of the war and events leading up to the quarrel between Agamemnon and Achilles; the five scrolls of the *Aethiopis*, named after Ethiopian Memnon, told of events immediately subsequent to the *Iliad*, concluding with Achilles' death and funeral and possibly the suicide of Aias. The four scrolls of the *Little Iliad* and two of the *Sack of Ilion* told of the final events in the war. The *Nostoi*'s five scrolls told of all homecomings except Odysseus', which was left to Homer's *Odyssey*. The *Telegony*'s two contained a sequel to the *Odyssey*. The *Telegony*, which is almost certainly post-Homeric, became popular for its thrillingly dreadful fulfillment of the Odyssean prophecy that Odysseus' death would come "from the sea" (*Od.* 11.134): in it, Telegonos, son of Odysseus and Circe, comes to Ithaka to find his father, but in a case of mistaken identity kills him with a spear tipped with the barb of a sting ray. Telegonos then marries Penelope while Telemakhos marries Circe. This astonishing denouement apparently captured the popular imagination and doomed the *Thesprotia*, the earlier epic it was based on, to near oblivion.

The loss of these cyclic epics is greatly lamented by classicists, but perhaps need not be by the general reader. If Aristotle is to be believed, only Homer's *Iliad* and *Odyssey* qualify as masterpieces, and every other epic in existence in his day is either misnamed or fatally flawed.[4] What Aristotle meant by this is that Homer's plots are the only ones that resemble those of Athenian tragedy, which Aristotle felt was the highest art form. From the fragments that do exist it appears that epic cycle events were presented less dramatically; that is, they were narrated with fewer speeches, less emotion, and a flowing loosely structured action. Despite what may appear to be long digressions and, in the *Iliad*, endless battle scenes, both Homeric epics are tightly constructed. Both contain little that is extraneous to the main action: Achilles' tragic movement toward death in the *Iliad*, and in the *Odyssey*, Odysseus' progress toward reunion with his family and native city. In this they are as different from their forbears as the *Epic of Gilgamesh* is from the five Sumerian Gilgamesh poems.

The Gods

The human heroes of epic songs were taller, stronger, braver, handsomer, and occasionally smarter than contemporary men and women because they were more closely related to the gods via mothers or grandmothers (more rarely, fathers) who had been the objects of divine lust. The list of heroic superiorities, however, does not necessarily extend to morality. Indeed, the gods themselves were not usually portrayed as morally superior, but they were subject to the same passions as human beings and were woefully prone to believing that might makes right. Judging by extant stories and fragments, only three things could control divine or heroic will in the ancient tales: a physically stronger being, an oath, or a social compact. In the human world oaths were enforced by the gods, but social compacts only by peer pressure, which usually appears not to have been highly effective. The attempt to create a moral universe against this background will be part of the problem set by the poet(s) of the *Iliad* and *Odyssey*.

Although most of the gods are neither wiser nor more moral than human beings, they must be worshiped because it is they who shape the world – with plague, music, war, sex, wine, with storms, medicines, favoring or ill winds, healthy or sickly children, with inspiration and impulse, and so on. Sacrificing to the gods is a way of showing respect for all aspects of an unpredictable environment, an environment that somehow keeps life going despite the passing of individuals and generations. The gods' several wills, even as they clash, embody a kind of cosmic order that, even if not benevolent, is better than no order at all. Zeus, whose reign represents the final stability of the universe, is the only guarantor of human cultural codes, such as the necessity to respect the suppliant and atone for murder, theft and adultery.

Even Zeus's morality is called into question in the tragic world of the *Iliad*. Menelaos may be convinced that Zeus Xenios "Protector of Guest-Relations," will punish the Trojans for their failure to fear his wrath (*Il.* 13.623–625), but the audience knows that Zeus loves Troy no matter what its king has done and that what will destroy Troy is Hera's hate (*Il.* 4.17–49). The poet also makes it clear that Hera is willing to sacrifice her own three favorite cities in order to achieve vengeance for Paris' insulting decision (*Il.* 4.50–54). Humans can count on gods to retaliate when they or their priests are insulted or their favorites are killed, but they cannot count on what from the human perspective might be regarded as comprehensive justice from the gods. In the *Iliad*, it is almost entirely up to humankind to carve out its own codes of moral justice.

Although Zeus vindicates Achilles' just claim against Agamemnon, he does it not for the sake of justice, but because he owes Thetis a huge debt for her having saved him from being "bound" (the immortals' equivalent of death) by Hera, Athena, and Poseidon in the past (*Il.* 1.397–406). Zeus's intervention establishes Achilles' importance and value, but that is all. It is through his fellow humans – Nestor, Agamemnon, Phoenix, "Kalchas," unnamed Greek soldiers – and, above all, Achilles' own persuasive logic that Homer establishes the justice of his hero's cause.

In the *Iliad*, the partisan human-like passions that cause passing annoyance or joy on Olympos have drastic effects on the human beings with whom the gods are portrayed as totally preoccupied. The *Odyssey* is different. In a discussion at the beginning of the epic, the poet has Zeus deny that gods are responsible for human ills, and the poet makes sure that on the whole this is true. The *Odyssey* creates a more moral universe by limiting the number of important gods to two, Zeus and Athena, and making them guarantors of civilized values. Although Poseidon twice intervenes in the manner of the Iliadic gods, that is, for vengeance at cross-purposes with the hero's supporters, Athena and Zeus successfully mitigate his damage and make sure that virtue is rewarded. Warring gods do not add to the sorrow that continues to define human life; instead, Athena and Zeus acting in concert, intervene benevolently on behalf of Odysseus and his family. Here there is no doubt that Zeus's epithet Xenios, "Protector of Guest Relations" has force. Zeus's final intervention stops a civil war that has just begun, the very opposite of what he does in the *Iliad* when he yields to Hera's desire for revenge.

In both epics the gods frequently intervene in human affairs. Modern readers may feel that such intervention takes away characters' responsibility for their actions, but ancient Greek audiences did not interpret it that way. Every human action or thought is both natural to a particular human and is motivated by a specific god. What does it mean that Hera inspires Achilles rather than Agamemnon to call an assembly in Book 1? Basically, that Achilles has the qualities of a leader – intelligence and initiative – to know that an assembly is necessary, while Agamemnon does not. What does it mean that Athena grabs Achilles' hair as he is about to kill Agamemnon in the assembly? That Achilles has the inherent wisdom to take the more prudent or rational course of action. This is not to say that Athena is merely a symbol of Achilles' wisdom – she is a goddess who embroiders, weaves, drives chariots, fights, feasts, and hates – but there is a natural affinity between the goddess of Wisdom and a man prone to think things out before acting.

Does it remove blame from Pandaros that Athena persuades him to break the compact in *Iliad* Book 4? No. Athena targets Pandaros because he is the kind of man who would like the idea of underhandedly eliminating Menelaos in order to get a reward from Paris. He is, in other words, doubly motivated by his own nature and supernatural incitement.

We may feel a little queasy about Athena after this episode, but Pandaros must bear responsibility for his action. Similarly Achilles and all whom the gods help retain the credit for theirs.

The clearest example of the affinity that binds a human being and a particular god is the relationship between Athena and Odysseus in the *Odyssey*. Pleased at his having told her a strategic lie when she is in disguise, she affectionately asserts their similarity: "you by far surpass all mortals in strategy and stories and I am famous among all the gods for cleverness and cunning." She again approves when he says he doesn't trust her, declaring "This is why I cannot abandon you when you are in trouble: you are intelligent, shrewd, and self-controlled" (*Od.* 13.296–299, 331–332). Homeric double motivation is an archaic forerunner of the proverb, "God helps those who help themselves."

Throughout the *Iliad*, Homer deploys the deathless gods to heighten the seriousness of human action, as, for example, in Book 1 when he follows Achilles' and Agamemnon's deadly quarrel in the Greek camp with a comic one between Zeus and Hera in Olympos. I call it comic because it begins with Zeus, great king of the gods, worrying about his wife's nagging, develops into threats of nasty physical violence and fear, and ends in laughter, reconciliation, and sleep. The gods' quick shift from anger and fear to laughter acts as a foil to the human quarrel with its enduring emotional and physical consequences. It illustrates by means of contrast the deep implications of living a human rather than divine existence.

Many scenes of divine interaction in the *Iliad* have this comic and contrastive element. The *Odyssey*'s divine interactions are less frequent and more serious. There are three scenes on Olympos in which there are only two speakers, Zeus and Athena, who plan positive intervention in the human world. There is only one comic scene, and this is distanced from the main action by being put into a poem within the poem. I refer to the "Ballad of Aphrodite and Ares" by Demodokos, court bard of the Phaiakians, which presents a comic view of adultery. The worst that happens to Ares and Aphrodite and the clever husband, Hephaistos, who catches them *in flagrante*, is a few minutes of ridicule and embarrassment. This divine fable stands in stark contrast to the disaster that has ensued from the adultery of Klytemnestra and Aigisthos and the disaster that will ensue if Penelope takes another husband before Odysseus gets home. Like the Olympian scenes in the *Iliad*, it points up the difference in consequence between actions of beings who exist outside of time and those whose life is circumscribed by death.

The Homeric poems are totally focused on the human actors. The gods give these creatures of a day cosmic resonance, assuring them that what they do matters in a largely unfathomable universe. To rephrase John Milton, Homeric epic uses the gods to justify the ways of man to man.

Note on Spelling of Proper Names

Traditionally, Greek proper names came into English through Latin, whose alphabet does not contain all the Greek letters and whose common word endings are different. Greek uses K instead of C, and since the Latin C is pronounced K, it was easy to make this substitution: Hektor simply became Hector. The masculine ending in Greek is -os, that in Latin is -us, which also makes for easy substitution: Patroklos becomes Patroclus. Sometimes the ending changes slightly more: Meleagros becomes Meleager. In all the above cases, I retain the retain the Greek spelling.

In other names, substitution produces substantial changes in how names are pronounced in English. For example, C in combination with E and I is always pronounced K in Latin, but in English we pronounce it as if it were an S, as in "certain" and "circumstance." The Greek X (pronounced KH) became "CH" in Latin (for example, Telemakhos became Telemachos). In English, where ch is normally pronounced softly as in "children," this shift creates a problem for the unwary. With the most well-known names like Circe and Achilles, I use the Latin spelling, but with lesser known names like Telemakhos and Andromakhe, I use k or kh to indicate the best pronunciation.

Latin transliterates the Greek I as either I or J depending on whether it is used as a consonant (Y) or vowel and also on the letter that precedes and follows it. The English J is always pronouned "je," and thus Iason, the leader of the Argonauts, becomes Jason, Troian becomes Trojan, and Aias becomes Ajax. The dipthong "ai" (pronounced "aye") becomes "ae" in Latin, which in English rhymes with "nay" or "ski"). Thus Aineias, son of Aphrodite, becomes Aeneas. With well-known names, I use the Latin.

Further Reading

John Miles Foley, ed., *A Companion to Ancient Epic* (Oxford, 2005) and Robert Fowler, ed., *The Cambridge Companion to Homer* (Cambridge, 2004) offer excellent collections of essays by leading scholars on all aspects of the Homeric poems. Barry Powell's *Homer* (Oxford, 2004) offers an accessible and comprehensive introduction to Homeric epic that is especially interesting on the history of the texts and Homeric language. Powell also offers an extensive well-annotated bibliography for further reading.

History and Archeology

For a well-documented argument that the *Iliad* reflects an historical Trojan War see Joachim Latacz, *Troy and Homer: Towards a Solution to an Old Mystery (Oxford, 2005)*. Susan Sherrat's "Archaeological Contexts" does not accept the historicity of the Trojan War, but gives an excellent account of how and when different items entered the epic tradition (in Foley 2005:119–141). Robin Osborne's "Homer's society" also gives an excellent summary of the differing sociopolitical systems that made contributions to the poems (in Fowler, 2004:206–219). Walter Burkert's *The Orientalizing Revolution: Near Eastern Influence on Greek Culture in the Early Archaic Age*, translated by M. E. Pinder, (Cambridge, MA, 1992) and Martin West's *The East Face of Helicon: West Asiatic Elements in Greek Poetry and Myth* (Oxford, 1997) give full accounts of how and when material from West Asia entered Greek culture. Part I of Barry Powell's *Homer* (Oxford, 2004) presents examples of what early Homeric texts looked like and gives useful background on bards, religion, and civic life. Ian Morris presents a picture of what Homer's late eighth-century audience was like in "The Strong Principle of Equality and the Archaic Origin of Greek Democracy," in *Dēmokratia*, J. Ober and Ch. Hendrick, eds. (Princeton, 1996), 19–48. Two archaeological works that are easily accessible are *Troy c. 1700–1250 BC* by N. Fields, D. Spedaliere and S. Sulemsohn Spedaliere (Oxford, 2004), which illustrates its findings about the history of Troy's fortifications with excellent drawings and photographs, and *A Guide to the Palace* of Nestor, *Mycenaean Sites in its Environs, and the Chora Museum* by C. W. Blegen, M. Rawson, J. L. Davis, and C. W. Shelmerdine (Princeton, NJ, 2001), which illuminates Mycenaean life with the help of watercolor reconstructions by Piet de Jong and numerous photographs of landscape and artifacts.

Oral Formulaic Poetry

To read more about the significance of repeated scenes such as lamentation and feasting, the signification of groupings of words that form 'words', and how the name-epithet combination often summons up the full traditional biography of a hero, see J. M. Foley, *Homer's Traditional*

Art (University Park, PA, 1999). M. Nagler's *Spontaneity and Tradition* (Berkeley and Los Angeles, 1979) is also excellent on this subject. The groundbreaking work of Milman Parry has been collected and brilliantly introduced by his son Adam in *The Making of Homeric Verse: the Collected Works of Milman Parry* (Oxford, 1971).

Epic Cycle

M. L. West discusses and beautifully translates all surviving fragments in *Greek Epic Fragments from the Seventh to the Fifth Centuries BC*, Loeb Classical Library vol. 497 (Cambridge, MA, 2003). J. S. Burgess, *The Tradition of the Trojan War in Homer & the Epic Cycle* (Baltimore, MD, 2001), argues convincingly on the basis of art and references in other literature that the stories in the Epic Cycle existed independently of the Homeric poems before the poems in which they originally appeared were cropped to fit around the *Iliad* and *Odyssey*. He argues that a story of the wrath of Achilles against Agamemenon existed in the *Kypria*, but Homer took it and developed it at length in a more realistic style. Burgess gives a nice summary of his argument about the Cycle in Foley (2005), 344–352. In *Poetry as Performance: Homer and Beyond* (Cambridge, 1996), Gregory Nagy uses two Greek metaphors, weaving and carpentry, to analyze the epic tradition; he takes the original meaning of "cycle" as a chariot wheel and makes a convincing argument that when applied to groupings of epic poetry it is a metaphor from the master carpenter's art of joining.

Jasper Griffin's pioneering article "The Epic Cycle and the Uniqueness of Homer," *Journal of Hellenic Studies* 97 (1977), 39–53 offers a somewhat outdated but still outstanding comparison between the episodic style and romantic content of the Cycle poems versus the more realistic, tightly structured Homeric ones. Gregory Nagy, *Best of the Achaians: Concepts of the Hero in Archaic Greek Poetry* (Baltimore, 1979), 168–207, discusses and contrasts the immortality of traditional epic heroes as described by Hesiod and other poets with the fate of heroes in the *Iliad* and *Odyssey*.

Susan Woodford's *The Trojan War in Ancient Art* (Ithaca, 1993), H.A. Shapiro's *Myth into Art. Poet and Painter in Classical Greece* (London and New York, 1994), M. J. Anderson's *The Fall of Troy in Early Greek Poetry and Art* (Oxford, 1997), and A. M. Snodgrass's *Homer and the Artists: Text and Picture in Early in Greek Art* (Cambridge, 1998) provide excellent reproductions and discussions of ancient vase paintings that illustrate incidents from the Epic Cycle and Homeric poems. Margaret R. Scherer's *The Legends of Troy in Art and Literature* (Phaidon Press for the Metropolitan Museum of Art, 1963), which is out of print but still available used, offers reproductions of art from classical Greece and Rome through the Middle Ages and Renaissance to the 1950s as well as discussions of literature and music based on Trojan themes.

The Gods

Richard Janko, *The Iliad: A Commentary, vol. III: Books 13–16* (Cambridge, 1992) has an excellent section on the gods and double motivation. W.F. Otto's *The Homeric Gods*, translated by M. Hadas (New York, 1954), is no longer in print, but it is worth tracking it down in a library or used bookstore. Jasper Griffin's *Homer on Life and Death* (Oxford, 1980) offers useful chapters on the gods and on religion in the *Iliad*, as does Seth Schein's *The Mortal Hero* (Berkeley, 1984).

Notes

1   Odysseus shares this one with the god of crafts, Hephaistos (*Il.* 21.355).
2   This epithet occurs only twice in the *Odyssey*, but since the poet can delay naming the hero until line 21, it must have been joined firmly with Odysseus in the tradition. Scanning short-long-short short, for metrical reasons *polutropos* must be separated from the name Odysseus (short-long-long), which makes it less useful than the other words denoting craftiness. *Polútlas*, "much-suffering" or "much-enduring," occurs 42 times, while epithets denoting craftiness occur 110 times.
3   Hesiod's *Theogony* (1011–1018) alludes to two sons by Kalypso and two by Circe. Other sons appeared in the *Thesprotia*, which told of Penelope's giving birth to Ptoliporthes ("Citysacker") and probably recounted the birth of Polypoites, future king of Thesprotia, during Odysseus' sojourn with the Thesprotian princess Kallidike. Later, possibly after the Homeric poems had gained prominence in the sixth century, Eugammon, a poet from Cyrene, adapted the *Thesprotia*, renaming it the *Telegony*, after the new name of Odysseus' (single) son from Circe, and renaming the son of Odysseus and Penelope *Arkesilaos* to please a line of Cyrenian kings named Arkesilas (see Burgess, 2001, p. 11).
4   A later "biography" of Homer indicates that four poets were ranked along with Homer as the "most powerful" writers of epic. Of these poets, Aristotle would not rank Hesiod's didactic *Works and Days* and genealogical *Theogony*, which survive in substantial portions, as epic poems; he seems to rank Pisander's and Panyassis's, epics about Herakles as grossly inferior (*Poetics*, 1451a); and he does not mention Antimakhos or his *Thebaid*, which was ranked just after the *Iliad* and *Odyssey* by Pausanias (*Description of Greece* 9.9.5).

3

The *Iliad*

Sing, goddess, the wrath of Achilles, Peleus's son,
deadly wrath that caused the Akhaians thousandfold woes;
it sent countless strong souls to Hades, souls of
heroes, and rendered their bodies spoil for dogs
and birds to dine on; and the plan of Zeus was fulfilled.
[Start] from where those two stood hostile, quarreling,
Son of Atreus, king of men, and godlike Achilles.

(*Il.* 1.1–7)

Wrath is the first word of the epic and the *Iliad*'s subject. Compare the *Epic of Gilgamesh*, whose first words ("He who knew the depths . . .") indicate that the epic will be celebrating the cultural achievements of an extraordinary man.[1] The *Iliad* does not ask the Muse to celebrate the man who brought victory to the Greeks by killing Hektor, but instead focuses on a deadly emotion that greatly harmed Greek society. Instead of producing cultural achievement, Achilles' wrath makes human bodies into "dinner" for animals, thus confusing friend and enemy, nature and culture.

Achilles' wrath also confuses human and divine. It is not just heroic wrath but *mênis*, "divine wrath," an absolute, punishing anger experienced in epic poetry only by gods – mostly Apollo and Zeus – aside from Achilles. *Mênis* communicates Achilles' strong link with the gods, but its immediate association with human death and cultural implosion signals the epic's concern with the fragility of human life and culture. The hero's divine potential, inherited from his goddess mother, will be trumped by his humanity: his own mortality and that of the people he loves. Despite constant contact between gods and human beings, in the *Iliad* the gap between mortal and immortal is ultimately unbridgeable, and as in the *Epic of Gilgamesh*, this gap turns turns linkage between human and divine into a tragic condition.

The poet aligns the deadly results of Achilles' *mênis* with the plan of Zeus. Although important action is always credited to the gods by characters who seek to explain the inexplicable, the solemn coda invoking Zeus does more than merely explain. It elevates the poem's action and hero to cosmic importance, and it assures the audience that Zeus will in fact vindicate Achilles in his quarrel with Agamemnon. At the same time, for an audience steeped in traditional epic poetry, information that countless deaths fulfill "the plan of Zeus" may evoke a troubling idea from the legendary beginning of the war. According to an ancient commentator, Zeus started the Trojan War as a strategy to control population, and when "heroes kept being killed in Troy, the plan of Zeus was fulfilled" (Scholia to *Il*. 1.5). The "plan of Zeus" therefore implies both a strategy to honor Achilles and one that serves a dire purpose indifferent to the hero.

The concluding lines of the proem pinpoint the origins of the wrath in what was probably a well-known quarrel between Achilles and Agamemnon. The poet juxtaposes traditional name-epithet formulae – "king of men" and "godlike" – to create a quarrel between a man who possesses supreme social power and a man with supreme personal ability. He thus sets up an opposition between external and internal value, inherited social position and innate worth. Subsequent events will reveal the political problem that this opposition embodies: there is a disjunction in the Greek army between political power and ability. In an ideal world, the most able man would also be the supreme leader, and there would be no contest between the "king of men" and the "best of the Akhaians" (1.243–244, 411–412; 16.273–274).

The Quarrel

The Greek audience would have been familiar with Achilles' extraordinary martial prowess, which would have been quite enough to certify his status as "best of the Akhaians" in tradition.[2] The *Iliad*, however, explores "best" in ways that put the political question at the center of Achilles' and the Greeks' unfolding tragedy. Book 1 does this partially by contrasting Achilles' proactive behavior on behalf of the community with the passivity and self-serving behavior of Agamemnon.

Agamemnon's first action in the epic is to abuse a suppliant, dishonor a priest, and counteract the wishes of his community (1.22–32). The result is an entirely predictable disaster: Apollo punishes the dishonor with a plague that rages for nine days while Agamemnon does nothing. It is not the commander in chief, but Achilles, inspired by Hera, who calls an assembly and asks the Greek priest of Apollo, Kalkhas, the cause of Apollo's *mênis* and what they can do to appease it (1.55–67). Then, when Kalkhas reveals that the remedy for dishonoring Apollo's priest is to return the daughter without ransom and perform a costly sacrifice of one hundred animals, Agamemnon's response is violent anger and name-calling (1.103–108).

Although Agamemnon agrees to give the woman back so that the army won't perish, in the next breath he creates a new crisis for the community by demanding immediate compensation from the army in the form of a replacement "gift of honor." By this he means he wants another talented beautiful noblewoman captured from one of the cities that the Greeks, led by Achilles, had conquered. This demand provokes a heated response from Achilles, who calls him a "supremely greedy," "utterly shameless," "dog-faced" "king-who-devours-the-community" (1.122, 149, 158–159, 231). Achilles' extreme response is understandable only when the full implications of Agamemnon's demand are understood.

The word *géras*, which I translate above as "gift of honor," denotes an item that has value beyond its intrinsic worth because the community awards it to individuals (including respected elders, royalty, great warriors, and the dead) as their due. For example, when the spoils of a conquered city were divided, each leader would receive a *géras* by common consent. This *géras* confers *timé* – the honor or prestige that gives meaning to and increases the enjoyment of what would otherwise be a purely biological life. We see how it works when, in the middle of battle, two Trojans pause before making a final push toward the Greek camp. Sarpedon reminds his friend Glaukos that their people honor them with "the best seats, meat, and drink" because they "confront scorching battle . . . in the forefront" (12.310–321). Since their lives are short, they must enjoy them to the full by obtaining *timé*: "if there were a possibility of living forever," he says, "I wouldn't urge you to fight in the foreranks, but since a human being cannot escape death at some point, let us go" (12.322–328). Meaning comes to the lives of heroes through the admiration and material things, the *timé*, that their community awards them.

Timé contributes not only to the enjoyment of life but also to the hero's desired form of immortality after death. The Homeric afterlife is a state in which ghosts wander about longing to be among the living; heroes retain some power to affect the actions of the living through their *kléos*. Though often translated as "fame" or "glory," *kléos* is more accurately "a story in epic song about admirable achievement." In the *Iliad* it refers strictly to stories of how a hero has won *timé*. All heroes, therefore, strive for *timé*, and the Greek heroes at Troy depend on their community of fellow warriors to make sure that their achievements receive the value they deserve. *Timé*, often awarded in the form of a *géras*, is the glue that holds the society of warrior princes together.

When Agamemnon demands that the Greeks immediately find him another *géras* because it is not "fitting" that he be the only leader without one (1.135–139), Achilles asks him to wait until they sack Troy because it would not be "fitting" for the community to take back an already awarded *géras* in order to find him one (1.123–129). Agamemnon continues to insist on immediate compensation, threatening first to take Odysseus', Ajax's, or Achilles' own *géras*. In effect claiming that what is right for him overrides what is right for the group, Agamemnon's threat, if successful, would seriously compromise the system of communal valuation that turns possessions into *timé*.

The *Iliad*'s audience would have known that Achilles, unlike other warriors bound by their oath to Helen's father, came to Troy solely to win *timé* and *kléos*. The poet underscores Achilles' voluntary presence in the Greek army by having the hero say explicitly that he has no quarrel with the Trojans and came only as a favor to win *timé* for Agamemnon and his brother (1.150–160). When Achilles questions why he or anyone should continue to fight under Agamemnon's leadership, he begins a theme that will be explored repeatedly in Books 2–8 and developed more fully in Book 9: what motivates men to fight this war? Now he says, "If I am to be without *timé*, I do not think I will stay to heap up riches and wealth for you" (1.170–171).

Agamemnon's response evokes what appears to be a traditional theme of contention between the commander in chief and his most powerful warrior. "Cut and run if you want to," sneers Agamemnon, "others will stay and give me honor, especially Zeus." He belittles the divine genes that give Achilles his personal power and claims the highest divinity, Zeus, as the source of his own more consequential political power (1.173–178). To prove his greater power, he asserts that he will personally take the woman Briseis, Achilles' *géras*, for himself. His avowed purpose for doing this is to establish his superiority "so that other men will shrink from addressing me as an equal and vying with me face to face" (1.182–185).

Kings are supposed to accept criticism in assemblies. In a later assembly Diomedes prefaces strong criticism of Agamemnon with "I will be the first to combat your foolishness, King, as is customary in assembly. Do not get angry" (9.32–33). Nestor also reminds Agamemnon that a king should "both speak and listen, and act on the advice of another whenever [he speaks] for our welfare" (9.100–102). Agamemnon's denial of equal speech to Achilles, therefore, is another example of his grossly deficient leadership skills.

Achilles accuses the other leaders, in addition to Agamemnon, of destroying both the space in which everyone has a right to speak and also the system that gives value to deeds. The elderly Nestor, who represents the wisdom of long tradition, may try to dissuade Agamemnon, but he still yields to him (1.280–281). Achilles calls the other kings "nothings" (1.231) because they surrender their right to disagree; he refuses to become that kind of "nothing" (1.293). For allowing Agamemnon to take his *géras*, he condemns them all with "you (plural) take her who gave her" (1.299). The destruction of these social systems motivates Achilles' choice to leave the Greeks to destruction by withdrawing from the battle and requesting Zeus to help the Trojans (1.240–244 and 1.408–412).

Achilles has more at stake in preserving communal custom than do his fellows, for his goddess mother has told him that if he chooses to fight at Troy he will die there. The other heroes risk their lives but still hope for homecoming. Achilles has only the expectation of *kléos*, the story of how he won great *timē* as the Greeks' greatest fighter.

Homer waits until Book 9, after many moving descriptions of young men dying, to make Achilles' choice explicit. In response to the embassy from Agamemnon, he says,

> if I remain here and fight around the city of Troy, my homecoming is lost, but I will have undying *kléos*; if, on the other hand, I go home to my own country, my noble *kléos* is lost, but I will live a very long life. (9.412–416)

Achilles had chosen a short life with immortal *kléos* when he chose to come to Troy. Corruption of the system of *timē* has reopened the subject.

When the embassy from Agamemnon arrives, Achilles is singing and playing a beautiful lyre taken from the spoils of a sacked city, pleasuring his heart with epic lays, the "*kléa* (plural of *kléos*) of men" (9.186–189). Since *kléa* are exemplary stories of previous heroes meant to influence the actions of living heroes (compare Phoinix's "*kléa* of heroic men" at 9.524–525), we can envision Achilles' singing as equivalent to reviewing

Greek cultural history to help him understand his present situation. This intensely private singing exemplifies the paradox of Achilles' situation – he is alienated from his community because he is, or was, committed to its professed values. It functions as a prelude to Achilles' working out in the embassy scene the answer to an urgent question: is there any kind of *kléos* worth dying for?

A story about gaining possessions is emphatically not worth the sacrifice of his life (9.401–409). Because Agamemnon has not returned his *géras* with an apology but is merely offering Briseis and other gifts as an incentive for future action, Achilles has good reason to assert that "the coward and the brave have the same *timé*, and both die alike" (9.318–320). Recognizing what is unspoken in Odysseus' speech, that the offer requires him to "yield" to Agamemnon as the "superior king" (9.160), Achilles refuses to be, in essence, a mercenary, subject to a paymaster.

Achilles moves on to the justice of the war as a possible motivation for fighting. Achilles draws a parallel between Menelaos's loss of Helen and his own loss of Briseis, terming the latter his "wife" and asking, "Why must the Argives fight with the Trojans? Was it not on account of fair-haired Helen? Are the sons of Atreus the only ones who love their wives?" (9.336–340). His answer to the last question – a strong declaration that he deeply loved Briseis in the same way "every good and sensible man loves and cares for his wife" (9.341–343) – creates two effects. First, it marks Achilles as a man capable of true affection in contrast to Agamemnon, who clearly does not love and care for his own wedded wife (1.112–119). More importantly, it creates a parallel between Agamemnon and Paris that shifts the argument to a principled one about the purpose of the war.

Achilles' words likening Agamemnon's action to Paris' imply a moral equation between Greek and Trojan. This shift from chauvinist to universal thinking reflects the wide vision of the poem as a whole, but it isolates Achilles further from his community. Ajax, for example, cannot understand why he stays so angry over "one young woman" while being offered "seven excellent ones" (9.636–638). Rejecting his society's apparently arbitrary definitions of right and wrong and finding nothing that would impel him to return to the Greek army, Achilles declares he will return home on the morrow (9.356–363, 428–429).

Phoinix, Achilles' former tutor, attempts to change Achilles' mind. He asks Achilles to honor Prayers of Entreaty, personified as daughters of Zeus, and begs him to give up his *ménis* in return for the gifts Odysseus has enumerated (9.496–524). He concludes with a story drawn from the *kléa* of ancient heroes, a story intended to illustrate the wisdom of giving up righteous anger in return for magnificent gifts. Achilles, however, draws a different lesson from the story.

The story is that of Meleagros, who was cursed by his mother when he killed her brother during a struggle over who was to be awarded the head of the giant Kalydonian Boar. When Meleagros withdrew because of the deadly curses, the quarrel spread to an attack on his city, and no amount of promised gifts and entreaties from town elders, kin, or friends could get him to fight. Not until the attackers set fire to the city towers did Meleagros yield to his wife's personal plea to stave off destruction. At that point, the city was saved, but Meleagros no longer had any claim to the gifts. Phoinix advises Achilles not to be like Meleagros, not to wait until the ships are burning to change his mind and fight without gifts, for then his *timé* will be less (9.529–605).

Although Achilles replies that he doesn't need the Greeks' *timé* since he has Zeus's, his purpose is affected by Phoinix's pleas. After sternly telling the old man not to "confuse his mind with lamenting and groaning," he adds, "when dawn comes we will consider whether we will go home or stay" (9.607–619). Then, after agonizing over Ajax's later appeal to ties of friendship, he specifically chooses to follow Meleagros' example. Achilles cannot fight to save his friends since that would mean yielding to the hateful Agamemnon, but he will await the Trojan champion Hektor by his own ships. If Hektor gets close enough to set fire to a Myrmidon ship, Achilles will join battle with him there. In other words, the *kléos* for which he will be willing to exchange his normal life span is a story about conquering a personal enemy, not a communal one (9.650–655).

As it turns out, that personal motivation will be not fire on his ships but grief for his beloved friend, Patroklos, whose name is almost identical to that of Meleagros' wife, Kleopatra. The choices that lead up to this grief will all stem from the compassion for friends that Achilles overtly rejects as sufficient motivation to rejoin the army when Ajax asks. Concern over a wounded friend (11.601–614) will begin a sequence of events that will result in Patroklos' begging Achilles to help the Greeks as Hektor fires Ajax's ship (16.30–45). Torn between his human sympathies and his ideals, Achilles will make the tragic choice to allow Patroklos to wear his armor to scare the Trojans off. Once in that armor, gentle Patroklos will turn into a fighting machine, ignore Achilles' orders to return as soon as the Trojans retreat, and be killed near the Trojan wall by Apollo and Hektor. Achilles' new quarrel with Hektor will make the original quarrel over who is "best of the Akhaians" irrelevant to him.

Motivations for War

"Why should anyone follow avaricious Agamemnon?" asks Achilles in Book 1. "Why should anyone fight in this war?" he asks in Book 9. Questions of leadership and motivation for fighting appear to be also on the mind of the poet, who returns frequently to these issues in the books leading up to Achilles' decision making in Book 9. Books 2–8, which introduce the Greek and Trojan armies and plunge into actual warfare, depict the supreme leaders, Agamemnon and Priam, as incompetent and out of touch with their people, and they reveal that no one, except an elite group at the top of each hierarchy, believes this war is worth its cost. By frequently raising the vain possibility that the war can be stopped, the poet can present a wide variety of motivations and reasons for its continuance. Desire for *timé* and reward, passion for revenge, and fear of punishment are the aggressors' motivations; familial love and desire to protect homes motivate the defenders. Since the poet is careful to disconnect these motivations from larger issues of right or wrong, the audience's response to them will depend for the most part on their own culturally conditioned views of what a war is worth fighting for.

Motivations: The Greek Army

In Book 2, Zeus sends Agamemnon a false dream that tells him exactly what he wants to believe: he will take Troy the very next day. "Fool," comments the poet (2.38), and, indeed, subsequent events show how divorced from reality the king is. When Agamemnon tests the army's spirit by advising them to accept the shame and bad *kléos* of defeat and go home, his thinly disguised appeals to honor go unheeded as almost everyone, noble and commoner alike, immediately runs for the ships.

Then, says the poet, all would have been lost if Hera and Athena had not inspired Odysseus to act. Odysseus grabs Agamemnon's scepter, the explicit symbol of Zeus-sanctioned authority (2.100–108), and uses it to stop the stampede. Threats about the potential anger of the king it represents are enough to stop the upper-class warriors from fleeing, but with the common people Odysseus wields the scepter as a physical weapon, striking them with it as he orders them to listen to their betters (2.198–199). In addition to illustrating the class hierarchy of the epic world, this use of the scepter demonstrates that inherited authority, even when divinely sanctioned, is powerless when not supported by compelling physical force.

Odysseus uses the scepter again against Thersites, a man who likes to amuse the Greeks by constantly railing at those in authority.[3] Despite his ugly character and body, every reproach Thersites hurls at Agamemnon strikes home, and there is no possible refutation except to deprive him of the authority to speak (2.255–266). The scene thus functions as a foil to the quarrel in Book 1, further illustrating the failure of Agamemnon's autocratic leadership. Using the golden scepter to raise a graphic welt on Thersites' back and reduce him to tears, Odysseus does to this weak comic "Achilles" what Agamemnon could not to the real Achilles.

After this display of physical force, Odysseus deploys his persuasive power, recalling a long-ago omen that signified the Greeks would take Troy in this very year. Nestor takes up the cause next, offering both a carrot and a stick to keep the men focused on the war: he first reminds them that there will be Trojan widows to rape and then threatens to kill anyone who tries to leave (2. 354–359). At long last Agamemnon enters the conversation: he commends Nestor, tells the men to eat and get ready for battle, and concludes with a more extreme version of Nestor's threat: anyone who lingers by the ships will become food for birds and dogs (2.391–393).

The repeated physical coercion creates the impression that there is not much popular support for the war among the Greeks. The common people fight only because they are forced to. Upper-class warriors may fight to maintain their status by winning *timé* and *kléos*, but even they are forced to fight: they fear Agamemnon and would have to pay a fine if they chose not to be part of the army (13.669–670). This fine, which is mentioned only once, may reflect the oath that obligates them to Helen's husband. Although the poem does not mention the oath specifically, it implies twice that if Menelaos dies everyone will leave (4.155–182, 5.565–567). It is obvious that with no Greek husband to claim her, Helen's former suitors will be released from their oath, and in that case desire for *timé* and *kléos* will not be sufficient to keep them in Troy.

Although Agamemnon and other Greeks several times refer to Zeus's promised victory, only Menelaos expresses Zeus's promise in terms of justice. In Book 13 he declares that Zeus *Xenios*, "Zeus Protector of Guest-Relations," will destroy the city of the "evil Trojan dogs" because they failed to fear his *ménis* (13.623–625). But a previous conversation between Zeus and Hera undercuts this moral certitude. In Book 4, once the duel between Paris and Menelaos has taken place, Zeus proposes ending the war. If everyone could agree, he suggests, "the city of King Priam might remain habitable and Menelaos might take Argive Helen home" (4.17–19). Hera and Athena emphatically do not agree. "What?!" Hera fumes, "Waste all my efforts to bring evil to Priam and his children?" To which Zeus expresses wonder that losing a contest could matter so much: "What great evil has Priam done to you to merit your determination to destroy his city?" He suggests that her anger would be appeased only if she could "eat Priam, his children, and all Trojans raw" (4.35–36). This statement, which Hera does not deny, confounds divine will with bestial instinct, bypassing cultural codes entirely. Despite his claiming to honor Troy and Priam above all other cities, Zeus immediately yields (4.37–49), and his yielding is specifically said to be a gift to her, not a matter of justice. Unlike the Zeus of Hesiod (compare *Works and Days*, 256–273), the *Iliad*'s Zeus is not a figure of justice, and the Trojans are apparently not guilty of failing to fear his wrath. What keeps the war going is Hera's primal hate.

Motivations: The Trojan Army

The Greeks may not be fighting a just war, but Troy is not therefore innocent. Paris is guilty of a grave breach of hospitality, and Priam is guilty of allowing Paris to keep Helen. Homer emphasizes this guilt by having them repeat in Books 4 and 7 the choices they originally made at the beginning of the war. Troy's guilt, however, is limited to its ruler, one of his sons, one courtier named Antimakhos, whom Paris corrupted at the beginning of the war, and Paris' fellow archer Pandaros. Hektor and the mass of Trojans are kept carefully separate from Paris' criminal breaches of social compacts.

The very first words the poet puts into Hektor's mouth denounce his brother Paris as "a woman-mad cheat," whom he wishes "had never been born and had died unmarried" (3.39–42). Hektor reproaches Paris for carrying off a woman who has spear-fighting in-laws, "a great pain for your father, your city and the whole populace, a joy to enemies, and shame for yourself" (3.46–51). "Were the Trojans not so fearful," he concludes, "you would be clothed in stones for the great wrong you have done" (3.57–58). Hektor's dislike is so strong that he speaks similarly even before their mother, adding, "If only I might see him enter Hades, then I could say my heart had been freed from its wretched anguish" (6.281–285).

Every Trojan except Paris' father Priam seems to share this view. When Paris and Menelaos agree to end the war by dueling for Helen, an event that reprises what would likely have happened at the beginning of the war, both Greeks and Trojans pray Zeus to give death to "whichever of the two men is to blame for the war" (3.320–322). Since the Trojans know that Paris is to blame, this prayer confirms Hektor's wish for his death. Further confirmation comes after the duel. After Aphrodite whisks the about-to-be-killed Paris off the battlefield and into Helen's bed, Homer indicates that the Trojans want Menelaos to find him, "for to all of them he was as hateful as black death" (3.451–454).

Although the vast majority of Trojans hate Paris, Athena finds one Trojan leader, Pandaros, who is willing to curry favor with the prince by shooting an arrow at Menelaos (4.94–99). Thus hostilities restart. Later, in Book 7, the Trojans hold a council to decide what to do about the oath Priam swore to return Helen and all the wealth taken with her if Paris lost the duel. In this council, "sensible" Antenor urges that they return Helen and her treasure so as not to falsify their oaths (7.347–353). When Paris, however, refuses to give up Helen, agreeing only to return the treasure and pay Menelaos extra compensation, Priam makes the fateful decision to let Paris have his way (7.362–378). Idaios, the Trojan herald, adds his own commentary when he reports this decision to Menelaos and Agamemnon: "Paris is willing to give back the treasure he brought to Troy – *would that he had died first*," but he will not give back Menelaos' wife, "*although the Trojans are asking him to*" (7.389–393). The second comment creates a parallel between Paris and Agamemnon – like Paris, Agamemnon's refusal to heed community sentiment and return a woman has caused and will cause his community huge loss of life – and it thus prepares the way for Achilles' explicit analogy between the two as wife snatchers. As in Hesiod, the Trojan people, like the Greek soldiers, must pay for the recklessness of their kings (*Works and Days* 260–261).

The Trojans' motive for fighting is reluctant self-defense. They are not fighting to keep Helen in Troy; they are fighting because Priam's acquiescence to Paris has brought a huge army against them. The omen of victory that Odysseus recalls in Book 2, in which the Trojans are analogous to pitiful sparrows eaten by the a terrible blood-red snake (308–316) portrays the Trojan people as unfortunate victims of the devouring strength of the Greek army. Despite the guilt that taints and dooms their city, this dreadful omen, together with the poet's insistence on their innocence, makes the Trojans highly sympathetic as they arm for battle in Book 8, "determined to fight for their wives and children, forced by necessity" (8.55–57).

Motivations: Hektor

The most sympathetic of the Trojans is Hektor, eldest son of Priam and bulwark of his city, whose name expresses his essential quality: Protector. If Achilles is an idealist in search of an uncompromised system of values, Hektor is the civic-minded man devoted to preserving his community. Like all heroes, Hektor has learned to fight always in the foreranks, but he creates his *kléos* in different value system: not that of *timế* but of *aidố*, "societal and familial obligation." The *kléos* he seeks to win is as much for his father as for himself (6.444–446), and what keeps him in the front lines is respect for his city's opinion (6.442–443). However, like the mass of Trojans who march to war in Book 8, his primary concern is personal: his wife and child.

The audience learns these facts during Hektor's brief foray into Troy in Book 6, when he seeks out his wife and engages her in a lengthy and moving dialogue. Having already lost her father and seven brothers to Achilles and fearing that her husband's courage will get him killed also, Andromakhe asks him to marshal his forces closer to the wall and direct them from the safety of the tower. Andromakhe requests that he adopt this nonheroic style of fighting out of pity for her and their son, who will be utterly bereft as his widow and orphan. Although Hektor does feel pity, he rejects her request because he feels obligated to the Trojans and his father. There follows an utterly personal moment in which he envisions Andromakhe as a raped wife living in bondage to a Greek lord. He implies that this vision is the true core of his heroism: "may I be dead and buried in the earth before I learn from your cries that you are dragged off captive" (6.464–465).

After removing his terrifying helmet, Hektor picks up his baby son and kisses him while his wife smiles through her tears. His tragic vision fades as he prays that his son may grow up to be a warrior stronger than his father and "delight his mother's heart when he carries a dead enemy's bloody armor in from the battlefield" (6.479–481). Much as he appears to dislike it, Hektor accepts war as an inevitable fact of life just as the Greeks do (compare 14.85–87). He parts from Andromakhe, directing her to return to her women's work in the household while he returns to his man's work on the battlefield. Andromakhe does as ordered, weeping and turning back to look at him as he goes, and mourning him at home as if he were already dead (6.490–502).

This encounter between the Trojan hero, his wife and baby is perhaps the most memorable scene in the *Iliad*. Fighting not for a principle but for a city full of families and for one family with whom we have become intimate, Hektor is a champion far more accessible than the semidivine Achilles. He is someone we can identify with and like as well as admire. Likability or lack thereof may not have been a factor in traditional heroic poems, but in Homer's more realistic world it is a way of investing a man of lesser physical power with equal emotional interest. Clear-eyed, semidivine Achilles, constricted only by the mortality of self and loved ones, exemplifies the tragic *state* of humanity. Fully human Hektor, vision clouded by hope, embodies one individual man's exemplary tragedy.

Hektor's last stand will take place in the context of his family and city. Fired by previous victories and the impatient hope of finally ridding his city of the Greek invaders, he will dismiss wise advice to move the army back inside the walls now that Achilles has returned to the Greek army (18.284–309). He will then await Achilles before the Skaian Gates while his father begs him to come inside the walls, offering him a vision of families destroyed, civilization itself destroyed as the family dogs feed on their master's dead body (22.38–76). His mother will plead, holding out a breast and reminding him of his duty to the mother who loves him (22.82–89). He will ignore them, ashamed to take refuge after making a mistake that has cost the lives of many Trojans. Once the arrogance that warped his mind in the heat of battle departs, Hektor will show the true hero's ability to take responsibility. It will be his *aidós*, his sense of failed responsibility, that gives him the courage to wait for almost certain death. By the time that courage fails and he turns to run from the fiery super hero who approaches, the audience will be so much on his side that it will feel it is running with him, caught in the nightmare with him.

The Battlefield

Two armies of bronze-clad soldiers come together in the field, shield against shield, spear against spear, strength against strength. There arises a great tumult of "painful howl and triumphal shout" as "men kill and are killed and blood flows on the ground" (4.446–451 = 8.60–65). Then the killing and dying, wailing and boasting become specific.

Weapons enter bodies in graphic detail, ripping through foreheads, eyes, mouths, necks, shoulders, chests, stomachs, buttocks, thighs, arms, to mutilate and kill. Soldiers die, falling like slender poplars (4.482–487) or drooping like rain-wet poppies (8.306–308) or screaming as death enfolds them (5.68). The gleaming armor of an army at work "turns white in rising dust," as white as a pile of chaff on a threshing floor (5.498–502). Elaborate similes invite the audience to compare and contrast the mayhem to scenes of agriculture and other peaceful human endeavor, nonheroic scenes from everyday life. Harsh or gentle natural processes like dying flowers, tempest, wild animal attacks, and wildfire naturalize but do not neutralize the terrifying violence of war or the pathos of a young life annihilated.

Someone hurls a spear that takes a man's life. The friend of that dead man first feels grief and then anger. The anger impels him to aim his spear at the enemy who killed his friend. His spear takes a life; a friend standing near feels grievous anger and then hurls his own spear. And so it goes, the main variations being the place the spear enters the body, the brief biography or simile chosen to add either pathos to the death or fierceness to the killing, the treatment of the body and its armor. The momentum and the brutality increase as this pattern repeats in waves during the Great Battle that extends from Book 11 through Book 17 (see especially 14.458–505). The nastier characters cut off heads and flaunt eyeballs on spear points, and even admirable characters like Odysseus vaunt that their victim's bodies will be eaten by animals (11.452–454). Hektor too changes from civilized soldier to vicious killer eager to cut off Patroklos' head and feed his body to dogs (17.125–127). One of the lessons imbedded in the *Iliad* is that no one can control the course of war or the psyche of the warrior.

Fire and animal imagery suggest the shift into inhumanity that happens to all warriors when they leave the ordered world of civilization for the battlefield. Fire, which burns throughout the *Iliad* in metaphor and narrative fact, represents extraordinary, that is, divinely inspired, martial success. For example, Athena kindles fire around Diomedes' helmet and shield (5.4–6), as she will do later around Achilles' head (18.205–214). This flame imagery is often accompanied by images of its opposite: predatory animals representing an unbridled killer instinct equally necessary for success on the battlefield. Hektor at his fiercest, when Zeus and Apollo drive him relentlessly toward the Greek ships, is like "a deadly fire raging in the mountains" and is "lit up with fire" (15.605–606, 6.623). At the same time, however, he "froths at the mouth" (15.607). Earlier, Poseidon had described him as "a rabid dog like a flame" (13.53).

The most important of the predatory images is the lion. Only the three greatest heroes – Achilles in the *Iliad*, Odysseus in the *Odyssey*, and Herakles in both – receive the epithet "lionhearted," but all major heroes have lion-like qualities vivified by similes. Lion similes image both noble courage and savage mercilessness. When Diomedes is wounded by Pandaros, for example, he turns on his attackers with tripled rage; just as a lion wounded by a shepherd ravages the sheep flocks, killing heaps of them, so Diomedes mercilessly ravages the Trojan ranks, leaving heaps of corpses (5.136–160). Aeneas is "like a lion confident in his strength" when he later protects Pandaros' body (5.299).

Occasionally the action stops as warriors confront each other with words, not swords. Sometimes it is to exchange identities and boasts, sometimes it is to ask unsuccessfully for mercy. We know that Achilles took prisoners for ransom in previous battles (see 21.100–102, 24.750–753), but no one does in the *Iliad*. A defeated soldier begs Menelaos to take him prisoner instead of killing him. Menelaos is about to grant this, when Agamemnon intervenes, urging vengeance instead of mercy: let no Trojan survive, he urges, not even the male baby in his mother's womb. Menelaos yields, and Agamemnon stabs the begging man (6.37–65). Shortly after this brutal scene there occurs a scene at the opposite pole of warfare. Diomedes and Glaukos exchange genealogies, discover hereditary ties of friendship, and agree to exchange armor instead of fighting (6.119–136). The pairing of these two scenes shines a harsh light on Agamemnon's character, as does the scene in Book 11 when Agamemnon kills two brothers who are explicitly said to have been spared by Achilles before (11.104–112). It also juxtaposes two views of warfare: one in which the category "enemy" wipes away all other distinctions, and one in which enemy opponents can be respected as individuals.

Domestic Space: The Women

Several wives and mothers who will never receive their menfolk back from the war are briefly evoked in the biographies of the dead and dying. These women, together with the women characters who are either Trojan women or enslaved concubines taken from the twenty-three allied cities Achilles has sacked, focus the cost of war on families. The enslaved women represent the future of the women in Troy, while the women in Troy give insight into what the slaves have lost. Semidivine Helen of Argos, now Helen of Troy, is an exception, for she will always be a wife, never a slave, but she nevertheless shares the same domestic world, the same dependence on men, as the others. Scenes involving all these women develop male and female realms as polar opposites, much as they have been in Anglo-American culture until relatively recently.

Hektor's interactions with the women of Troy in Book 6 show these opposing realms most clearly. On his arrival in Troy, he is surrounded at the gates by women who want news of their "sons, brothers, relatives, and husbands" (6.237–240); he gives many of them bad news, directs them to pray to the gods, and passes on to his mother. Hekabe, solicitous, offers him wine to revive his strength (6.261), but he rejects it on the grounds that it may make him weaker and forget his courage (6.265); he gives her instructions for propitiating Athena and leaves. He moves on to Paris' house where Helen invites him to sit and rest for a moment; he refuses, asks her to speed his self-indulgent brother back to the battle-field, and leaves to find his wife. Andromakhe too, like Hekabe and Helen, offers Hektor something: advice on how to prosecute the war (close to the city, and *not* in the front lines). After affectionately rejecting this advice, Hektor directs her back to the house, where she will spend her time weaving, caring for her child, and warming the bath water for her battle-weary husband (6.490–493, 22.440–448). A woman's contribution to war is limited to prayer, encouragement, and the care of her husband's house when he is not fighting. Any other efforts – offers of refreshment, rest, advice – are regarded as a danger to his heroism, restraining him from quickly returning to the frontlines of battle. As a wife to be protected or retrieved, she may be the *cause* of heroism, but she has no part in it.

She may also be, like Achilles' Briseis, the reward for heroism, the sexual victim of the men who kill her family. Briseis' lament for Patroklos is instructive: she grieves for Patroklos because he was kind to her after Achilles killed her husband and three brothers and sacked her city; the best she could hope for after that disaster was to become Achilles' wedded wife instead of a slave (19.282–303). Through Briseis, Homer illustrates poignantly why women like Andromakhe try to keep their menfolk close to home: unable to act on their own behalf, their well-being depends on the survival of their fathers, brothers, and husbands.

Even Zeus's daughter Helen, who is not dependent on the survival of any one husband, has power only through men. Hers is the power of Aphrodite, the power to charm men into loving her, but in the *Iliad* she uses this power only out of fear. In Book 3, Helen resists joining Paris in bed after Aphrodite saves him from Menelaos. At this, Aphrodite threatens to hate Helen as much as she now loves her, and Helen gives in (3.414–417). This interaction between goddess and woman exemplifies psychological realism. Because Helen is disgusted with the man she fell in love with and with herself, she scorns Aphrodite, goddess of the sexual lust that caused her to follow Paris to Troy. When she yields, it is out of fear that her charismatic beauty will disappear and that the Trojans and Greeks will stop desiring her and start hating her for the war she has caused. What if the town elders, who already believe that she should be sent back (3.156–159), should cease to believe that her awesome likeness to a goddess takes away blame? Disgusted or not, Helen must use her beauty and sex appeal: she must yield to Aphrodite, if she wishes to go on living. Aphrodite is the only power a woman has.

Women's final function in the heroic world is to mourn the dead. In the *Iliad* they are the eternal mourners: Andromakhe and her household women mourn Hektor before he is dead (6.500–502), and Thetis mourns her son's short life throughout the *Iliad*. Andromakhe leads the lament for Hektor at his funeral, followed by Hekabe and Helen (24.722–776). The women's lament is the counterpart to the male bard's *kléos;* but while *kléos* is celebratory and is intended to keep the hero's achievements alive, the focus of mourning is loss, and achievement is mentioned only to highlight the loss. Women's focus is concrete, not abstract. Here again Helen is an exception in that she participates in realms of both *kléos* and lamentation: she laments her personal loss of Hektor in Book 24, but she also weaves a tapestry of the Trojan War (3.125–128) and envisions herself and Paris as subjects of song (6.357–358).

There are three mourning mothers in the *Iliad*, Thetis, Hekabe, and Andromakhe.[4] Andromakhe's fear that her son will be an orphan contributes to her attempt to block her husband's heroism in Book 6. Hekabe's anticipatory grief leads her to assert maternal claims against her son's heroism in Book 22. Only in Thetis, the divine mother, does maternal grief not interfere with male heroism. Totally supportive of her son, lamenting his sorrows with him, interceding with Zeus for him, procuring a new set of divine armor, and informing him of his choices but not trying to keep him alive at the cost of his *kléos*, Thetis exemplifies ideal motherhood within the heroic ethos. Her sorrow, however, is portrayed as even greater than the human mothers'.

Achilles recalls that Thetis once saved the king of the Olympians from being deposed by Hera, Poseidon, and Athena (*Il.* 1.397–406). Although the story about her saving Zeus is obscure, it brings to mind the key role Thetis unwillingly played in ending cosmic struggles over divine succession. Had Thetis married a divine suitor, either Zeus or Poseidon, her son would be immortal like herself and his power unlimited. Thetis' constant grief over her son's destined brief life thus highlights his mortal condition in contrast not only to her own immortality but also to what might have been. The fact that immortality has in some sense been *lost* in this particular case sharpens the pathos that attends every warrior's death, intensifying this mother's grief and giving it exemplary status.

Temporarily Like Achilles: Diomedes

Diomedes, who functions as both surrogate and foil to Achilles in the first half of the *Iliad,* offers a picture of what the Achilles of pre-Iliadic epic might have been like. Diomedes' martial prowess, his desire not to mince words, and his faith in his own powers (7.399–402, 9.46–49, 696–703) make him similar to Achilles, but Diomedes has no trace of tragedy about him. His deference to the commander-in-chief in the face of gratuitous insult (4.367–418) makes him the ideal team player that Achilles is not. In Diomedes, Homer offers the audience an unproblematic "best of the Akhaians" while Achilles is off the field.

In Book 5, Homer gives Diomedes an extended period of triumphal fighting that is called an *aristeía,* from the Greek word *áristos,* "best." Exuding the seductive joy of uninterrupted victory, Diomedes' *aristeía* demonstrates the heroic ideal: the divinely inspired warfare of one who fights because he loves doing what he is good at. Although his *aristeía* accomplishes little of significance except to kill the truce-breaker Pandaros, it establishes for its Greek audience the basic superiority of the Greek army and its gods. Diomedes' encounter with Glaukos, in which he exchanges bronze armor for gold (6.234–236), contributes to that superiority.

Diomedes' exuberant *aristeía* establishes patterns of fighting, imagery, and behavior against which the audience can later compare the tragic *aristeías* of first Patroklos and then Achilles. One of the most interesting features to compare in each *aristeía* is the hero's interaction with the gods. All heroes are helped by gods, who intervene constantly on behalf of their favorites, but only Achilles will provoke divine involvement comparable to Diomedes.

In addition to giving Diomedes added strength and curing his wound, Athena gives him the extraordinary power to recognize the gods, who normally operate in human disguise and are known, if at all, only after they leave. Furthermore, she encourages Diomedes to wound Aphrodite, and she drives his chariot herself to help him wound Ares. Since attacking gods is dangerous – those who fight with the gods normally do not survive (5.406–415) – these attacks ought to carry intimations of coming tragedy.

The audience, however, knows from the *Nostoi* that Diomedes will make it home safely and that there will be no repercussions.[5] Diomedes' consequence-free wounding of gods is of a piece with his whole *aristeía*: it is the stuff of high romance, comparable to today's superhero comic books.

The lack of consequences in Diomedes' interaction with Apollo contrasts sharply with what happens to Patroklos later in Book 16. Diomedes, who can clearly see Apollo protecting Aeneas, nonetheless attacks three times, and is three times physically repelled. On the fourth attack, Apollo orders him back, reminding him he is a god, whereupon Diomedes falls back "a little" in order to avoid his *mênis* (5.439–444). Diomedes continues fighting elsewhere, and Apollo does not harm him. In Book 16, Patroklos is unable to see Apollo guarding the towers when he attempts to scale Troy's wall; having beaten him back three times, the god commands him to stop on his fourth attempt (5.438–439 = 16.705–706). In a verse nearly identical to that used with Diomedes, Patroklos falls back "a lot" in order to avoid Apollo's *mênis* (16.710–711). This more respectful deference to the god does not save him. Patroclus' *aristeía*, which has been unrelentingly grim and marked with moments of high tragedy and brutality, ends in a terrifying divine assault. As Patroklos murderously charges the Trojans elsewhere, Apollo's invisible hand stuns him without warning, knocks off his helmet, shatters his spear, breaks his corselet, and renders him helpless. A second-rank warrior spears him, and Hektor stabs him in the stomach. The difference between Diomedes' high-spirited *aristeia* and this horror story, with its emphasis on human mortality and blindness, illustrates well how Homer transformed traditional stories of adventure to fit into the tragic arc of the *Iliad*.

Achilles' *aristeía* will be three times as long as Diomedes' and Patroklos' and will provoke a corresponding increase in divine intervention. In Book 21, a terrifying assault on Achilles by the river Skamandros will provoke action by Hephaistos, who in a reversal of natural processes burns the river's waters as elemental fire. Unlike Diomedes' victories, the result of this elemental battle will be highly significant: the surrender of the river to fire is a precursor of the day that Troy will burn and the river waters will be unable to help (21.373–376). The comic Battle of the Gods, in which Athena sends Ares and Aphrodite sprawling and Hera boxes Artemis' ears, will give little relief from the horror of human bodies saturating the ground with their lifeblood. The final divine intervention, that of Athena, will be felt as tragic, not to Achilles but to his doomed opponent Hektor and the city that depends on him. Hektor, blind to the goddess like Patroklos, will be felled by forces he cannot comprehend until the very end. Achilles' final triumph over Hektor will be the tragic opposite of Diomedes' final triumphs. Here there will be no healing in Olympos, no exchange of armor. Achilles will strip his own despoiled armor from Hektor after dispatching him to Hades "lamenting his fate" as Patroklos had, "and leaving youth and manhood behind" (22.361–363 = 16.855–858).

The Best of the Akhaians: Achilles

Grief and rage drive Achilles into this terrible *aristeía*. When in Book 18 he makes his definitive choice to fight and die in Troy, his choice has become one between a long life without vengeance or short life with vengeance. He has no interest in continuing to live "unless Hektor should die stricken by my spear and pay back the despoiling of Patroklos." When Thetis tells him that his own death is "fated straightway after Hektor's," he replies, "I wish I could die immediately, since I was not there to help when Patroklos was killed" (18.90–99). Achilles' sense of guilt is clear in this verse and the following ones, especially when he berates himself for not being "a saving light for Patroklos or many other companions killed by Hektor," and calls himself "a useless burden on the earth" (18.102–104). Although he still feels wronged and angry with Agamemnon, he nonetheless forces himself to put their quarrel behind him (18.107–113). Achilles' taking responsibility for his actions contrasts greatly with Agamemnon's later plea of "temporary insanity" (19.78–89). His guilt and repeated acceptance of death win him the audience's sympathy, a sympathy that holds, even while sorely tried, during the horrific slaughter that follows.

At the request of Thetis, Hephaistos makes Achilles new armor to replace the armor Hektor took from Patroklos. As the poet describes its making, the new shield seems to come alive before our eyes. Celestial bodies – sea, earth, sky, sun, moon, stars – cluster in the center (18.483–489). Just outside them are two cities, one at peace, with scenes of marriage and civil judgment (490–508); and one at war, with scenes of debate, defense, deadly ambush, and battle (509–540). Agricultural scenes depict ploughing and harvesting, with a king watching over reapers, and young people dancing and singing as they bring in the vintage (541–572). Sudden death intrudes into a pastoral scene as two terrible lions attack a bull at the front of the herd. Sheep flocks in a beautiful meadow and an intricate dance scene complete this miniature world, which is encircled by Ocean at the rim of the shield. What Hephaistos has created is a vision of generic human life in all its myriad changes.

The two other shields described in the *Iliad*, one divine, one human, are both intended to petrify opponents with fear. Strife, Prowess, chilling Pursuit, and the terrible Gorgon's head (5.739–742) adorn Athena's aegis. An image of a staring Gorgon flanked by Fear and Panic embellish Agamemnon's shield, while a coiled three-headed serpent holds its strap (11.36–40). In contrast to these monstrously fearsome shields, Achilles' shield invites the audience to ponder the wonder of life and the poignancy of having to lose it.

Although he is the best warrior, Achilles has been portrayed as far from single-mindedly warlike. In addition to playing the lyre and singing epic lays, he is the only character to create similes about himself (9.323–324, 16.7–10) and he is the only warrior besides Asklepios' sons to have a professional level of skill at healing, having learned it directly from Kheiron, the teacher of Asklepios (11.829–831). He is thus portrayed as having a poet's ability to put events in perspective and the physician's ability to save life despite war's best effort to take it. In addition, Andromakhe portrays him as having greatly respected the body of her father (6.414–427), and he is the only warrior in the *Iliad* who is said to have spared captives (11.104–106, 111–112; 21.100–103, 24.751–753). His character is as complex as the shield Hepahaistos creates for him.

Book 19 shifts Achilles progressively away from this complex humanity. When Achilles receives the divinely made armor from his mother, his delighted eyes blaze with increased anger and his focus on vengeance intensifies. He immediately calls an assembly to begin battle against Hektor. He is uninterested in the gifts Agamemnon offers, and when Odysseus insists that not only must he take the gifts, but he must allow time for the soldiers to eat breakfast, Achilles refuses to recognize this human need, insisting that all he cares about is "killing and blood and grievous groaning." Homer emphasizes the contrast in perspectives by having Odysseus again insist that the men must eat in order to fight (19.145–237). Odysseus wins the debate, but since Achilles still refuses to give in to the needs of his body, Athena feeds him intravenously with nectar and ambrosia (19.352–354). This divine feeding signifies two contradictory things at once: it acknowledges Achilles' human need for sustenance, but it also suggests that his agonized anger is shifting him away from humanity toward superhuman status.

Images of fire reinforce Achilles' shift into inhumanity. Achilles puts on his immortal armor, shining like fire and the sun (19.364–399); during his *aristeía*, he rages like a fire that sweeps wildly through the mountain forest (20.490–492); he drives forward like a firewall just before he takes twelve Trojan youths to sacrifice on Patroklos' pyre (21.12–14); he is aided by divine fire when Skamandros attacks; he races toward Troy like a divinely sent conflagration destroying a city (21.522–524), and, as he finally approaches Hektor, his armor shines like the bright, fever-bringing Dog Star (22.26–31). This fire imagery reinforces the perception that Achilles' relentless force is superhuman, powered by a new *ménis* as implacable as the gods'.

Images of predatory animals signal another level of inhumanity. Highly personified lion similes had imaged Achilles grief and rage as he mourned over Patroklos' body (18.318–322) and as he entered battle (20.164–173). At the point of his climactic duel with Hektor, a self-generated lion simile marks his furious behavior as subhuman. Achilles rejects the contractual obligation that characterizes a civilized duel: whoever wins shall return the loser's corpse to his people (7.76–91 cf. 22.254–259). Instead he portrays himself as a beast outside social systems: "As there are no trustworthy oaths between lions and men . . . so there will be no oaths between me and you, until one of us is dead" (262, 265–267). He corroborates this beastliness when he wishes he could hack the flesh off Hektor's corpse and eat it raw (22.346–347). Achilles' "lion-ness" has superseded his human-ness; his ascent to the superhuman is simultaneously a descent to the subhuman.

The mourning that greets Hektor's death is "most like what would happen if all lofty Troy were consumed top to bottom in fire" (22.410–411). This simile circles back to Priam's prediction that if Hektor is killed, "Zeus will destroy me wretchedly, after I have seen many evils: my sons killed and my daughters dragged away, . . . innocent children thrown to earth in terrible warfare, and daughters-in-law dragged off, . . . and at the end my own dogs will eat my raw flesh" (22.60–67). These framing references make Hektor's destruction equivalent to the destruction of Troy, and they thereby prove Achilles' claim to be "best of the Akhaians." However, Achilles' inhumanity together with Priam's vision of civilization being overtaken by savagery puts the audience's sympathy wholly with Hektor and Troy. It is possible, therefore, to reserve judgment on whether heroic victory does, in fact, constitute the highest criterion of human worth.

Achilles returns only partially to the human world in Book 23. Following Patroklos' cremation, Achilles presides over funeral competitions that form a structural balance to the quarrel scene in Book 1. Disputes arise and are solved, apologies and extra prizes are forthcoming where necessary. Achilles awards Agamemnon a prize without allowing him to compete for it, which is a socially viable way of showing contempt under the guise of showing respect. The geniality of the games, however, is framed by continued signs of inhumanity: before the pyre is lit, Achilles kills the twelve Trojan captives as a sacrifice to Patroklos (23.175–176); after the games, his grief prevents him from eating or sleeping; and on the following day he continuously drags Hektor's body around Patroklos' tomb (24.1–18).

Achilles' attempt to mutilate Hektor's body provokes divine intervention. On Olympos, Zeus listens to arguments that oppose and support Achilles' behavior, each by denying his humanity. In Apollo's view Achilles is behaving like a lion rather than a human being, for he is without the patience and respect for others that characterize men (24.40–45). As in Achilles' own simile at 22.262, Apollo creates an explicit contrast between human beings and lions that locates Achilles in the bestial category. Hera counters by locating Achilles in the divine realm: "Achilles is born of a goddess" (58–59), and Hektor, therefore, need not receive equal consideration. The two are not to be held in equal *timê* (57).

Zeus begins the process of bringing Achilles back to humankind by asking the goddess mother to persuade her son to ransom the body according to human custom (74–76). The appearance of Thetis evokes, as always, Achilles' mortality. Zeus's messenger finds her "lamenting the fate of her son, who is going to die in Troy" (85–86); she wears a black veil, as if he were already dead (93–94). When she comes to Achilles, she chides him for neither eating nor sleeping, and advises him to "lie in love with a woman, for . . . already death and strong fate stand near" (24.128–132). Her advice begs to be compared to Sarpedon's exposition of the heroic code, in which the inevitability of death impels men to risk life for *timê* and *kléos*. For Thetis, impending death calls not for heroic but for basic human activity: eating, sleeping, and sex. Achilles will accept all three before the poem ends.

Achilles yields and from this point takes the lead in distinguishing humankind from both god and beast. In addition to his mother, he is moved to this task by his worst enemy, the father of the man who killed Patroklos. Grief has reduced Priam too, to something seemingly less than human: Homer describes him rolling in dung, maltreating guests, and abusing his surviving sons for not having died instead of Hektor (24.163–165, 237–262). Hermes guides him mysteriously through the night, into Achilles' compound as if to the land of the dead. In this compound, outside of all communities, the two men fated soon to die find a bare minimum of comfort in the sharing of a common human sorrow.

Priam supplicates Achilles as a father and asks Achilles to remember his own father (486–492, 504). The two weep together, Priam mourning Hektor while Achilles mourns "his father and also at other times Patroklos" (509–512). A simile in Book 23 that depicts Achilles grieving "like a father" (23.222–223) suggests that Achilles' loss of Patroklos is equivalent to a parent's loss of a child.[6] When Achilles weeps with Hektor's father, therefore, he grieves both for and as a father. This comprehensive grief transcends each man's anger at what the other's kin has done.

The grief that mingles their tears asserts their common humanity in opposition to the carefree existence of the gods. Achilles makes this clear in a parable about two urns that sit on Zeus's threshold, one holding bad things, the other good. The gods, he says, receive only good things, but the best that human beings can hope for is to receive a mixture of both. He uses both Peleus and Priam to illustrate this truth, and he posits himself as the evil in their two otherwise fortunate lives. Peleus "has no generation of strong sons in his house, /but fathered only one child . . . Nor do/I care for him as he grows old, but very far from my fatherland/I remain in Troy, causing pain to you and your children" (24.525–542). Useless to his father, killer of Priam's sons, Achilles incarnates the sorrow that differentiates human life from that of the gods.

After attending to Hektor's body and placing it on Priam's wagon, Achilles persuades Priam to stop grieving long enough to eat. Then, they prepare for the sleep that neither has enjoyed since the deaths of Patroklos and Hektor. Returned to his human nature and to humankind, Achilles' last appearance in the poem shows him in bed reunited with Briseis (24.675–676).

Before Achilles retires to his bed, he offers Priam something neither he nor Zeus had requested: time to perform complete funeral rites for Hektor. These funeral rites will conclude the poem with a high tribute to both Hektor and Achilles. Just as Hektor had hoped to gain *kléos* from the tomb of a man he wanted to kill (*Il.* 7.84–91), so his own tomb will create *kléos* for the man who killed him. But the *kléos* Homer establishes with Hektor's tomb is more than that of conquering an enemy in combat: the tomb exists only because Achilles conquers his own hate in shared suffering. Because the Achilles who killed Hektor is portrayed as inhuman, but the Achilles who offers the funeral is wholly and definitively a man, the audience of the *Iliad* may well conclude that though Achilles may be "best of the Akhaians" through martial prowess, it is compassion that earns him the enduring *kléos* of supreme human excellence.

The Tragic Arc

The trajectories of the *Iliad* and *Gilgamesh* are similar in some important ways. Both Achilles and Gilgamesh are semidivine heroes who begin by believing that immortal stories about their superhuman deeds will in some way ameliorate the fact that they must eventually die. When they actually experience death through the loss of a beloved companion, both discover that death's reality is utterly unbearable and that nothing their cultures have to offer – statues, stories, honor – provides any comfort or compensation. Both respond by crossing the limits of the civilized world, by temporarily becoming wild men who are both less and more than human. Both are compelled at the end to acknowledge and accept their humanity.

There are, of course, substantial differences in their tragic arcs. Gilgamesh responds to his new understanding of death by refusing to accept that he too is mortal and by beginning a quest for physical immortality. Achilles, on the other hand, becomes utterly careless of death, his own or any other's. He becomes the very incarnation of blood-hungry Ares in a quest for vengeance. Although neither hero finds comfort in his quest, when Gilgamesh returns from his journey, it is to a city that he has built and over which he rules. There is some consolation in his proud description of this city and in the understanding created by the proem that Gilgamesh will himself soon write the story of how he brought back knowledge from his journey. The *Iliad* too ends with an affirmation of culture, the funeral of Hektor, but there is little hint of consolation. The funeral is very important for the audience's response to the hero, but Achilles himself acknowledges no comfort. His return to full humanity produces only a tragic redefinition of humanity as a vessel of sorrow. He remains emotionally alienated from his social group, which continues to follow an unworthy leader. Achilles' final jibe at Agamemnon and those who collaborate with him (24.650–655) reaffirms earlier indications (18.113, 19.66, 23.890–894) that no true reconciliation has taken place.

The heroic ideal remains fissured. The world goes on in its compromised way. War is a fact of life, nothing more nothing less. But out of broken social codes and the impossible human desire for permanence, the poet of the *Iliad* has wrested a beauty that, for a while, transcends the grief of Achilles and Priam, the lament of Andromakhe. The flame of martial heroism burning to ash in the funeral pyre of Hektor allows us to touch the divine but delivers us finally to the very quick of humanity.

Further Reading

What follows is an extremely small selection of the numerous excellent books and articles available.

Translations and Texts

Richmond Lattimore's translation of the *Iliad* into stately iambic hexameter (Chicago, IL, 1951) gives the best sense of the Greek text. Most general readers will prefer the livelier new versions by Robert Fagles (New York, 1990), Stanley Lombardo (Indianapolis, IN, 1997), and Ian Johnston (Arlington, VA, 2006). All three have useful maps and glossaries of names with guides to pronunciation; Lombardo's offers in addition an index to speeches and a catalogue of battlefield deaths. All three capture the vigor and excitement of Homer's text; Johnston's, however, is somewhat more removed from the formal aesthetic of the Greek poem. Fagles' translation offers an excellent introduction by Bernard Knox, Lombardo's an equally excellent one by Sheila Murnaghan.

The Greek text on which I have based my translations is T. W. Allen and D. B. Munro (eds.), *Homeri Opera: Ilias* (1920). I have benefited greatly from the recent six-volume commentary to the Greek by G. S. Kirk, J. Hainsworth, R. Janko, M. Edwards, and N. Richardson (eds.), *The Iliad: A Commentary* (Cambridge, 1985–1993).

Interpretation and Commentary

Seth Schein's *The Mortal Hero: An Introduction to Homer's Iliad* (Berkeley and Los Angeles, 1984) gives an accessible literary interpretation of the epic as well as essential background information. E. T. Owen's *The Story of the Iliad* (Toronto, 1946) comments insightfully on the narrative technique book by book. Barry Powell's *Homer* (Oxford, 2004) has a succinct section on the *Iliad*. See also the first chapter in K. King's *Achilles: Paradigms of the War Hero from Homer to the Middle Ages* (Berkeley and Los Angeles, 1987). James Tatum's *The Mourner's Song* (Chicago, 2003) is an eloquent reading of the *Iliad* alongside other literary and physical memorials of war, especially the American Civil War and the Vietnam War.

For the more advanced reader there are many excellent book length studies of the *Iliad*, among them Cedric Whitman's *Homer and the Heroic Tradition* (Cambridge, MA, 1958), whose chapter on "Fire and Other Elements" has been especially influential; and Mark Edwards's *Homer: Poet of the Iliad* (Baltimore, MD, 1988), which offers an introduction to Homeric aesthetics in the first half and a book-by-book commentary in the second half. Oliver Taplin's *Homeric Soundings: The Shaping of the Iliad* (Oxford, 1995) argues many perceptive points with performance always uppermost in mind. P. Vivante's *Homeric Imagination* (Bloomington, IN, 1970) is excellent on Achilles' inward journey.

The very advanced reader skilled in both Homer and literary criticism will find the following studies well worth while: Richard Martin's *The Language of Heroes: Speech and Performance in the Iliad* (Ithaca, NY, 1989); Pietro Pucci's *Song of the Sirens* (New York and Oxford, 1998), especially the final chapter on "Honor and Glory in the Iliad;" Peter Rose's "Ideology in the *Iliad*: Polis, Baileus, Theoi," *Arethusa* 30.2 (1997) 1–38, gives a meticulously researched Marxist reading of the epic.

The following books and articles, many of which have greatly influenced my arguments in this chapter, will be useful for thinking more deeply about specific issues. **Warfare and the Heroic Ethos**: Ch. Segal, *The Theme of the Mutilation of the Corpse in the Iliad* (Leiden, 1971) began the discussion in Homeric scholarship about the increasing savagery which war releases. J. Redfield's *Nature and Culture in the Iliad* (Chicago, 1975) uses anthropological theory to argue that the warrior is poised in margins between nature and culture. Sheila Murnaghan's "Equal Honor and Future Glory: The Plan of Zeus in the *Iliad*" in

Roberts, Dunn, and Fowler, eds., *Classical Closure: Reading the End in Greek and Latin Literature* (Princeton, NJ, 1997), 23–24, presents a detailed argument that Zeus's plan to keep mortals dying in warfare includes many shorter plans like that supporting Achilles' wrath. Gregory Nagy's *Best of the Achaeans. Concepts of the Hero in Archaic Greek Poetry* (Baltimore and London, 1979) brilliantly discusses various heroes' claims to be "best of the Achaeans" on pp. 26–41. A. Parry's "Have We Homer's Iliad?" *Yale Classical Studies* 20 (1966), 177–216, discusses the *Iliad* as a critical exploration of "the heroic concept of life." Simon Weil's "The Iliad or the Poem of Force" (1940) and Rachel Bespaloff's "On the Iliad" (1943), which both read the *Iliad* through the lens of World War II, are now conveniently paired in *War and the Iliad*, translated by Mary McCarthy (New York, 2005). **Kléos**: For the importance of *kléos* as keeping the hero's agency alive, see Damian Stocking, "*Res Agens*: Toward an Ontology of the Homeric Self," *College Literature*, Special Issue 34.2: *Reading Homer in the 21st Century* (Spring 2007). See also J.-P. Vernant "A Beautiful Death" in *Mortals and Immortals: Collected Essays*, ed. F. Zeitlin (Princeton, NJ, 1991). **Similes**: Carroll Moulton, *Similes in the Homeric Poems*, (Gottingen, 1977) is an excellent book-length discussion of the similes. **Gender**: Marilyn B. Arthur, "The Divided World of Iliad VI" *Women's Studies* 8 (1981) 21–46 (*Reflections on Women in Antiquity*, ed., Helene P. Foley [New York, 1981]: 19–44) discusses the relationship of women to war and martial heroism. L. Slatkin *The Power of Thetis* (Berkeley, 1992) discusses how Homer shapes the role of Thetis as traditional nurturing goddess, transforming her from one who seeks to extend the life of her loved one to one who helps him become the exemplar of mortal heroism. H. P. Foley, "Women in Ancient Epic" (J. M. Foley, 2005), 105–118; and N. Felsen and L. Slatkin, "Gender and Homeric Epic" (Fowler, 2004), 91–114, offer excellent discussions of the role of women in both the *Iliad* and *Odyssey*.

Modern Adaptations and Revisions

Elizabeth Cook's *Achilles* (New York, 2001) uses epic cycle events as well as the *Iliad* in a lyrically moving short novel about the life of Achilles. Christopher Logue's arresting free-verse adaptation of the *Iliad* in is still in progress; *War Music: An Account of Books 1–4 and 16–19 of Homer's Iliad* (New York, 1997); *All Day Permanent Red: The First Battle Scenes of Homer's Iliad Rewritten* (New York, 2003); *Cold Calls: War Music Continued* (New York, 2005).

Notes

1 I refer to Sin-leqe-unninni's version. The Old Babylonian version, which begins "Surpassing all kings," indicates that it will tell about the remarkable deeds of an extraordinary king.

2 Agamemnon is called "best of the Akhaians" by virtue of his having the biggest and best individual army (2.577, 580), but the poet undercuts this praise almost immediately. Achilles and Nestor both say that Agamemnon claims to be the "best of the Akhaians" (1.91, 2.82), but in fact he never does so directly.

3 It is not really important to know whether Thersites is a man of the people or a man of the upper class. In either case he speaks without a scepter and he speaks only what he "knows" will cause laughter (2.215). He is an anti-Achilles in that he is the ugliest in the army as Achilles is the most beautiful (2.216–219; 2.673–64), he is physically weak, he really does like to quarrel for its own sake, and he models his reproaches on Achilles' accusations in Book 1.

4 Aphrodite's son Aeneas is destined to survive the war, so laughter-loving Aphrodite can stay in character. She, attempts to save Aeneas once, but despite her saying that he is dearer than anything to her (5.378) he is not her main concern in the *Iliad*.

5 Linkage between Diomedes' wounding of Aphrodite and his troubles after reaching home seem to be a much later invention, probably Roman.

6 There are three other parent–child similes that contribute to this effect: see 9.323–325, 16.7–10, and 18.318–322.

4

The *Odyssey*

Tell me, Muse, of that versatile man, he who
wandered far and long after sacking Troy's holy city.
He saw many men's cities and learned their ways of thought,
and he suffered much woe on the sea, blows to his spirit,
while striving for his own life and the homecoming of his companions.
But although he tried hard, he did not save his companions,
who perished because of their very own recklessness,
silly fools; they devoured the cattle of Helios, son of Hyperion,
and he took away from them their day of homecoming.
Pick a place to start, divine daughter of Zeus, and tell us too the story.
(*Od.* 1–10)

"Man" (*ándra*), the first word of *Odyssey*, stands in stark contrast to *mênis*, the first word of the *Iliad*. "Man" and "divine wrath," even without their important modifiers "versatile" and "deadly," immediately signal the immense difference between the two epic worlds. The *Iliad* uses a semidivine hero to explore the defining differences between man and god, leading to the tragic recognition that even the most clear sighted of men, one who possesses the strongest link to the divine, cannot control the life-destroying plan of Zeus. Extraordinary intelligence makes the *Odyssey*'s hero *like* the gods, but his intelligence owes nothing to divine or even semidivine parentage, and he fully comprehends human reality from the start. With this fully human hero, the *Odyssey* celebrates the power of human resourcefulness, the ability to rebound from unexpected misfortune. Furthermore, its hero's desire coincides with the life-affirming plan of an ethical Zeus.

Although the poet is careful to evoke his hero's martial status as a warrior who participated in the sack of Troy, the stated goal is survival and homecoming (*nóstos*), not the *timé* and *kléos* of the *Iliad*'s heroes. While Achilles boasts of sacking twenty-three cities in his career as *timé*-seeking warrior (*Il.* 9.328–329), the *Odyssey* announces a less destructive relationship to the many cities its hero sees and studies on his way home. Like that of the *Epic of Gilgamesh*, the *Odyssey*'s proem stresses its hero's intellectual response to the world. This hero's ability to see, learn, and adapt is as fundamental to his attaining homecoming as Achilles' martial prowess is to attaining *timé*.

The hero of the *Odyssey* is in many ways the polar opposite of Achilles. Achilles is a complex character, but he is always straightforwardly himself; never disguising his thoughts or emotions, he speaks without regard for consequences and hates the man "who says one thing while hiding another in his heart" (*Il.* 9.309, 311–312). The *Odyssey*'s "versatile man," who is supremely skilled in the art of deceit and disguises, is precisely the kind of man Achilles hates. Instead of vainly attempting to make the world live up to its ideals, Odysseus accepts as given a world of deceit and treachery, and his skill in coping with this imperfect world is viewed as equal to Achilles' semidivine prowess on the battlefield.

The *Odyssey*'s proem highlights a second, analogous, contrast between the abilities of the two epic heroes. When it describes its hero as one who *suffered* much woe, it is hard not to recall Achilles, the warrior who *inflicted* much woe (*Il.* 1.2). Whether in a storm at sea (*Od.* 5.291–379) or the cave of a cannibalistic giant (*Od.* 9.287–461), Odysseus' characteristic ability to suffer without losing his head or giving in to despair is a key component of his success, equally as important as his resourcefulness. Although Achilles in fact suffers deeply, and Odysseus inflicts a fair amount of pain,[1] nonetheless, these opposing verbs in the proem present a striking difference in the strengths most valued in the two epic worlds.

The *Odyssey* poet turns a potentially blameworthy fact – his hero's failure to achieve homecoming for his companions as well as himself – into something that reflects positively on the hero's endurance. The poet brings the failure up early and then emphatically places responsibility for it on the companions' "very own recklessness" (*Od.* 1.6–7). As Book 12 will reveal, it will be the companions' inability to endure distress, their overwhelming desire to take the easier way and to assuage their bodies' pain, that destroys them. Although they are not evil, they are morally weak. They fail to be heroic in a situation where heroic endurance is required; they lack the strength and conviction to risk death in order to do what is right. Their leader possesses these heroic qualities, but his heroism cannot preserve them the way it might have on the battlefield. In the *Odyssey*, every individual is responsible for himself or herself.

The *Odyssey*'s moral program, signaled in the proem by tying the companions' death to their own recklessness, strongly differentiates it from the *Iliad*, where death is ubiquitous and conceived more as a consequence of being human than as a consequence of moral error. When moral error does lead to group disaster in the *Iliad*, it is always the error of a leader, and it often involves the *mênis* of a vengeful god, which sweeps away the innocent along with the guilty. Like the *Iliad*, the *Odyssey* takes for granted that evils will be mixed into every human life, but it bases its ethics on a sense that individuals, not the gods or leaders, are responsible for their own ultimate success or failure. As Zeus says, explicitly confirming what the poet implies in the proem, human beings wrongly blame the gods for the bad things that happen to them, incurring pain beyond what is fated through their "very own recklessness" (*Od.* 1.32–34).

The proem associates the companions' recklessness with eating what they should not (the cattle of Helios). This association links their recklessness with the behavior of the suitors, who, as we will hear repeatedly, have spent three years "eating up" Odysseus' household. What, how, and why one eats is an important issue throughout the poem. As Odysseus indicates in Book 8 (208–221), filling the belly is necessary for basic biologic survival, one of the necessities that differentiate human beings from gods. Eating, however, can also differentiate human beings from animals. Human modes of eating are throughout the *Odyssey* associated with self-restraint, the ability not to yield to the body's demands until properly prepared food is available and the proper rituals followed.

Proper preparation of food mainly means cooking, which necessitates both technology and restraint from eating raw, but it also includes rituals of serving and of sacrifice to the gods. These rituals tie the motif of eating to the larger theme of hospitality (*xeínia*), the reciprocal relations of a host with a guest (*xeínos*), who is by definition away from home. The norms of hospitality are the ancient substitute for international law and are enforced by Zeus, who has a special epithet, *xeínios*, to signify his concern. They require a host to provide proper food in a proper setting to any wanderer who comes to the door. They require a guest to eat no more than what the host offers. In the *Odyssey*'s moral program, adherence to the norms of hospitality differentiates bad and beastly beings from civilized, fully human beings.

In contrast to the *Iliad*, whose tragic plot focuses on the limitations of humans in comparison with gods, the *Odyssey* celebrates human potential to surpass the limitations of beasts. Proper eating and the rituals of hospitality are one way this superiority is shown. Proper sexual relations, or marriage, is another.

Marriage is the foundation of the basic social unit, the patriarchal *oîkos*, or household.[2] Without it there can be no inheritance through the father. Monogamous marriage (monogamous for the wife, at least) goes a long way toward relieving uncertainty such as Telemakhos voices over whether he is, in fact, Odysseus' son: "My mother *says* I am his, but I don't know, since no one really knows who fathered him" (1.215–216). Because it permits knowledge of father as well as mother, the institution of marriage is fundamental to the archaic and classical Greek understanding of culture. A challenge to this patriarchal understanding may have been posed by distant memories of long-past matrilineal inheritance, memories that surface in the *Odyssey* in the uncertainty over whether Odysseus' wealth will pass to Penelope's new husband or Odysseus' son. The epic, of course, raises the issue only to dispel it firmly, confirming patrilineal inheritance largely by making the theme of proper marriage central to its narrative.

When the Muse is invited to start the story of homecoming wherever she likes, she chooses to set the scene with a vision that couples homecoming with marriage: Odysseus, the poet says, longs for homecoming and his wife, but he is kept in a cave by a goddess who desires him for husband (*Od.* 1. 14–15). For reasons that are explored in Book 5, the human Odysseus is not the proper husband for Kalypso, whose name means the Hider, nor is she the proper wife for him. As it turns out, Kalypso represents only one of many marriages that tempt Odysseus to forgo homecoming and remain where he is in painless oblivion. Homecoming in the *Odyssey* is predicated on the reunion of true spouses, which is fundamental to reconstituting the *oîkos* (household) at the core of Odysseus' identity and power on Ithaka.

The idea of being justly destroyed through one's own "recklessness," introduced in the proem through the companions' unrestrained eating, will tie the theme of marriage to that of hospitality. When Zeus inveighs against those who "recklessly" bring destruction on themselves, his prime example is the adulterer, Aigisthos, who married Agamemnon's wife, Klytemnestra, and then killed Agamemnon when he returned from Troy; Agamemnon's son, Orestes, some years later killed Aigisthos and took back his inheritance, just as Zeus had warned Aigisthos he would

(*Od.* 1.35–43). Soon after Zeus's words about Aigisthos, the suitors, who are frequently called "reckless," are described as continuously feasting on Odysseus' sheep and cattle (*Od.* 1.91–92). Throughout Books 1–4, they are depicted as morally equivalent to Aigisthos, wooing the absent king's wife, sensing danger in the maturing son, and threatening to overpower the rightful husband if he returns. Their "recklessness" combines the moral errors of both the companions and Aigisthos: they eat up the household and they attempt to adulterate it as well.

The extended proem foregrounds issues of character, temptation, and self-restraint, alluding to traditional martial heroism only briefly at the beginning. Only at the very end of the proem, as part of the transition to narrative action, does a traditionally epic opponent, a hostile god, appear. "When the time came in which he was divinely fated to return home to Ithaka," the poet says, "all the gods pitied him except Poseidon, who raged unceasingly against Odysseus until he reached his own country" (*Od.* 1.20–21).

Poseidon does not merely represent the uncontrollable dangers of the sea that threaten all mariners. Angry at Odysseus for blinding his Cyclops son (*Od.* 1.68–75), he also embodies, alone among the *Odyssey*'s gods, the same kind of amoral personal vengeance that drives much of the *Iliad*. Poseidon's wrath is necessary to the *Odyssey*, both to certify that the hero's endurance and resourcefulness are truly heroic and also to justify the long inaction of Zeus and Athena, moral gods more suited to the *Odyssey*'s ethical universe.

The Olympian gathering that initiates the action of the *Odyssey* is quite unlike the contentious assemblies of the gods in the *Iliad*. Poseidon is conveniently away dining in Ethiopia, and the only two gods to speak are in harmony. While the best the *Iliad*'s Zeus could do in return for Hektor's sacrifices was to ensure a funeral (*Il.* 24.66–76), this Zeus repays Odysseus' with life and homecoming. Athena, dutiful daughter, carries out their joint plan rather than raging in rebellion. This divine concord is necessary for the epic's moral program and the unfolding of the kind of human story we label comic: that is, a story ending in marriage and stability rather than in death and/or chaos.

Telemakhos

Before the epic starts the story of Odysseus's return, it takes its audience to Ithaka, the home to which he will come. There it shows the effects of

Odysseus' long absence on his wife, his son, his father, and his city, and it shows matters coming to a crisis. Telemakhos, his nineteen-year-old son, is on the brink of manhood but is having a hard time making the transition without a father to guide him. Penelope, his wife, has used her weaving and unweaving to trick the suitors for three years, but she has been found out and is being pushed hard to choose a husband among them. Laertes, his aged father, has moved from the palace to the remote countryside. The suitors continue to party riotously, but their mood towards Telemakhos shifts from condescension to hostility when, under the prompting of Athena, he shows signs of finally growing up. In addition to this domestic crisis, there is a civic one: no assembly has been held since Odysseus left, and the people are anxious for the many men who have not returned from Troy. All these things illustrate the need for the father, the husband, the son, and the king to return to Ithaka.

When Athena arrives in the palace to "rouse up" Telemakhos, she finds him staring off into space, dreaming of his father returning and driving off the ubiquitous suitors (1.113–117). He is totally helpless. Athena, disguised as an old friend of his father's, sets out to give him confidence. She assures him that he looks like his father, insists that Odysseus is still alive, and gives him advice. This advice includes standing up to the suitors, denouncing them in an assembly, traveling to Nestor and Menelaos to find news, and then devising a way to kill whatever suitors remain in his household, "either by cunning (*dólos*) or openly," for he must stop being a child (1.187–297). By doing the first three of these things during what is called the "Telemachy" (Books 1–4), he will in fact mature enough to help his father accomplish the fourth.

On the level of plot, Telemakhos' initial weakness is necessary to create a sense of crisis, and his growing up is necessary so that he can help Odysseus kill 108 suitors with some verisimilitude. On the level of art, the poet's following Telemakhos for four books creates a pleasing symmetry between father and son as they both become strong and active after a period of passivity (Telemakhos in 1–4, Odysseus in 5–8). In addition, the *way* in which his maturation is depicted creates an ideological result as Telemakhos becomes a replica of his father, worthy of inheriting the kingship when the time comes.

Loyalty to the father is the first goad to the son's maturation. Immediately after giving him the above advice, Athena reminds him of the exemplary story of how Agamemnon's son Orestes won *kléos* by killing his father's murderer (1.298–300). This *kléos* is analogous to the epic lays (*kléa* of men) that are meant to guide behavior in the *Iliad*. The

Oresteian story of adultery, murder, and filial vengeance is the single paradigm for the *Odyssey*'s story of domestic crisis, and as such it is told not once but several times, by Nestor (3.261–310), Menelaos (4.412–437), and Agamemnon himself (11.404–434). It is not laid to rest until after Ithaka's would-be murderers tell their own new paradigmatic story to Agamemnon in Hades (24.200). There are, of course, three exemplary elements in this story: in addition to Orestes' behavior as model for sons, Aigisthos' behavior is a foreboding paradigm for the suitors, and Klytemnestra's is a foil for the virtuous Penelope. For the moment, however, I would like to focus on the *kléos* of Orestes.

In the *Iliad*, a poem of war, the bond between father and son is fractured. Achilles laments that he, an only son, will give no aid to his father as he grows old. His relationship with his commander-in-chief, which ideally would be like that of father and son (Odysseus, after all, is a "father" to his people, *Od.* 2.234), is instead portrayed as a rivalry between men whose personalities could not be more different. The only "father" Achilles relates to is Priam, who is an enemy and whose own son he has killed. Add into this mix Achilles' tutor, Phoinix, who was cursed and exiled from his paternal home because he took his mother's side against his father.

Although patrilineal succession is the ideal in the *Iliad*, at the poem's heart there is a tension around how it works in the real world, at least as it relates to kingship. Fathers can be estranged, and even when they are not, Agamemnon is living proof that he who inherits kingship is as likely as not to be unworthy of it. An important subtext of the *Iliad* is that another of the aristocrats, or all of them collectively, might better occupy his position. The issue is not resolved in the *Iliad*, but it will be in the *Odyssey* precisely though the restored filial bond.

The *Odyssey* stresses that Orestes won his throne through loyalty to his father. The act that won him the throne also involved disloyalty to the mother, a fact to which the poet alludes even as he, with characteristic decorum, avoids saying explicitly that Orestes killed her (see *Od.* 3.306–310). A son in a less conflicted family need not make such drastic choices, but it is interesting that immediately after Athena boosts Telemakhos' confidence that he can be like his father, he asserts independence from his mother, apparently for the first time. It happens when the bard, Phemios, begins to sing of the Greeks' "wretched homecoming" from Troy. Penelope enters weeping and asks Phemios to stop because it makes her too sad. Totally without sympathy, Telemakhos tells her "to steel her heart to listen" and "to go into the house and attend to her own work: the loom and the distaff and oversight of the servants' tasks; for speech is men's concern, all men's but especially mine, since I am in charge here in this house" (1.353–359). Not surprisingly, Penelope is astonished and retreats upstairs to weep herself to sleep.

Like Penelope, many critics are astonished at Telemakhos' rudeness here, one critic even suggesting that the lines must be an interpolation. However, in addition to being a realistic depiction of teenage behavior, they initiate an important assertion of the masculine self against the mother who would keep him a child. This assertion continues in Telemakhos' trip away from home against his mother's wishes, a trip that cements his identification with Odysseus via the comments and stories of surrogate fathers, Nestor and Menelaos. By the time he comes back home, he has won, as Athena tells Odysseus, "noble *kléos*" (13.422–423), and he has grown almost into his father's sandals. He has gone a long way toward proving that he will be one of the few sons who equal their fathers (2.276–277), a feat that requires great effort in addition to a genetic base.

When the time is right, Athena prods Telemakhos to return home by putting suspicions about Penelope into his head: Athena portrays her as about to marry the evil Eurymakhos and about to take Odysseus' property with her. "For you know women," whispers Athena in the night, "a woman wants to increase the household of the one she marries and does not remember her earlier children nor think of her once beloved husband when he is dead. When you get home," she advises, "turn all your property over to the best of the servant women until the time you marry" (15.20–26). Since Athena follows up this unfair characterization with true advice about the suitors waiting in ambush, Telemakhos – as well as the audience, which has had no direct interaction with Penelope since Book 4 – is left wondering. This plot device, whose purpose is to motivate Telemakhos' return as well as to create suspense about the situation in Ithaka, also demonstrates Telemakhos' new maturity. His road to becoming like his wary father begins with mistrust of his mother, a mistrust that, when he is back in Ithaka, will divert him to that father in the swineherd's hut before returning to his mother in the palace.

The Suitors

Penelope's cousins Helen and Klytemnestra furnish exemplars of the kind of woman Athena warns about. Helen took many possessions with her to Troy, possessions that feature prominently in the *Iliad* (3.70, 281–285; 7.350, 363–364, 389–390), and which it took ten years' fighting to retrieve. When Klytemnestra married Aigisthos she transferred the kingship to him, proving that she cared more about her new husband than about protecting her son's property rights or even, in some variants, his life. Helen's and Klytemnestra's infamous actions illustrate alternative dangers to the household of Odysseus and his son: if Penelope leaves with a new husband, she could take her sizeable dowry with her, or, worse, she could stay and transfer kingship in Ithaka to her new husband.

Though the suitors mostly claim to value Penelope's personal excellence, they seem equally to seek the wealth and power that might come with her. Odysseus appears to be the highest ranking aristocrat in Ithaka, occupying the position that is usually translated as king.[3] The issue of whether or not his rank will be inherited by his son is raised in Book 1, when Telemakhos reveals his anger to the suitors for the first time. Antinoös (whose name means "Hostile Minded") says explicitly that he hopes Telemakhos will never be king in Ithaka, "though it is your paternal inheritance by birth" (1.386–387). Telemakhos responds that although he wouldn't mind being king, since kings get wealthy, there are other nobles in Ithaka who can have the kingship; all he wants is control over his own household (1.390–398). Eurymakhos, a smooth-talking hypocrite, says that the matter of kingship lies with Zeus, but he hopes no one will ever carry off Telemakhos' possessions by force (1.400–404). This exchange indicates a tension in the political system, one that may well reflect an historical tension between a system of kingship and one of aristocrats who share power equally. Since the suitors are "the best men" in Ithaka (23.121–122), that is, precisely the ones who would compete for the highest political power, this tension deepens the crisis within Odysseus' household and doubles the danger to Telemakhos: in addition to diminishing his possessions, the suitors threaten his rank in Book 1 and his life in Books 2, 4, and 16.

The suitors do not threaten Telemakhos's life until he matures enough to threaten them. Then their complete intentions in courting Penelope become clear. After Telemakhos asserts that he will seek help to kill them if they do not decamp from his house, they mock him in threatening tones. One of them imagines out loud that if Telemakhos perished on his voyage, "we could divide his possessions among us and give the dwelling to his mother and the man she marries" (2.335–337). In Book 4, Antinoös actually devises a plan to ambush and kill Telemakhos on his way back from Sparta, alleging as motivation Telemakhos' possible revenge upon his return. Just in case preventing revenge might possibly be seen as a legitimate motive, the poet clarifies the issue in Book 16 by having Antinoös offer his fellow suitors a stark choice: either kill Telemakhos or give up hope of getting hold of Odysseus' possessions; either kill him or stop "eating" his property, and start courting Penelope from their own homes (16.383–392). They choose not to kill him when Amphinomos balks at killing one of "kingly family" without positive omens from Zeus, but they never seriously consider the alternative of ceasing to consume his property.

In addition to consuming Odysseus' livestock and wine, some of the suitors also sexually corrupt his serving women while pressing for married sex with Penelope. The possible consequences of such corruption are illustrated in the story of the swineherd Eumaios, who, originally the son of a king, was kidnapped by his nurse after she took a sailor as her lover (15.430–75). Sex with a woman without her male overlord's approval unfailingly suborns her loyalty. Melantho, the serving woman who sleeps with Eurymakhos, scorns the woman who has reared her "like a daughter" and thinks only of pleasure with her lover (18.322–325). It is she or one of the eleven others who sleep with suitors who betrays the secret of the web (2.108–110; 19.153). In the patriarchal world of the *Odyssey*, Melantho and her sisters are Helens or Klytemnestras writ small, giving the suitors the inroad into the household that Penelope refuses them. This is the reason they suffer such a severe punishment, one that repels most modern readers.

The suitors refuse to accept or impose any constraints on their behavior. They exemplify disorder, greed, self-indulgence, and lack of self-reliance – the very opposite of the qualities the *Odyssey* posits as requisite both for survival and for kingship. They do not attempt to earn wife, wealth, and power, but wait for them to fall in their laps. They do nothing but play games all day and party all night, disregarding the norms of hospitality obligatory for both hosts and guests. When young Telemakhos sees and takes care of the disguised Athena in Book 1, the orderly ritual of giving her a seat, water, food, and wine functions as a foil to the "arrogant dining" and "disgraceful acts" of the noisy suitors that surround him (1.132–229). The two ringleaders, Antinoös and Eurymakhos, commit the most egregious violation of hospitality, for they are courting the wife and attempt to kill the son of a host who, as Penelope reminds them, established bonds of guest-friendship with their fathers when they themselves were still children (16.418–447). In violating these norms, they show themselves to be as uncivilized as the Cyclopes or Laistrygones, monsters who eat their guests during the adventures Odysseus recounts in Books 9–12.

The huge size of the Cyclopes and the Laistrygones protect them from consequences. Likewise, the suitors feel immune from consequences because of their large numbers. As Leokritos says, even if Odysseus were to return, he would be unable to prevail against their greater number (2.244–251). The disguised Odysseus raises the issue when he unsuccessfully warns Amphinomos, the one relatively decent suitor, not to rely on the group to get away with reckless acts (18.138–142). The suitors' failure to fear divine retribution and respect community norms is clearly tied to a failure to take personal responsibility for their acts. Their "recklessness," like that of the companions and of Aigisthos, condemns them as a group to die, and they die at the hands of four men – Odysseus, Telemakhos, Eumaios, and Philoitios – who exemplify individual responsibility.

Odysseus

At roughly the same moment as Athena goes to Telemakhos, Hermes goes to Kalypso's island to instruct her to let Odysseus go. As helpless as his daydreaming son and as miserable as Penelope weeping in her room, Odysseus laments on the beach, looking out over the sea and longing for homecoming (5.151–158). Kalypso has offered him immortality as her sexual partner, but, the poet says, "she no longer pleased him" (5.153). Despite Penelope's physical inferiority to the beautiful ageless goddess, all he can think about is returning to his *oîkos* (5.215–220). The huge distance and dangers that lie between give him no hesitation when his chance to leave comes.

Hermes's words to Kalypso help to explain why Odysseus rejects immortality to return to Ithaka. "Why would anyone choose to come here?" he says frankly to Kalypso, who has mentioned his infrequent visits. "One has to cross endless stretches of sea, and there is no city nearby where mortals perform sacrifices" (5.100–102). Since sacrifices are made only with domesticated animals and harvested grain, Hermes' words imply not only a lack of society but also of agriculture. In other words, Kalypso's sensuous island lacks the political life and labor that make human life worth living. Without them, there is only biological existence, and it is this that Odysseus rejects. Homer excluded immortality as a possibility for heroes in the *Iliad*, and here in the *Odyssey*, he has the hero himself reject it in favor of a fully human life.

The poet deftly establishes Odysseus' character in his first conversation with Kalypso. Odysseus responds with mistrust to Kalypso's sudden offer to help him leave, insisting on an oath before he will believe her. Kalypso is not angry at this mistrust, but smiles and strokes him, which is identical to the way Athena responds to similar mistrust in Book 13 (5.180–181, 13.287–288). Wariness is as great a virtue in the *Odyssey* as was the ability to kill in the *Iliad*.

Another facet of his character is revealed in his preparations to leave the island. In order to cross the water that stretches endlessly before him, Odysseus must build a raft, a task that Homer describes in great detail. This detail shows that Odysseus is no stranger to hard work and he is skilled in technology as well. Since both work and technology characterize human life, this task represents his return to the human condition.

In Odysseus, skill and willingness to work exist on a heroic level, part of the versatility mentioned in the proem. The storm he encounters in the next episode reveals another characteristic, his great endurance. The immense Poseidon-driven storm is terrifying, and Homer does not shrink from showing his hero in momentary despair. As the winds blast from all directions, roiling the sea, Odysseus wishes he had died in Troy, for then he would have received a funeral and *kléos* rather than the obliteration he now faces. This was exactly the sentiment of Telemakhos when he first spoke with Athena: "I would not so lament for him had he died in Troy . . . for all the Greeks would have built him a tomb, and he would have left behind great *kléos* for his son; but now the storm gusts have snatched him away without *kléos*" (1.236–241). These statements recall the Iliadic economy that makes a heroic death the price of *kléos,* an economy that will be reiterated and finally laid to rest in Book 24 by Achilles and Agamemnon in Hades. Although both father and son initially invoke Iliadic *kléos* in the face of obliteration, they will not do so again. A new Odyssean *kléos* is just beginning, one that celebrates heroic living in various situations rather than death on the battlefield.

Odysseus has no intention of dying no matter how desperate his situation seems. In an exciting action sequence, he is swept from the raft, manages to swim back to it, hangs on to it until it is completely broken up, and then starts to swim, aided by a sea goddess's veil. After swimming for three days on the open sea and being battered against coastal rocks, he finally makes it to land on the island of Skheria. Swollen, encrusted with salt, and exhausted, he does not simply fall asleep on the beach.

Instead, he goes inland a short way and "covers" himself in leaves against the cold, like a man burying an ember in ashes to keep it alive for morning (5.388–391). The verb for "cover" or "hide" is *kalúptō*, identical to Kalypso's name. The man who was "hidden" against his will, now acts to hide himself and keep his spark of mortal life burning.

The place where he sleeps is beneath entwined olive trees, one wild, the other a cultivated variety. The olive, a tree essential to Greek civilization, marks the distance Odysseus has come, just as it will mark every stage of his return home. No olive tree appeared in Kalypso's groves of poplar; on Skheria the wild and the cultivated are inextricable; and on Ithaka, which is fully in the real world, there are two: one near the coast, where Odysseus is dropped off sleeping (13.122), and another in his marriage chamber (23.190–124). When he "*kalúptō* "s himself in olive leaves to sleep, the verb indicates he has gone from passive to active; the olive leaves, that he has come from a paradise of nature toward the real world of humankind. As we see later, when Odysseus tells his story "as skillfully as a bard" in this island's city (11.368), he has also moved from biological immortality to cultural immortality in *kléos.*

The Phaiakians who inhabit Skheria are highly civilized. They have a walled city with houses and temples, cultivated orchards and gardens, art, music, dances, and athletic games (6.9–10, 7.112–28, 8.244–249). The men have perfected the art of seafaring and the women are expert in weaving (7.108–111). Their bard even knows stories of the Trojan War, and sings two involving Odysseus before Odysseus has identified himself. Here is a place that is tempting indeed, and many another hero might have married the king's pretty daughter and stayed.

That pretty daughter is the first person Odysseus meets upon awakening. Nausikaä, who has just reached marriageable age, has come to wash the royal clothes so that they will be ready whenever she marries. She thinks it is her own idea, but really it is Athena's, who has begun to intervene. No scene in the epic is more charming than this one. First the girls wash and play ball, and then Odysseus emerges naked from the bushes "like a lion," with only a leafy branch to cover his privates. The other girls run, but Nausikaä, who is well schooled in the rules of hospitality, waits to hear what the wild-looking stranger will say and then offers bathing supplies, clothing, food, and escort to the city (6.186–210). Odysseus flatters her, comparing her to Artemis and saying how lucky her future husband will be. He extols the value of a harmonious marriage (6.149–85). After he bathes and Athena enhances his looks, Nausikaä suddenly sees potential husband material (6.242–245). She manages to let him know that she is courted by all the finest Phaiakian men (6.276–289), and then gives him instructions as to how to find her father, Alkinoös, and how to supplicate her mother, Arete. Odysseus says nothing after his initial speech, allowing her to continue the flirtation but not getting himself in any deeper.

When Arete asks him to identify himself and say where he came from, Odysseus skirts the truth by starting his story only with Kalypso. He does not mention that he is married, thus keeping his potential as bridegroom alive. Alkinoös likes him as much as their daughter does and immediately offers her in marriage (7.311–315). Odysseus does not say yes, but he also does not say no. Much later, after he is completely sure of their goodwill and begins to reveal who he really is, he turns down the marriage without addressing the proposal directly. Kalypso and Circe had both desired him as husband, he says, but they could not persuade him because "there is nothing sweeter than fatherland and parents" (9.29–36). He delays mentioning a wife until he is about to board ship in Book 13 (42–43). Between Odysseus's careful speech and Alkinoös' perfect civility, no one gets hurt in this marriage dance.

"To a man who has any brains at all, the stranger and suppliant is like a brother," says Alkinoös (8.546–547), thereby setting the standard for the perfect host. An analogue of Menelaos when he hosted Telemakhos in Book 4, and forerunner of Eumaios, who hosts Odysseus in Books 14–16, Alkinoös knows when and how to feed and entertain a guest, when to question him, and when to send him off with guest gifts. The greatest gift is transportation home in one of the Phaiakians' seemingly magical ships that can speedily travel great distances on automatic pilot (8.555–563). With this gift Alkinoös raises hospitality to an heroic level, for long ago the Phaiakians had been given an oracle saying that they would someday incur Poseidon's anger for transporting people and that the god would then turn a ship to stone and pile a mountain over the city (8.564–569). Despite this terrible threat, the Phaiakians have chosen to be good hosts for years. Unfortunately, conveying Odysseus will trigger the punishment (13.125–183), whereupon contact between the utopian Phaiakians and the normal world will cease forever.

Odysseus finally identifies himself so that the Phaiakians can program the ships to take him home "I am Odysseus, son of Laertes," he begins, " known to all men for my guile (*dólos*), and my *kléos* rises to the heavens" (9.19–20). *Dólos* is the same word Odysseus used when he asked Phemios to sing the story of the Trojan Horse (8.494), and he will himself now recount a story of postwar dangers, endurance and *dólos* that no bard yet knows. These adventures, which are often called the Great Wanderings, are part of his self-identification. All but the first are set in a folktale world of monsters and the supernatural, which retains a strong connection to the real world via key themes: mindfulness struggling against oblivion, the cost of wrong eating, and hospitality.

The world of the Great Wanderings is a liminal one between nature and culture, in which characters are just human enough to highlight modes of behavior and states of existence as being either bestial or human, either savage or civilized. Alkinoös asks Odysseus to tell which of the peoples he met were "harsh, savage and unjust, and which were good hosts with god-fearing thoughts," thus dividing the world into good and bad hosts (8.575–576, and see 6.120–121). Bad hosts are extraordinarily bad in the Great Wanderings: Polyphemus and the Laistrygones eat their guests instead of feeding them, while Circe turns them into pigs, or food animals. The Sirens' song binds men to oblivion and death. Even good-willed hosts can be dangerous: the Lotus Eaters offer improper food that makes men forget homecoming, induces oblivion. Odysseus once (with Circe) is able to turn a bad host into a good one through a magic herb given him by Hermes, but all he can do with the others is escape.

Some of Odysseus' adventures have become proverbial, such as having to choose between Skylla and Kharybdis, the man-eating monster on one side and the ship-swallowing whirlpool on the other. This particular adventure has no moral lesson to teach, but it is a wonderful image for situations that are totally unmanageable. Most adventures teach the value of restraint and caution, of refusing the easy way, especially when it comes to eating. It is a lesson Odysseus' men do not learn, and it is why all of them perish in the end. Because they are weary, they insist on stopping on the island of Thrinakia even though they have been warned of disaster if they do. When they are trapped there for a month, they decide to eat Helios's cattle, even though they know the animals are sacred. They think they will be able to pay the god recompense when they get home, a thought they share with the suitors, but they also think that a slow death by starvation is worse than a quick one the god might send (12.340–352). In other words, they would rather die with a full belly than endure with an empty one. And so they do: the ship is struck by a lightning bolt as soon as it leaves the island, and Odysseus, the only one who refused to eat, is the only survivor.

One adventure is fully epic: the journey to Hades to consult the seer Teiresias about how to get home. Herakles, the greatest of Greek heroes, had made just such an epic journey to bring back Cerberus, the three-headed hound, and trips to the underworld would become part of many heroes' quests in later epics. All that Odysseus will bring back is information, and he does not actually go underground or by himself; nonetheless, his journey is depicted as parallel to what the poet has Herakles call his most difficult labor (11.623–624). After speaking with Teiresias about how to get home, Odysseus then learns from his mother, who seems recently dead, about what awaits him at home. He learns that Penelope weeps, that his grieving father sleeps in the dirt at the farm, and that Antikleia herself died through longing for him (11.181–203). Similar to what the audience learned in Books 1–4, his mother's words indicate how much he is needed in Ithaka.

After talking with his mother, the ever curious Odysseus lingers to converse with as many shades as he can, first those of women, which greatly pleases Arete, and then those of Agamemnon, Achilles, and Ajax, whose martial *kléos* obviously gives them no happiness in the afterlife. Ajax refuses to talk with him, still angry over the judgment that valued intelligence over physical strength; Agamemnon describes his horrible end, which, like Ajax's, seems to have vitiated his previous *kléos* (see 9.264–266); and Achilles, who received supreme *kléos* for dying as a hero ought, finds it no consolation for the fact of being dead. Odysseus urges him to look on the bright side: "Achilles, no man ever was or will be more fortunate. For before while you were alive, we Argives honored you equally with the gods, and now again in this realm you wield great power among the dead." (11.482–486). Achilles will have none of it. "I would rather be above the earth as a servant to another in the house of a landless man who had little substance than to rule among all the withered dead" (489–491). Their exchange highlights the difference in their character that was visible in the *Iliad*: versatile Odysseus tries to make the best of any situation, while Achilles, the extremist, focuses on limitations, in this case the help he cannot give his father, the *timé* he cannot protect. Odysseus is able to make Achilles happy only by telling him a story of the living: how his son won a noble *géras* for his heroic fighting (11.506–537). Living is what matters in the *Odyssey*.

The qualities of endurance, guile, and restraint that ensure his survival in the Great Wanderings are also those that ensure victory at home. Odysseus' false identity in the Cyclops incident buys him the time he needs to escape; five equally clever false identities in Ithaka buy him time and provoke the action he needs. The ability to endure pain and to postpone acting until the time is right enables him to escape the

Cyclops's cave, overcome Circe, and refrain from eating Helios's sacred cattle; in Ithaka Odysseus endures the insults and physical assaults of the suitors and their henchman without losing his temper (esp. 17.235–238, 20.183–184); he hides his sorrow over his faithful dog Argos (17.304–305), and he holds firm against his pity for Penelope's weeping (19.209–211).

At the same time, the bad hospitality so clearly associated with bestial savagery in the Great Wanderings imbues the suitors' behavior with that same savagery. Polyphemos, the Cyclops, mocks the norms of hospitality by giving Odysseus the "guest gift" of being eaten last; Ktessippos, the suitor, throws a "guest gift" – an ox hoof – at the disguised Odysseus's head (20.296–300). The beef the companions eat on *Thrinacia* signals sacrilege by lowing as if it were alive (12.395–396); the meat the suitors eat signals bestiality by bleeding as if it were raw (20.348); both portend divine punishment. By the time Odysseus comes to kill them, the poet has made the suitors seem like animals, which readies the audience to accept the coming slaughter.

Odysseus moves by stages from the coast to the swineherd's hut to his courtyard to the dining hall of his palace, securing allies as he sets about winning back his *oîkos*. With the help of only his old nurse and two faithful servants who become family, he, Telemakhos and Athena kill the suitors. The *oîkos* will not really be his, however, until he wins his wife.

Penelope

Penelope is the archetypal faithful wife. The ghost of Agamemnon exclaims, "How good were the thoughts of blameless Penelope, daughter of Ikarios! How well she remembered Odysseus, her lawful husband! The *kléos* of her virtue will never die, but for earth-bound men the gods will fashion a song to grace the prudence of Penelope." How different is the "song of hate" that will arise from Klytemnestra's murder of her lawful husband to give a bad reputation to all "female women," even those who are good (24.191–202). Apparently, Penelope's *kléos* will grace only her, while Klytemnestra's will taint all women. All women are under suspicion, that is, unless and until they accomplish something truly heroic.

For her action to achieve heroic status, Penelope needs a heroic husband. If Odysseus did not return, and return in precisely the way he does, Penelope's endurance and wiles would be to no avail. On the other hand, if Penelope were not both faithful and clever enough to stall the suitors, Odysseus would not have a home and son to return to. This husband and wife, who are matched as closely as their different genders allow, exemplify the perfect marriage that Odysseus describes to Nausikaä in Book 6: "There is nothing stronger or better than this, when a like-minded man and woman maintain a household, a source of pain to their enemies but joy to well-wishers" (6.182–185).

Helen and Menelaos' marriage is not like this. Far cleverer than her husband, the daughter of Zeus interprets instantly things that Menelaos has to ponder (4.116–119, 140–144; 15.169–177); she also has mood-changing drugs that make her akin to the dangerous Circe. The stories she and Menelaos tell Telemakhos about Odysseus further demonstrate strains in their marriage. At the end of her story about helping Odysseus when he came to spy in Troy, she claims that by that time she wanted to return home, regretting the ruinous madness of Aphrodite "who led me away from my homeland, my daughter, my chamber and a husband who lacked nothing in brains and good looks" (4.249–264). Menelaos, though unfailingly polite, counters with a story about how only Odysseus' cleverness and endurance saved the men inside the Trojan horse from responding to her when she called to them in the voice of their wives; he includes the detail that she was accompanied by Deipho-bos, her second Trojan husband (4.269–289). So much for wanting to return to her perfect husband! Adulterous Helen can never be trusted, and her flawed marriage, like her sister Klytemnestra's murderous one, is a foil to the perfect match awaiting Odysseus.

Penelope's endless weeping expresses both her faithfulness and her genuine membership in Odysseus' family. Odysseus weeps frequently; Telemakhos, Eurykleia, Eumaios, Philoitios, Laertes, and the faithful servants weep copiously when they think of Odysseus and when they are reunited with him. As in the *Iliad*, weeping is connected with full human-ity, that is, with the grief and longing that stem from human caring and suffering. In the fabulous world of Odysseus' adventures, the Phaiakians do not weep, Circe does not weep, Kalypso does not weep. In Ithaka, the suitors neither weep nor pity Penelope's tears. In Sparta, semidivine Helen administers nepenthe ("no pain"), a drug that prevents weeping, to keep dinner guests cheerful while listening to war stories (4.221–225). When Penelope and Odysseus hear war stories, however, they are helpless to stop tears (1.336; 8.82–92, 521–531), and one suspects that if they were Helen's guests, they would refuse her drug.

Penelope needs as much endurance and *dólos* to cope with the uncivilized suitors for three years as Odysseus needs to cope with the monsters and allurements that hinder his return home. Her goal is to keep her identity as both Odysseus' wife and Telemakhos' mother intact, and she must negotiate between marriage to a suitor and the death or impoverishment of her son. The poem several times suggests that if Odysseus were in fact to be dead, she would be expected to remarry (1.292, 19.158–159); it also suggests that until she knows for sure, the virtuous choice is not to remarry (2.125–6, 16.75, 23.149–151). Her personal desire is clearly not to remarry, but once her son is grown, her love for him pushes her toward doing so. Like Odysseus in the storm at sea in Book 5, she must decide when it is time to abandon the raft; just as he does, she waits until the very last minute.

Penelope deploys her feminine tool, the loom, to delay having to make a choice for three years. Having persuaded the suitors to wait until she finishes weaving Laertes' shroud, she weaves by day and unravels by night. With this *dólos* (2.93), which is as clever as any Odysseus thinks up, she gains three years. She also deceives the suitors individually, "rousing hope in all and making promises to each" (2.91–92) to keep them all in competition with each other. She must do this because telling them that she is disgusted by their behavior and still loves her incomparable husband, which she does often (for example, at 16.409–433, 18.250–273, 21.331–333), fails to deter them. Penelope's "rousing hope" in the suitors is similar to Odysseus' gentle manipulation of Nausikaa and the Phaiakians in Books 6–9. The difference is that Odysseus' interlocutors are civilized and respect the laws of hospitality, while Penelope's are not.

Penelope is most famous for her weaving ruse, which is described at length no fewer than three times in the *Odyssey* (2.93–109, 19.137–155, 24.128–145). Within the epic's unfolding time, however, she performs another equally important stratagem to thwart the suitors: the contest of the bow. The dead suitors believe that it is a *dólos* contrived in collusion with Odysseus, but it is not so contrived, at least not consciously. Why does she do it? Homer does not say explicitly, but he gives clues. First is her comparing her night-long anxiety to the grief of the nightingale, who once mistakenly killed her son (19.518–523).[4] Since she knows the suitors are planning to kill Telemakhos, it is logical for her to feel that if she does nothing, she might be contributing to his death. Second is her dream about the geese and the killer eagle who turns into Odysseus (19.536–54). Dreams are a source of important information for Penelope, who does not have much access to the outside. In Book 4, Athena sends the dream that tells her Telemakhos is all right (4.795–829). In Book 20, with Odysseus actually sleeping in the palace close enough to hear her cry out, she dreams she is sleeping next to him (88–90). Her dreams, which truthfully predict the future, are equivalent to what we today would call feminine intuition and are the basis of her correct action. Third, even if her intuition is wrong, the contest will weed out anyone who is not as strong and skilled as Odysseus, which, as anyone could guess, probably means all the playboy suitors.

The reunion of Penelope and Odysseus famously depends on another trick, the trick of the bed. She tests the man who claims he is her husband by casually asking Eurykleia to move their marriage bed to the hall. Only she and Odysseus know that one post of the bed is a living olive tree, a mark of the fundamental importance of marriage to the household. For the first time in the epic, Odysseus is tricked into losing his temper, outsmarted by his wife. Then, after the two fall into each others arms, their weeping is described by a simile that cements their equality: "Odysseus wept as he held his soul mate, his loving wife. As welcome as land appears to swimmers whose well-built ship has been wrecked by Poseidon, by the pounding of waves and wind, and few escape from the gray sea by swimming to land, and much salt crusts on their skin, but welcome they climb onto land, escaping harm, so welcome did her husband appear to her when she looked upon him . . ." (23.232–239). The poet fools the audience into thinking the simile is about Odysseus and then switches to Penelope at the end. Just as in Book 8 Odysseus transcended gender by weeping like a woman whose husband has been killed and city destroyed (8.521–531), so Penelope weeps like male sailors whose experience mirrors her husband's.

Conclusion

The reunion of husband and wife concludes with lovemaking and long storytelling, each spouse fully informing the other about their experiences in the last ten years. Many readers feel that the story should end here, with the two of them finally falling asleep near the end of Book 23. But there is still much to resolve in Ithaka. The house is now in order, but the community is divided. Wedding songs are only temporarily effective against the discovery of the 108 bodies stacked in the courtyard, and vengeance will follow. Few are the fathers who will agree that a boorish son merits capital punishment, and some Ithakan fathers, like Aigyptos, have an additional grievance over the sons Odysseus did not bring home from Troy (2.15–23). Odysseus, therefore, goes back out of the palace to reunite with his own father and then to deal with the suitors' fathers.

One early Greek thought was that a whole community might be destroyed because of the guilt of one of its members, or saved because of the excellence of its leaders. But, as we heard at the beginning of the poem, both Odysseus' companions and Aigisthos, killer of Agamemnon, died through their own ruinous recklessness. Odysseus was not destroyed when his companions paid for their actions, nor could he, great and good and beloved of the gods though he was, save them.

The opposing point of view is expressed often in the *Odyssey*. Theoklymenos, Telemakhos' suppliant, is fleeing his home because he killed a man (15.272–278). Odysseus' first fictitious identity is that of a man who is in exile because he is a murderer (13.259–275) even though no one saw the murder. Before he killed the suitors, Odysseus seemed less worried about accomplishing the deed than about its aftermath (20.41–43), and he reiterates the problem afterwards: "when someone kills a single man in a community, a man who does not leave many helpers behind, he flees, forsaking kin and fatherland" (23.118–121). Belief that murderers automatically flee forms the basis of the suitors' relatives' assumption Odysseus will flee and thus perhaps escape their vengeance (24.430–435). Despite the fact that Medon certifies that Odysseus had the support of the gods, and despite Halitherses' reminding the fathers of their failure to stop their sons' recklessness (24.445–458), a majority of Ithakans support this world view (24.463–464).

It takes a fiat from Zeus, the moral Zeus who opened the poem with words about individual responsibility and who is worshiped by Eumaios as protector of strangers and punisher of wrongs, to resolve the head-on conflict between these two modes of consciousness at the end of Book 24. Zeus decrees three things: first, that there will be a treaty and Odysseus will be "always be king;" second, that there will be a "forgetting" of the murder and a resumption of friendship between Odysseus and the relatives of those he has justly slain; and third, that there will be peace and prosperity (483–486).

The poem does not end with the fiat. Before Athena executes Zeus's peaceful will on earth, she first helps Odysseus' family symbolically defeat the proponents of the other code of conduct. Laertes, energized and rejuvenated by Odysseus' return, is inspired by Athena to kill Eupeithes, the father of Antinoös. Odysseus and Telemakhos attack the front line until Athena's shout causes the Ithakans to turn and flee back to town. Odysseus keeps on until Zeus's thunderbolt warns him to desist. When Athena administers the treaty, therefore, the poem is celebrating the triumph of a social order that privileges the individual and the individual household over the community as a whole.

Odysseus started the poem as generic male humanity on Kalypso's island. At the end of the poem he has won his full social and familial identity as father, husband, son, and king. Furthermore, a powerful male family line has come into being, as Odysseus stands between his father and son, all three in full armor and competing in prowess, to face the angry Ithakans. It would appear that the *Odyssey* has resolved tensions about who will succeed Odysseus as king of Ithaka through the firm establishment of patriarchal hereditary monarchy.

Since Zeus has promised peace and prosperity, the audience can envision Odysseus as continuing to create *kléos* as a righteously ruling "blameless king" (19.109–114); Penelope, whom Odysseus earlier compared to such a king, recedes into her chambers. Her *kléos* is, as she predicted, "greater and more beautiful" now that her husband has successfully come home (19.127–128), because now heroic epic can celebrate her along with him. That the poet chose to do so in the way he did, giving her a central role as partner in a genre focused on male achievement, is extraordinary. But in the end, Penelope disappears as the *Odyssey* returns to the epic norms that discourage equating women with kings. Her like will not appear again, not in the *Argonautika*'s clever but terrifying Medea, nor in the *Aeneid*'s Creusa and Dido, who are tragically denied partnership with the questing hero. Without the *Odyssey*'s Penelope, however, Virgil could not count on his readers knowing just how much Aeneas must sacrifice to the overwhelming masculinity of Rome.

Further Reading

Text and Translations

Richmond Lattimore's *The Odyssey of Homer* (New York, 1967), in iambic hexameter, is closest to the Greek and has an excellent introduction. Most general readers will prefer the lively recent translations by Robert Fagles, *The Odyssey* (New York, 1996), with an excellent introduction by Bernard Knox; Stanley Lombardo, *Odyssey* (Indianapolis, IN, 2000), with an excellent introduction by Sheila Murnaghan; and Ian Johnston *The Odyssey* (Arlington, VA, 2006). Fagles and Lombardo give excellent suggestions for further reading. Robert Fitzgerald's fine translation has been reissued with an introduction by D. Carne Ross (New York, 1998).

The Greek text on which I base my translations is *Homeri Opera* second edition, vols. III and IV, ed., T.W. Allen (Oxford, 1917, 1919). I have benefited greatly from the commentary of W. B. Stanford, ed., *The Odyssey*, second edition, 2 vols. (London and New York, 1965), as well as by the three-volume *A Commentary to Homer's Odyssey*, Vol. I: Books I–VIII, A. Heubeck, S. West, J. B. Hainsworth (eds.); Vol. II Books IX–XVI, A. Heubeck, A. Hoekstra (eds.); Vol. III Books XVII–XXIV, J. Russo, M. Fernandez-Galleano, A. Heubeck (eds.) (New York and Oxford, 1988–1992).

Interpretation and Commentary

Seth Schein's *Reading the Odyssey* (Princeton, 1996) presents important essays that interpret the epic from a variety of approaches plus an excellent introduction by Schein. All the essays reward reading, but among them I would especially recommend the two short pieces by J.-P. Vernant (pp. 55–61, 185–189) and the essay by Charles Segal on "*Kléos*" (pp. 201–221).

G. Dimock's "The Name of Odysseus" *Hudson Review* 9 (1956), 52–70 (reprinted G. Steiner and R. Fagles, eds., *Homer* [Englewood Cliffs, NJ, 1962]) discusses Odysseus as "Trouble." H.P. Foley "Reverse Similes and Sex Roles in the *Odyssey*" *Arethusa* 11 (1978), 7–26 (reprinted J. Peradotto and J. P. Sullivan, eds., *Women in the Ancient World* [Albany, 1984], 59–78) and Ch. Segal's *Singers, Heroes, and Gods in the Odyssey* (Ithaca, NY, 1994) offer fine close readings and superb insights. K. J. Atchity's "Greek Princes and Aegean Princesses" in *Critical Essays on Homer* (Boston, 1987) is a flawed but nonetheless strong argument that the evolution from matriliny and to patriliny in the period 1650–1250 underlies some of the tension around Penelope.

The more advanced reader will find the following essays and book length studies rewarding: N. Austin, *Archery at the Dark of the Moon* (Berkeley, 1975), which uses a structuralist approach; J. S. Clay, *The Wrath of Athena* (Princeton, 1983); A. T. Edwards' "Homer's Ethical Geography," *Transactions of the American Philological Society* 123 (1993), 27–78, which discusses the reversal of the normal epic hierarchy between city and country in the second half of the *Odyssey*; Sheila Murnaghan

Disguise and Recognition in the Odyssey (Princeton, 1987), which, with special attention to Penelope, analyzes how motifs of disguise and recognition elucidate the values of the *Odyssey*'s world; M. Nagler, *Spontaneity and Tradition* (Berkeley, 1974), especially Chapters 3 and 4 (pp. 64–130); P. Pucci, *Odysseus Polytropos* (Ithaca, NY, 1987), which analyzes the relationship of the *Odyssey* to the *Iliad*; W. G. Thalmann, *The Swineherd and the Bow* (Ithaca, 1998), which discusses representations of class in the *Odyssey* through close textual analysis with the aid of archaeological evidence and anthropological theory.

There are many excellent studies of gender. Start with Beth Cohen, ed., *The Distaff Side* (Oxford, 1995), which offers excellent essays on the representation of female characters from the perspectives of art history and history as well as classics; it includes 60 illustrations of art works from the seventh century BCE to the first century CE. Other excellent works include Ann Bergren's "Helen's Good Drug" in S. Kresic, ed., *Contemporary Literary Hermeneutics and Interpretation of Classical Texts* (Ottowa, CA, 1981), 201–214; Barbara Clayton's *A Penelopean Poetics* (Lanham, 2004), which looks at Penelope's weaving as a gendered discourse that embraces multiplicity and ambiguity; L. E. Dougherty *Siren Songs* (Ann Arbor, 1995), which examines gender, narrators, and implied audiences; Marilyn Katz's *Penelope's Renown* (Princeton, 1991); Nancy Felson Ruben's *Regarding Penelope* (Norman, OK, 1997), which shows how the poet deploys alternative plot patterns around Penelope's behavior, and of which an important excerpt is reprinted in Schein, above, pp.163–183; and Nancy Worman's "This Voice Which is not One: Helen's Verbal Guises in Homeric Epic" in A. Lardinois and L. McClure, eds., *Making Silence Speak* (Princeton, 2001), 19–37.

Modern Adaptations, Revisions, and Responses

Edith Hall's *The Return of Ulysses* (London, 2008) is a highly readable but learned exploration of the influence of the *Odyssey* on literature from late antiquity to modern times. It is a very welcome addition to W. B. Standford's classic *The Ulysses Theme* (1968), which was written in a prefeminist, pre-postcolonial critical world.

Drama: Mary Zimmerman, *The Odyssey* (Evanston, IL, 2003).
Film: Joel and Ethan Coen used the framework and many episodes of the *Odyssey* to create their comic *O Brother Where Art Thou?* (2000).

Novels: Margaret Atwood, *The Penelopiad* (New York, 2005). James Joyce's *Ulysses* (Paris, 1922) is a masterpiece in its own right.

Poetry: Derek Walcott's *Omeros* (New York, 1992) is a lyric postcolonial Caribbean epic that contains an *Iliad* within an *Odyssey*. Linda Paston has written a series of seven poems, "Re-reading the Odyssey in Middle Age," in *The Imperfect Paradise* (Norton, 1988). To read many poets' responses to the *Odyssey*, see Nina Kossman, ed., *Gods and Mortals: Modern Poems on Classical Myths* (Oxford, 2001), 253–274.

Jonathan Shay, a psychiatrist with the Veteran's Administration, offers in *Odysseus in America* (New York, 2002) a fascinating interpretation of Odysseus as brilliant strategist but poor officer in charge of troops, and argues that the poem as a whole can be interpreted as an allegory of what happens to many combat veterans when they return home.

Notes

1 The names of both heroes may be etymologically connected to woe and pain. The first part of Achilles' name is undoubtedly connected to *akhos*, the Greek word for grief (for a full discussion, see Gregory Nagy, *the Best of the Achaeans*, Baltimore, 1979, 69–83). Homer links Odysseus' name to pain via the words of his grandfather: "since I have come causing pain (*odyssamenos*) to many, both men and women throughout the fertile earth, let his name be Odysseus" (19.407–409).

2 *Oikos* means "house," "home," and "family."

3 The Greek word that is translated as "king," *basileús*, means someone who has authority over a group. All the heroes in the *Iliad* are "kings." Just as there are several kings in the Greek army, so too there are many kings in Ithaka, with Odysseus being the one with overarching authority. These kings make up the aristocracy.

4 Before she was a bird, Aidon was a queen with one son. Angry at Niobe's pride in her numerous sons, she attempted to kill Niobe's oldest while he was sleeping but killed her own son by mistake.

5

The *Argonautika* of Apollonios of Rhodes

The Alexandrian Context

Epic poetry flourished in the 400 years between Homer and Apollonios, but, except for fragments, it has all disappeared. Gone, too, are the earlier epics that sang the voyage of the Argonauts, the labors of Herakles, and the Theban cycle of hubris, infanticide, incest, and fratricide. The *Iliad* and the *Odyssey* survived because they were early recognized as exceptional, and written copies became the prize possessions of some wealthy cities. Around 400 BCE, Antimakhos of Kolophon even produced a scholarly edition. For the illiterate, which was most of the population, there were public performances. Rhapsodes called the Homeridai, a guild of poets from Khios, claimed the *Iliad* and *Odyssey* as their special area of expertise and traveled throughout Greece singing the poems competitively and for hire. In Athens, large parts of both poems were sung every four years at the Great Panathenaic celebration of Athena, and by at least the early fourth century, as Xenophon tells us, recitations were available daily – perhaps performed by the equivalent of today's sidewalk singers. Some who had enough leisure and memory even memorized the poems for themselves (*Symposium* 3.5–6).

Alexander the Great carried the poems beyond the geographical confines of Greece – on his expeditions of conquest, we are told, he slept with the *Iliad* beneath his pillow (Plutarch, *Alexander* 8.2). After he died in 323 BCE, the poems had a natural home in the Greek communities that formed in the cities he had founded. They were as much a part of the heritage of Hellenistic poets as the lays of oral tradition were to Homer.

Hellenistic is the name given to the Greek culture that flourished over the area conquered by Alexander from his death until the Roman defeat of Kleopatra and Marc Antony in 31 BCE. Alexander's Greek generals divided up the conquered territory, ruling first as governors answering to Macedon, and then as self-proclaimed kings of four separate kingdoms. In this way, Ptolemy became king of Egypt in 305 BCE, and his son Ptolemy II, the first of fourteen successors named after their original progenitor, succeeded him in 283 BCE.

The Ptolemies' capital city was Alexandria, founded by Alexander in 331 BCE. Populated by Greek citizens, who had been recruited to immigrate, and by native Egyptian noncitizen residents, it was developed as a thoroughly Greek city. The Ptolemies grew fabulously wealthy on the huge revenues they received from trade into and out of Egypt, and they spent some of this wealth on building and maintaining a magnificent Museum, or Temple of the Muses, with an adjacent Royal Library. The Museum functioned as a research institute, with literary and scientific scholars in residence. The Library's purpose was to collect earlier Greek literature and make it the core of expatriate Greek culture in Egypt. The Homeric poems, archaic and classical lyric poetry, and the literary production – drama, history, oratory, philosophy – of classical Athens formed the bedrock of this culture. Obscure texts, too, were collected with the aim of preserving all of Greek literature. Greek texts were bought or borrowed from around the world, and at one point the Library held an astonishing 490,000 scrolls. Although precious originals were no doubt restricted to librarian access, the Library was open to all who knew how to read, which included most of the elite population.

Scholars from Athens and other centers of learning were enticed to Alexandria to become residents in the Museum where they would hold symposia, do research, and pass their skills on to a younger generation. Many worked in the Library, where they catalogued texts, supervised their copying, and studied them, noting variants and using their expertise to identify and eliminate scribal mistakes and changes to what they considered to be the original versions. Homer's texts were the prime object of study for many, including Zenodotos, the first chief Librarian.

Like Professor J. R. R. Tolkien in recent times, many of the literary scholars who worked in the Alexandrian and other libraries in the Hellenistic world (for example, at Antioch, Pella, Pergamum, and at the Academy and Lyceum in Athens) also wrote creatively. These scholar poets developed a new kind of poetry, one directed more to each other than to the public. Their poetry displayed the great learning of its writers, and it demanded of readers an equal amount of learning. To make old subjects fresh, rare words and obscure variants of myths were used. Much of the pleasure of reading apparently came from recognizing such obscurities as well as identifying frequent allusions to the literary predecessors that they all knew so well. Some of this poetry survives, but its demand for active reader participation can make comprehension difficult for even the most literate of today's readers – as it did indeed for most Alexandrian and Roman readers, who required handbooks of mythology and glossaries of obscure terms to cope with it.

The scholar poets wrote in a variety of genres on many subjects. We are told that Philetas of Kos, tutor of Ptolemy II, wrote a story in dactylic hexameters about Odysseus' stop at Aiolos's island, including a love affair with one of Aiolos's daughters; he also wrote narratives in elegiac meter (couplets consisting of one dactylic hexameter line and one five-beat dactylic pentameter line), and epigrams (short, pithy poems to commemorate the dead or dedicate something to a god or person). Asklepiades and Kallimakhos perfected the witty erotic epigram. Kallimakhos also wrote hymns, iambic poems, and a collection of elegiac poems called "*Aitia*" ("Causes"), which explained the origins of local cults and customs. Aratos transformed a prose treatise on astronomy into hexameter verse, the *Phaenomena*, which became widely influential and was translated into Latin by both Varro and Cicero nearly two centuries later. All of this poetry is characterized by tight construction and high polish, as are the pastoral vignettes of Theokritos of Syracuse, who was in Alexandria in the 270s. Theokritos wrote in dactylic hexameter, describing realistic scenes of city life in Alexandria or idealized life among lyric goatherds in the countryside. Love takes center stage, as Polyphemos the Cyclops sings his unrequited love for Galateia, housewives go off to the festival of Adonis, and a young woman tries magic to get her lover back. Perhaps because Theokritos was solely a poet and not also a professional scholar, his poems are more accessible than some of the others'.

I have given a sample of the genres and styles that were favored in order to illustrate what almost no serious poet wanted to do: write heroic epic or Athenian tragedy. The latter had been so intricately tied to the democratic city that its absence in the creative work of Alexandrian poets, who did not participate in political life, is not surprising. As for heroic epic, many of the scholar poets who admired and studied the

Iliad and *Odyssey* seem to have feared producing something on the level of the Epic Cycle poems or Antimakhos of Kolophon's *Thebaid* and *Lyde*, which, while popular, were judged by the avant-garde to be the very antithesis of art.[1]

Eschewing popular demand, cutting-edge Alexandrian poets chose to use Homer as a source, not a model, selecting out single episodes to elaborate and work into miniature epic. Such shorter narratives were more often than not elaborated through love themes or other nonheroic situations, as it appears Philetas did in his miniature epic about Odysseus on Aiolos' island. Similarly, Kallimakhos chose to elaborate an episode from within the story of Theseus' capture of the Marathon bull, to wit Theseus' visit with an old woman, Hekale, whom he encountered on the way to Marathon. Since the woman tells Theseus many stories about the origins of Attic cult, Kallimakhos is clearly using the epic form as an alternative way to present a collection of *aítia*. Other short epics told foundation stories, probably on commission from cities.

It appears that there was some artistic (as well as popular) pressure to write traditional narrative epic, and some poets regarded it still as the highest goal. Why else would the prolific and influential Kallimakhos need to declare he "hated the Cyclic genre" and famously defend his "slender Muse" and collections of short poems against some who disparaged him for not having written "a continuous poem with thousands of verses about kings and heroes" (*Epigram* 30, *Aitia* 1). Story tells that one of the disparagers was Apollonios of Rhodes, who did choose to write an epic poem with thousands of verses (5,835, to be exact) about kings and heroes. This epic, like *Lord of the Rings*, would be directed to a wide public, but it would not be a throwback to the old heroic poetics.

Apollonios was born in Alexandria, Egypt, around 300 BCE, and lived probably until the 230s BCE. He was educated either directly or indirectly by Kallimakhos. He is called Apollonios "of Rhodes" either because in his early manhood he spent several years in the island city of Rhodes writing poetry and teaching, or because he retired there. We do not know for sure. We know that he was tutor to Ptolemy II's son and that he was head of the Royal Library, probably from around 270–245 BCE. He produced critical works on Homer and Hesiod, as well as many foundation epics that seem to have exhibited the normal Alexandrian proclivity toward love, obscure myth, and origins of cities, cults, and customs. He also wrote the *Argonautika*, an epic on the traditional heroic theme of the first sea voyage from Greece to Asia.

The *Argonautika* before Apollonios

The story of the Argonauts, heroes who sailed on the ship Argo across the sea to the eastern end of the Black Sea to retrieve a golden fleece, was as old as stories of the Trojan War and had been told many times. It told of King Pelias's command to his young nephew Jason, rightful heir to the kingship of Iolkos, to bring the fleece as the price of the throne; and it told of the many heroes, most of them young like Jason, who came to join him from all over Greece, including Herakles, Orpheus, Kastor and Polydeukes, the twin sons of Boreas (the Northwind), and Peleus, Achilles' father. Building a ship strong enough to cross the ocean was the first heroic feat, and many more followed on the voyage to Kolkhis, the eastern margin of the known world. Clashing Rocks, nasty Harpies, recently "widowed" Lemnian ladies, and encounters with exotic natives tested the heroes' mettle in exciting ways. Once in Kolkhis, there were fire-breathing bulls to harness, earth-born giants to conquer, and a golden fleece to steal from its guardian serpent. On the way home they had to elude pursuit by killing Medea's brother, cross a desert with the ship on their backs, and slay a bronze giant. Once home, there was a treacherous king to deal with. All these events may not have been in the archaic epics (extant fragments do not allude to the desert or Talos the bronze giant, which were certainly there by the end of the fifth century), but even without them it would have been an exciting story filled with marvelous adventures.

The tasks in Kolkhis were for Jason alone, and to accomplish them he required the help of Aphrodite, the third goddess to come to his aid. Athena built him the first seaworthy ship; Hera made the first sea voyage possible by gathering the crew and navigating the Clashing Rocks; and in Kolkhis, according to Pindar, Aphrodite taught Jason the first love charm so that he could remove Medea's *aidōs* (sense of duty to her parents) and set her aflame with desire (*Pythian* 4. 216–219). Apollonios changes the "weapon" to Eros's arrow, but the effect is the same: Medea, madly in love, gives Jason a fireproof ointment and strategy for accomplishing the tasks her father has set. He in turn promises her marriage.

In at least one of the archaic versions, this marriage may have been part of an *aítion* or founding legend. Hesiod says, Medea "bore to Jason a son, Medeios, who was reared by Kheiron in the mountains"(*Theogony*

1001–1002), and in a tradition reported by the Graeco-Roman mythographer Apollodoros (1.9.28), Medea's son Medeios by Aigeus gave his name to the Medes, a people of what is now northern Iran. By means of such stories, Greek legend forged links with or asserted intrinsic superiority over peoples of eastern lands. The adventures of the Argonauts, which could be supplemented whenever the need arose, forged links at many places throughout the Aegean, Propontis (Sea of Marmara), and Black Sea. As such it was the perfect epic for a time of exploration and colonization in the early eighth century, and it was perfect too for the third century, when Alexander's huge empire was being sorted out by his Greek generals and the colonialist Greek communities they created. It was also ideally suited to combine the librarian's scientific interests in geography and ethnography with his more literary interests in romantic love.

Hesiod's *Theogony* and *Catalogue of Women*, at least two archaic Argonautic epics, one prose history,[2] Pindar's fourth Pythian ode, and Attic tragedy offered much material to Apollonios. Although only Euripides' *Medea* survives, we know that all three great Athenian tragedians wrote multiple plays on various parts of the legend. From these sources and from vase paintings, we know variants that Apollonios chose not to use. We also know what happened after Jason and Medea got back to Iolkos. Pelias refused to give up the throne, so at Jason's request Medea engineered his death in a most gruesome way. She tricked his daughters into killing and cutting him up into pieces, making them think that if they dropped the pieces into a cauldron of boiling herbs they would be rejuvenating their elderly father. (They had reason to believe her for she had demonstrated the procedure on a ram that turned into a lamb.) This repulsive strategy is reminiscent of what one variant of the myth said Medea had done to her brother Aspyrtos in order to deflect her father's pursuit: she killed him, cut him up, and dropped him limb by bloody limb into the sea so that Aieetes would have to stop to search for each piece of his son. After killing Pelias, Jason and Medea were expelled from Iolkos, whereupon they settled in Corinth for about ten years until Jason deserted Medea for a political marriage with the King of Corinth's daughter. At this point his "helper maiden"[3] became his destroyer, using her magic potions to kill his new bride, the king, and his two sons. When the Argo docks at the end of Apollonios' *Argonautika*, the audience knows what has been left out, what has been chosen and changed, and just what is still to come.

Apollonios' *Argonautika*

Beginning from you, Apollo, I will recall the epic stories (*kléa*) of
long-ago men, who drove the well-built Argo through
the mouth of the Sea and Black Rocks at the
behest of King Pelias, in quest of the golden fleece.
It happened because Pelias heard an oracle that
a dire fate awaited him from a man he would see
emerge from the people wearing one sandal.
And not long afterwards, just as the oracle said, Jason
[lost a sandal while crossing a river and appeared at a feast of Poseidon,
where Pelias recognized the danger and devised a dangerous sea voyage]
so that in the sea or
among foreign men he would lose his homecoming.

(1–17)

This extended proem contains a lot of information not just about the
subject of the poem but about the modern technique of the poet. The
poem opens as if it were going to be a hymn to Apollo, modeled on the
archaic "Homeric" hymn to Delian Apollo which begins "I will recall
Apollo the far shooter." But no, as the line continues it becomes clear
that the poet's real subject is "the *kléa* of men," a phrase that evokes the
Iliad's "*kléa* of men" (9.189 and 524) with only a slight change.[4] In
addition to shifting genre from hymn to epic, we note immediately that
the plural "*kléa* of men" signals that the poet is interested not only in a
multiplicity of heroes, but also in a multiplicity of stories. Aristotle, who
prescribed unity and consistency in epic, would have feared the worst,
and his fears would have been borne out.

You may have noticed that there is no Muse invoked. Does Apollo
perhaps take her place? No, because in line 5 the poet reveals that "beginning from Apollo" means he will start his story with the oracle that
caused Pelias to send the men on the quest. This kind of "beginning
from Apollo" again evokes the *Iliad*, where Apollo is said to have
caused the strife between Achilles and Agamemnon (*Il.* 1.9–10) just
before the terrifying god strode down from Olympos to shoot his
plague-arrows into the Greek army. Here Apollo disappears. He finally
makes an appearance in the middle of Book 2, but it is no more
than that, an appearance, accidental, as he passes by an island where the
Argonauts have landed. Although he is described in as awe-inspiring
terms as in the *Iliad*, he does not do anything but just floats away

anticlimactically (2.674–684). Heroic expectation is raised only to be transformed into something that feels no more unusual than an awesomely bright dawn.

The word in line 5 that I am translating as "oracle" (*phátis*) is a word that basically means "an utterance." Both "oracle" and "rumor" are possible translations. Apollonios chooses this word over one that more overtly carries religious significance.[5] Readers know to translate it as "oracle" because, if they have heard earlier epics or have read their Pindar or handbooks of mythology, they know that Apollo gave Pelias an oracle warning him that a one-sandaled man would cause his death. But at the same time, they can read the line as "It happened because Pelias heard a rumor," which gives the story an accidental quality that accords well with everyday life. Such fusion of the ordinary with the heroic characterizes the epic throughout.

A summary of essential background material concludes with a phrase, "would lose his homecoming" (17), which has a distinct Odyssean ring. Four lines later, after Apollonius (like Pindar) declines to describe the building of the ship, the words "heroes" and "wandering" again evoke Homeric epic and the *Odyssey* in particular. Again, the similarity points to a difference: the *Odyssey*'s proem pictured Odysseus suffering and learning on his wanderings, while the Argonauts will accomplish heroic deeds. Although the Argonauts will in fact suffer, their suffering is always brief and it is not a focus of the epic. This epic is an adventure story.

After he has asserted control over his poetic form and content, Apollonios finally asks the Muses "to prompt his song" (22) as a prelude to his catalogue of heroes. No reader could help being reminded of Homer's most famous invocation of the Muses for help with his catalogue of ships (*Il.* 2.484–92). Although most modern readers of the *Iliad* find little delight in Homer's catalogue and may find equally little in Apollonios', ancient Homeric scholars may have felt a frisson of intellectual pleasure when they noted how cleverly Apollonios matched the geographical distribution of his heroes' homes to that of Homer's ships. Much more delightful to most is the first hero to be described, one who has no analogue in the Homeric poems: the poet Orpheus, son of the Muse Kalliope. No poets appear among the warrior heroes of Troy (except perhaps Achilles, when he's not being a hero), and though there are some bards in the *Odyssey*, they are not heroes. Orpheus' talent, however, will be essential to this mission's success: his songs do not celebrate the glorious deeds of others, but are effective in themselves as, for example, when they create harmony among quarreling crew members and set the beat for the rowers' oars (1.494–515, 540–542).

Orpheus is a super hero in that his singing and lyre playing has the power to move even rocks and trees, and he can outsing the Sirens (1.26–31, 4.905–909). Other super heroes in the crew are Zetes and Kalais, sons of Boreas, who can fly by means of wings on their ankles (1.219–221); Lynkeus, who has x-ray vision (1.153–155); Periklumenos, shape-shifting grandson of Poseidon (1.156–160); Euphemus, son of Poseidon, who can run over water without getting his feet wet; and, of course, Herakles, who drops off the trussed Erymanthean Boar before playing hooky from his labors to join the adventure, (1.122–131). These super heroes mark an immediate difference from the Homeric world, aligning the poem rather with the Cyclic and other epics, which appear to have been concerned more with the marvelous than with the human condition.

Other demigod heroes like Zeus and Leda's son, Polydeukes, an invincible boxer (2.40–97), and several sons of Apollo, Hephaistos, Hermes, and Poseidon have extraordinary but not miraculous strengths and skills. Most interestingly, Jason, leader of the heroes, is not a demigod (he is at best the great-great-great-great grandson of Zeus or Prometheus) and has no particular strength or skill that we can see in the first two books of the epic. Unlike Pindar's Jason, who is "strong" and "mighty" (*Pythian* 4.236, 239) and is, as elsewhere, the automatic leader of the expedition, Apollonios' Jason is an ordinary guy who ends up leading the expedition for two unheroic reasons: he is the one who called them together, and he sets the terms of what the leader needs to do: "attend to details and be responsible for war and peace with foreign powers" (1.339–340).

In other words, the leader should be an organizer and negotiator. In one humorous scene, Apollonios contrasts Jason's abilities with those of traditional heroes by having the crew, against Jason's expectation, choose Herakles, who is the strongest if not the brightest, as leader. Only when Herakles declines this honor in favor of Jason do the others accept him as their leader. Many other versions of the story find ways early or late of getting rid of Herakles, whose prowess ought to make the others' skills superfluous and whose style of work is solitary, not social.[6] Apollonios will dispatch him by the end of Book 1, but until then, slender, introspective Jason must coexist with the bulkiest action hero of Greek mythology. This coexistence is not at all a bad image for the poetics of the *Argonautika*.

Jason

Jason's temperament and tactics are several times highlighted by confrontation with a more traditional heroic temper. Apollonios four times deploys for this purpose Idas, a caricature of the angry warrior who relies on his great strength to solve all problems. For example, on the eve of embarking and just after an elaborate sacrifice led by Jason, the heroes relax on the beach eating, drinking, and telling stories. "But there the son of Aison, helpless, brooded over every detail, the image of despair." Idas notices Jason's abstraction and picks a fight: "What are you devising? Or are you overcome by fear, fear that confounds cowards?" He brandishes his spear, asserting "this is what I rely on, and as long as you have me and my spear you need not fear even the gods" (paraphrase). When this blasphemy provokes the group's seer to rebuke him, Idas responds with mocking laughter and anger, and the quarrel can only be soothed by Orpheus' music (1.460–495). Jason's modern mode of operating, which is to ask others (including the gods) for help, is incompatible with Idas's old-fashioned heroic self-reliance.

Similar confrontations occur in Book 3. When Jason is faced with the impossible task of yoking King Aietes' fire-breathing bulls, plowing a huge field, and killing giants who will spring up from sown dragon's teeth, he quite reasonably accepts the offer of Medea's pharmacological help. After a positive omen – a dove lands in Jason's lap while a pursuing hawk falls on the stern of the ship – all other Argonauts accept her offer also. All, that is, except Idas who, raging, rails at them for calling on Aphrodite rather than Ares (3.471–488, 523–569). When Jason later gets a magic drug from Medea, everyone crowds around to see it except Idas, who, as if he were Achilles, sits apart by himself biting back his anger (3.1163–1170). After Jason applies the drug to his weapons and "tender" body, his weapons become invulnerable and he suddenly possesses "terrible indescribable strength." Idas, "implacably angry" as always, slices at Jason's annointed spear with his huge sword, only to discover that it is indeed invulnerable (3.1204, 1246–1255). In these four scenes in Books 1 and 3, Idas, the uncompromising Achilles figure, highlights Jason's more practical Odyssean temperament.

Jason, however, is only superficially like the Homeric Odysseus. Although he shares with Odysseus an ability to charm women, he is neither resourceful nor a heroic warrior. He fights well enough in Book

1 to mistakenly kill his ex-host (1030–1062), but this deed hardly qualifies as heroic. He completes Aietes' tasks, but he can do so only under the influence of Medea's drug. Most unlike Odysseus, he is at a loss for words when he needs them. For example, when they have left Herakles behind by mistake, a fierce quarrel arises as to whose fault it is. While the quarrel grows violent, Jason "dumbfounded by helplessness, did not say a word on this side or that, but remained sitting weighed down by doom, eating his spirit." Jason's inertia provokes fiery-eyed Telemon (father of the *Iliad*'s Ajax) to accuse him of using "cunning" (*mêtis*) and "craft" (*dólos*) to leave Herakles behind through jealousy of being outshone (1.1285–1296). With the words "cunning" and "craft" Telemon's "Achilles" is essentially accusing Jason of being an Odysseus, but the disparity between his accusation and what the audience knows to be true only points up the essential *difference* between the energetic eloquent Homeric hero and the passive tongue-tied Apollonian protagonist. This captain has lost control of his crew and mission, and it takes the intervention of the sea god Glaukos to get them back on track.

Since he is often afraid and anxious, some have called Jason an antihero. I feel that this word is too strong, for in fact he is occasionally brave – for example, he accepts Aietes' challenge even though he assumes he will die. In addition, he performs the ritual activity incumbent on a leader properly and often: his sacrifices and rituals, especially to Apollo, are the origin of many contemporary customs and landmarks. However, his one special ability, that is, the ability to inspire love in women, has never before been considered heroic in the epic tradition. Consorting with women has never been thought to be conducive to heroic endeavor – witness the need to keep Atalanta from joining the Argonauts (1.769–773). Though Odysseus manages to turn women's love to his own advantage in his quest for home – his manipulation of Nausikaä is masterful – his lingering for a year with Circe and his eight years with Kalypso are his least heroic moments. Apollonios uses these Odyssean episodes and key images from the *Iliad* simultaneously to heroize and ironize Jason's amatory exploits.

Who could forget Achilles' divinely made shield with its gorgeous depictions of the cosmos and human life (*Il.* 18.478–608)? In emulation of it, a sixth-century poet created an equally elaborate (less artistically successful) one for Herakles, grafting it onto an episode in the genealogical *Catalogue of Women* often ascribed to Hesiod. Given that a divine shield is *de rigueur* for the very greatest heroes, Apollonios does not allow his own to go lacking. Jason, too, carries a divinely wrought artifact, an artifact whose shining, similar in effect to Achilles' golden shield, blinds like the rising sun (compare 1.725–726 with *Iliad* 19.14–15). However, instead of hard refractive metal, its substance is soft sensuous cloth. As he heads into his encounter with Hypsipyle, queen of the murderous Lemnian women, Jason buckles on his shoulders a thick cloak woven and embroidered by Athena.

The robe's images are located only at its borders, perhaps an indication of Alexandrian interest in periphery, not center, in refinement rather than proliferation. It is difficult to derive symbolic meaning from the series of pictures, and perhaps they are, as one scholar has suggested, simply a brilliant example of current artistic technique and the illusionistic art so popular in Hellenistic times. Hellenistic poets liked to recreate pictures in words, a technique called *ecphrasis*, and what Apollonios has created for his modern hero is the "very latest Alexandrian fashion."[7] Three of the images do have some relevance to Jason's mission: Aphrodite appropriating Ares' shield as a mirror, the successful treachery of Pelops and Hippodamia's love, and a "conversation" between Phrixus and the ram whose fleece Jason is after. It is also possible to find a serious message in the substitution of cloak for shield: diplomacy is better than battle, or, as the antiwar slogan puts it, "make love not war." Humor, however, may be the cloak's most important effect. The incongruity between Jason's coming exploit in bed and those of his epic predecessors on the battlefield creates amused distance between narrative and audience, keeping it aware of artifice at the core of heroic story.

Similarly, both Odysseus and Achilles lurk behind Jason when he strides toward the meeting with Medea in which he will get the magic drug and give marriage pledges in return. As Athena beautifies Odysseus to impress Nausikaä (*Od.* 6.229–236) so Hera beautifies Jason (*Arg.* 3.919–925). With amusing hyperbole, the poet declares that Hera has made Jason incomparable to any hero that has ever walked the earth, both to look at and to talk with. Radiating charm, Jason moves toward Medea, who sees him springing toward her "like Sirius coming from Ocean, the star that rises bright and beautiful to see, but that comes as unspeakable woe to flocks; so came the son of Aison, beautiful to look on but in his looks the trigger of tormented love" (3.956–961). This image evokes a terrible scene in the *Iliad*. Medea is in the position of Priam watching in horror as Achilles comes bounding across the plain to kill his son, his armor all shining "like the star they call Orion's dog, the one that shines brightest but is a sign of evil and brings fever to wretched mortals" (*Il.* 22.25–31). The image bodes ill for Jason and Medea's union, but more importantly, the simile once again emphasizes that the sweet-talking lover has usurped the warrior's epic privilege. The vast gap between the heroics of Achilles and Jason and between the tragedies of Hektor and Medea startles the reader, possibly provokes laughter, and disrupts tragic identification. It is one more illustration of how Apollonios claims continuity with Greek epic tradition but refuses to be bound by its ethos.

The Gods

Like its hero, the gods of the *Argonautika* are both familiar and unfamiliar. The first thing to notice is that all active gods are female. Zeus is a distant presence, affecting the action only in Book 4 when he disapproves of sibling murder and insists on purification. Apollo is worshiped constantly but, except for oracles, intervenes only once to provide a dim light in a very dark night. The boy Eros shoots an arrow into Medea's heart, but he is under the direction of his mother. The only male divinities to affect the action are two minor sea gods, Glaukos and Triton, who briefly appear to give information and advice in Books 1 and 4. The gods who move the action are Hera in concert with Athena, Aphrodite, and to a lesser degree, Hekate and Thetis. Hera is behind almost everything that helps Jason complete his quest: she helps gather the Argonauts, she arranges for Medea to fall in love, she stills the winds and the sooty volcanoes on the voyage home, and she gets Thetis and her sisters to carry the ship past Skylla and Kharybdis. Athena builds the Argo and later physically pushes the ship through the Clashing Rocks. Aphrodite persuades her son Eros to make Medea fall in love with Jason. Hekate blesses Medea's drug for use on Jason's body.

This gender division perhaps allowed Apollonios' more secular Hellenistic audience to interpret Zeus and Apollo as equivalent to divine justice and reason while reserving the anthropomorphic goddesses to supply the expected divine machinery. It also, however, puts Hera apparently in control, most remarkably when she hurls lightning bolts, normally Zeus's prerogative, at pursuing Kolkhians (4.509–510). The female universe that results corresponds to the displacement of the warrior by the lover.

As in the *Odyssey*, the gods themselves do not quarrel with each other. The epic's one scene on Olympos involves Hera, Athena, and Aphrodite all eager to help each other (1.7–157). Gone is the Iliadic enmity between Aphrodite, patron of Trojan Paris and Helen, and Hera and Athena, patrons of the Greeks. In its place Apollonios creates a comic scene in which the three goddesses look like Alexandrian ladies chatting over tea. Athena and Hera brainstorm over how to help Jason. Athena, goddess of wisdom, is stumped. Why? Because the only answer is love, and Athena knows nothing of love. Aphrodite is astonished when Hera and Athena ask *her* for help – a subtle way to recall how out of place she was in the *Iliad* and how nonexistent in the *Odyssey*. After some comic complaining about how she cannot control her unruly son, Aphrodite agrees to ask him to shoot Medea. All is harmony on Olympos, and were this the world of the *Odyssey*, justice would soon prevail on earth.

Justice, however, is not a major component of the Argonauts' world. The scene in which Aphrodite cajoles Eros into carrying out the mission, is both comic and scary. A spoiled little boy who embodies uncontrolled desire (the word Eros means desire), whatever Eros does is in his own self interest. Through Eros, erotic love is introduced into the epic as demanding, ruthless, and selfish. This understanding of love, which we can label either tragic or realistic, is borne out by the narrative as the epic's focus shifts from super heroes and divine miracles to the powerful mysteries of the human psyche.

Hera herself is not entirely beneficent. Her character bears some similarity to her vengeful character in the *Iliad*. Although she claims to like Jason for his kindness to her when she appeared to him disguised as an old woman, her reason for helping him is not justice for him, but revenge for herself: Pelias left her altar "without a gift of honor" (3.64–65, 74–75). Jason is mainly the means of bringing Medea to Iolkos as "an evil for Pelias" (3.1134–1136), and to this end she manipulates Medea into accompanying him and helps preserve her from pursuers.

There is no intimate relationship between gods and humans in the *Argonautika*. Except for Thetis, who speaks briefly with her ex-husband, gods do not converse with humans, but manipulate them from afar. The difference between the Homeric world and Apollonios' can be illustrated by comparing Hera and Athena's visit to Aphrodite with Thetis's visit to Hephaistos in the *Iliad*. Thetis procures and brings invulnerable body armor for her son. Hera and Athena procure the same for Jason, but they do it indirectly via Eros and Medea's drug. They act through human emotions and human science rather than through epiphany.

Medea

Come now Erato, stand by me, and tell me how Jason
brought the fleece back from there to Iolkos
by means of Medea's love: for you yourself share Aphrodite's
sphere, you bewitch untamed maidens with the
pains of love, wherefore your lovely name!

(3.1–5)

Given Medea's importance to all versions of the Argonaut's story, it must
at first seem odd that Medea is omitted from the proem to Book 1.
Apollonios, it turns out, has something special in mind for her: a second
proem to mark her entrance into the poem and to mark a change in focus
from the deeds of a male cohort to the workings of the female psyche.
This second proem, as far as we know, was as unprecedented as was the
invocation of Erato, Muse of erotic poetry, in an epic poem. Erato's
contribution to Apollonios' poem quite literally changed the epic world,
paradoxically preparing the way for a successful return to high heroic epic
in Virgil's *Aeneid*.

Medea's falling in love is at one and the same time realistic and con-
ventional. The minute she lays eyes on Jason, Eros's arrow strikes her
"like a flame" and "burns coiling around her heart" (3.287, 296–297);
her "heart smoulders" and "flames" (3.446, 661). Alongside such con-
ventional imagery, realistic descriptions of her pain and anxiety reach for
scientific accuracy, even at one point representing something very much
like a migraine (3.761–765). Added to the mix are literary reminiscences
of Homer, as when torn between shame and desire, Medea tries three
times to leave her room and then on the fourth attempt, like Patroklos
stopped by Apollo (*Il.* 16.705–711), she falls writhing on her bed (*Arg.*
3.645–655). Did Nausikaä in Phaiakia behave like this behind the closed
doors of her bedroom after she left Odysseus on the edge of the city?
Unlikely, for Homer brings their flirtation to a gentle end once Odysseus
needs nothing more from her. The *Argonautika*'s bachelor hero needs
much more from his "Nausikaä" – readers are often invited to compare
the two episodes – and offers Apollonios full scope for his modern
interest in the psychology of love.

In Book 4 Apollonios explores fully the darker side of love, which he
had hinted at in Book 3. Another invocation of the Muse poses only two
alternative reasons for Medea's theft of the golden fleece and flight with
Jason, both negative: ruinous love-madness or shameful panic (4.3–5).

Though it is the poet that speaks them, these verses are apparently written from the perspective of Medea, who often laments her choice throughout Book 4. Her casting in her lot with the Argonauts is not presented as a happy flight from barbarism to civilization or from danger to happy ever after. Signs of future trouble have appeared already in Book 3. The first is Jason's deliberately misleading evocation of Ariadne's helping Theseus as an example for Medea to emulate (3.997–1006). Ariadne, as the audience knows – but Medea pointedly does not (3.1074–1076) – was abandoned by Theseus on the voyage back to Greece. The second is the noun-epithet phrase "deadly Eros" used when first Medea (3.307) and then Jason (3.1078) fall in love. This epithet comes from the same root as the word that describes Achilles' wrath in *Iliad* 1.2, and since Apollonios does not often use epithets, it links the lovers in a most inauspicious way.

The above hints of trouble are fully if inconsistently developed in Book 4. Although Jason twice reaffirms his vow and eventually does marry her, when he first must choose between the survival of the Argonauts and keeping her by his side, he chooses the Argonauts. When Medea discovers this betrayal, the gentle conflicted maiden of Book 3 suddenly transforms into the raging Medea of Euripides. The flame of her love turns to burning wrath: "She desired to set the ship on fire, to cut it to pieces, and to cast herself into the ravening fire" (4.391–393). What she ends up doing instead is help Jason to kill her brother. This dreadful act provokes the narrator to address Eros as "a great curse to humankind," using language that more fully recalls the description of Achilles' wrath in the *Iliad*'s proem (4.445–447). The murder of Aspyrtos unleashes the full implications of love's epithet, "deadly." Medea has chosen Jason over her father (3.619–632), her mother (4.8–31), her brother (4.452–479): the ties of blood kin are as nothing before the flame of her passion.

Later, in Book 4 Medea is again the helpless girl: when the Argonauts again look like they will have to hand Medea over, all she can do is plead for their aid. In the end it is Queen Arete who saves her and precipitates her marriage (4.1011–1169). As the Argo wends its torturous way through Europe, Italy, and Libya, she disappears from the narrative, contributing nothing to the Argonauts' adventures until they reach Crete. Then she suddenly reappears on deck and calls up spirits of death and hounds of Hades to subdue Talos, the rock-hurling bronze giant (4.1633–1672). She is positively terrifying in this scene, a full-blown, enraged sorceress. Once Talos falls, she is not mentioned again, and the epic closes with a few more aetiological episodes before quietly ending on the beach near Iolkos.

Many memorable images linger from one's reading of the *Argonau-tika*: the city of lusty Lemnian ladies, Herakles pulling a tree up by its roots or fighting six-handed giants, the drive through the Clashing Rocks, the birds of Ares who hurl their feathers as deadly darts, the fire-breathing bulls and dragon-tooth men, the golden fleece, the twelve-day portage across the Libyan desert. Most vivid for subsequent poets, however, has been the woman torn between duty and erotic passion, vividly struggling against a force beyond her control and, when she loses the battle, evolving into the murderous witch familiar from legend. Virgil will transform Apollonios's Medea into his tragic Dido, keeping the struggle and slide from virtuous woman to deadly paramour, but raising the erotic stakes to include empire.

Of equal interest, at least for Virgil, is the *Argonautika*'s portrait of a hero whose main function as leader is to perform ritual (when he is not charming women, of course) and who prefers negotiation to aggression. These traits as well as Jason's occasional unheroic helplessness will inform Virgil's Aeneas in the first half of the *Aeneid*. To me, however, one of the most appealing things about Apollonios's epic is its vision of a collective as hero, each of whose members contributes something essential to the success of the quest. This vision Virgil would not, or could not, use.

Further Reading

Translations and Texts

Two vigorous, highly readable prose translations have been published under the title *Jason and the Golden Fleece* by R. L. Hunter (Oxford, 1998) and E.V. Rieu (London and New York, 1971). Hunter's also provides an excellent introduction and explanatory notes.

Peter Green's verse translation in *The Argonautika by Apollonios Rhodios*, second edition (Berkeley, 2008), is lively. Green's introduction is very useful (literary and political scene, the myth before Apollonios), as are the 129 pages of commentary to specific passages. There are excellent maps plotting the course of the Argonauts' journey both to and from Kolkhis plus a very thorough glossary of names and places.

R. C. Seaton's 1912 translation has recently been published, with Greek and English side by side, by Forgotten Books as *The Argonautica. Jason and the Argonauts* (2007); it features large print and inexpensive price.

The Greek text on which I have based my translations is the Oxford edition of Eduard Fraenkel (1961).

Commentary and Analysis

R. L. Hunter, ed., *Apollonius of Rhodes: Argonautica Book III*. In addition to an extensive commentary to the Greek text of Book 3, Hunter offers an introduction that discusses the poet's life, the myth of the Argonauts before Apollonios, the poem as a whole and aesthetic features of Book 3.

Stimulating book-length studies include: Calvin Byre's *A Reading of Apollonius Rhodius* (Lewiston, NY, 2002), which argues for a poetics of uncertainty via detailed comparison with Homer. R.J. Clare's *The Path of the Argo* (Cambridge, 2002) examines language, imagery and narrative. James J. Clauss's *The Best of the Argonauts* (Berkeley, 1993) examines the redefinition of the epic hero from singular to plural in Book 1. Mary Deforest's *Apollonius' Argonautica: A Callimachean Epic* (Leiden, 1994) argues that Apollonios has created in the first two books an amusing conflict between would-be Homeric heroes and their Kallimakhean narrator but that when Medea steps in, the narrator steps out. R. L. Hunter's *The Argonautica of Apollonius: Literary Studies* (Cambridge, 1993) interprets the epic as an attempt to renew the epic genre through its creative and often disruptive dialogue with literary predecessors in many genres. Virginia H. Knight's *The Renewal of Epic* (Leiden, 1997) thoroughly analyzes allusions to the *Iliad* and *Odyssey* and demonstrates repetitions of patterns.

C. R. Beye has a delightful chapter on the *Argonautika* in his *Ancient Epic Poetry* (Ithaca, 1993; reprint New York, 2006), 187–218. J. J. Clauss' "Conquest of the Mephistophelian Nausikaa" in James J. Clauss and Sarah Iles Johnston, eds. *Medea* (Princeton, NJ, 1996), 149–177, analyzes the numerous evocations of *Odyssey* 6 in *Argonautika* 3. D. P. Nelis's "Apolonius of Rhodes" in John Miles Foley, ed., *A Companion to Ancient Epic* (Oxford, 2005), 353–363, provides an excellent survey of current scholarship and ways of thinking about the poem.

For background on the Hellenistic Age and Aesthetics, see Peter Green in *Alexander to Actium. The Historical Evolution of the Hellenistic Age* (Berkeley, 1990), which discusses the Museum and Library of Alexandria on pp. 85–91 and 155–186.

Adaptations and Revisions

Valarius Flaccus translated and adapted Apollonios' epic into Latin in the mid first century BCE, drawing on Virgil's *Aeneid* to develop Jason as leader; D. R. Slavitt has recently produced a highly readable translation (Baltimore, MD, 1999). Michael Wood's "Jason and the Golden Fleece" in *In Search Of Myths and Heroes* (Berkeley, 2005), 78–139, takes the reader on a tour across the Aegean through the Sea of Marmara and the Black Sea into the River Phasis in Georgia, discussing the Argonaut myth via ancient sources and gorgeous photographs.

Hollywood has produced two interesting versions: *Jason and the Argonauts* (Columbia Pictures, 1963) depicts Jason as a true hero and is famous for its battle of heroes against skeletons. A television movie *Jason and the Argonauts* (USA, 2000) has a thrilling sequence of the passage through the Clashing Rocks. Medea is a typical romance heroine in both.

Notes

1   Catullus, who followed Hellenistic poetics in his own Roman writing, alludes to Antimakhos' work as suitable only for fish-wrapping (Poem 95).

2   Eumelos' *Korinthiaka*, which dates to the sixth century, was a historico-genealogical epic focused on Corinth's kings (among which were Medea's father and subsequently Medea). The anonymous *Naupaktia*, which originated in either the sixth or fifth century, was a genealogical epic that contained an Argonautika. The relevant fragments can be found in M. L. West, ed., *Greek Epic Fragments from the Seventh to the Fifth Centuries* (Cambridge, MA, 2003), 238–243, 274–282. Pherekydes the historian wrote a prose version in the fifth century (*Fragments of the Greek Historians*, F. Jacoby, ed., 3).

3   The term is J. J. Clauss's. See "Conquest" in "Further Reading: Commentory" below.

4   *Phōs* solves the problem of having a word ending with a vowel leading into a word beginning with one, something Greek writers abhorred. Apollonios could have used the original phrase as an archaism, but his change cleverly solves the problem with the plus of signaling change itself. *Phōs* also has a less heroic ring to it.

5   *Báksis* in line 8 carries a primary meaning of "oracular utterance" but a secondary meaning of "rumor," the reverse of *phátis*.

6   Pherekydes (see Apollodoros 1.9.19) and Antimakhos (*Lyde*, Fr.58) had the ship, through its one speaking plank, refuse to carry Herakles past Thessaly because of his weight; Dionysios Skytobrakhion wrote a prose version around 250 BCE that rationalizes the story, removing the anthropomorphic gods and miracles, and has the heroes choose Herakles leader, because of his "manliness" (*andreía*) (Diodoros Siculos 4.40–56, esp. 41).

7   H. A. Shapiro, "Jason's Cloak" *Transactions of the American Philological Association* 110 (1980), 263–286; the quotation is on p. 271.

6

The Context of Roman Epic

Rome: Legendary Beginnings

In the eighth century BCE, around the time that archaic Greeks were using their new alphabet to record the *Iliad* and *Odyssey*, a cluster of villages near the western coast of Italy was gradually developing into the city of Rome. Most ancient Romans believed that their capital city was founded around 750 BCE, and most believed that the one who made it happen, the one who first built walls to enclose Rome's people, was Romulus, son of the war god Mars and a royal priestess named Rhea Silvia or Ilia.

At some point Romulus became linked to the famous Homeric texts by an ancestor, Aeneas, the Trojan warrior whom Poseidon saves from Achilles because he is fated to start a dynastic lineage to rule over the Trojan people (*Il.* 20.307–308). By the end of the third century BCE, Trojan kinship was being used advantageously in foreign diplomacy, and four major writers of the third and second centuries BCE – Naevius, Fabius Pictor, Ennius, and Cato – chose to begin their histories of Rome with Aeneas. Some writers considered this link with Troy so important that, ignoring the gap of at least 432 years between the traditional date at which the Trojan War ended (1184) and traditional dates for the founding of Rome, they made Aeneas himself either the father or the maternal grandfather of the founder. Virgil himself fudges the issue in the *Aeneid*, which makes Aeneas found "a city" that is the origin of "the walls of high Rome" (1.5, 7).

Aeneas was famous from at least the sixth century BCE for carrying his lame father from Troy just before it was sacked. Many early Greek and Italian vase paintings illustrate this scene,[1] which is described by the fifth-century Athenian tragedian Sophokles in a fragment from the lost *Laocoon*:

Aeneas, son of the goddess, is now at the gates, with his father on his shoulders . . . surrounded by a multitude from his household; there follows an unbelievably huge crowd of those who desire to emigrate with him from Troy. (Soph. *Fr.* 373).

There is numismatic evidence as early as 129 BCE that the Julian clan claimed descent from Aeneas' mother Venus, and in the first century BCE it becomes clear that this descent comes through Aeneas. Julius Caesar issued coins in 48 BCE with Venus on one side and Aeneas carrying his father on the other. Octavian followed his adoptive father's example by issuing similar coins in 43 BCE. The fact that powerful Julians claimed lineage back to this mother and son made it wise, at least after 31 BCE, to promote linkage between Aeneas and the founding of Rome.

Legend told that after Troy fell Aeneas sailed westward, founding cities in Thrace and Greece for those who did not want to go further and leaving behind temples to Venus at almost every stop. First-century versions all bring Aeneas to the Tiber River on the western coast of Italy, where certain omens tell him that this is where the gods would have him settle. He forms an alliance with **Latinus**, king of a city there, and marries his daughter, **Lavinia**. Either before or after his marriage, he helps Latinus defeat hostile neighbors, the Rutulians, led by **Turnus**. Aeneas founds his own city, Lavinium, but intermarriage and joint warfare eventually make Trojans and Italians all one people called Latins. After Aeneas' death, his son Silvius (by Lavinia) inherits Lavinium; thirty years later, his older son Ascanius/Iulus (by his former Trojan wife Creusa) builds a new city close by in Alba Longa. How these two lines coalesce (if they do) remains cloudy.

The action now shifts entirely to Alba Longa, where sixteen generations later, **Romulus and Remus** are born to an unmarried female descendant of Aeneas. Using the excuse that their mother is a priestess required to remain virgin, her cruel uncle, who has usurped the throne from her father **Numitor**, executes her and has the twin boys set adrift on the Tiber to die. Protected by Mars, they float ashore, and are nursed and protected by a wolf until some shepherds come along to rescue and rear them. When they grow up, they avenge their grandfather, Numitor, who gives them land and people with which to build a city for themselves. But, alas, the prospect of power changes brotherly love to hateful rivalry. Romulus ends up killing Remus, and the new city, which is named Rome after the surviving twin, is thus founded in fratricide and civil war. Romulus adds the Sabines to his city by some unorthodox methods, and then he reigns for thirty-eight years until one day he disappears into a cloud and reappears as the native god **Quirinus**. The hill upon which this apotheosis happened was renamed Quirinal.

The March to Empire

Archaeologists tell us that by 575 BCE, Rome had coalesced into a true city. Slowly it began to increase its sphere of influence, and by 275 BCE, when Apollonios was about to compose the *Argonautika* in Hellenistic Egypt, Roman power extended throughout the Italian peninsula. Having conquered Italy, Rome then began to spread its empire to other lands.

Its first target was Carthage, the expanding North African empire that ringed the Mediterranean from Libya across the northern coast of Africa up through southern Spain across to the islands of Corsica and Sardinia and down to western Sicily. Desiring to get Carthage out of Sicily, Rome provoked the first of three wars, which, together totaled forty-three bloody years (264–241 BCE, 218–202 BCE, 149–146 BCE). These are called the Punic Wars, after Carthage's original Phoenician founder. Although the Carthaginians lost all three of these wars, the second one, in which Hannibal crossed the Alps and came all the way to the walls of Rome, caused prolonged destruction and fear. So angry did this invasion make some Romans that they would not rest until Carthage was destroyed. In 146 BCE, at the end of the brief third war they had started for this purpose, the Roman army slaughtered the population and razed the surrendered city of Carthage so completely that until recently archeologists have found little to study.

In that same year, annoyed at the insolence of Greek states who had the temerity to insist on independence and the foolishness to declare war, Rome also razed Corinth. Romans thus brought the Greeks (and many masterpieces of plundered Greek art) into their empire. Since it had already reduced Macedon to a province in 148 BCE, Rome was now the dominant force in the western Mediterranean. The eastern Mediterranean soon followed, and by 27 BCE, when Virgil began to write the *Aeneid*, Rome was an empire that extended to Spain in the west, France in the north, Tunisia and Egypt in the south, and Turkey and Syria in the east.

Virgil's Jupiter promises the Romans limitless empire and an end to war after the Greeks are conquered and a "Trojan Caesar" becomes "rich with eastern spoils" (*Aeneid* 1.279, 286–294). This promise appears to describe the Rome in which Virgil wrote, for once Octavian conquered Marc Antony in Egypt, Rome's power seemed boundless, and the official "gates of war" were closed for the first time in 200 years. What remained to be seen was whether Romans would succeed in fulfilling the most important part of Jupiter's promise; that is, in binding the "impious fury" of civil war.

Civil War

Roman tradition told of the city's being governed by kings for nearly 250 years, starting with Romulus and ending with **Tarquin the Arrogant**, who was driven out after raping a nobleman's wife. From 510 onward, Rome prided itself on being a republic, with two leaders called consuls elected every year. Over the next 300 years, class strife gradually resolved itself into organized ways in which upper-class patricians and both wealthy and working-class plebeians could all participate in a government of elected officials and of decisions reached by vote. By the time Virgil began the *Aeneid*, however, Rome was a republic in name only, something to look back on with nostalgia.

What drained the republican constitution of meaning was a seemingly endless series of civil wars that erupted as powerful individuals contested for domination. Often, one of the contestants would champion the aristocracy and the other would take the masses of the working class as his power base. Though there was some mobility between the classes – a few wealthy plebeians could enter the nobility through election to the senate – the divergent interests of the rich and poor formed the basis of many a political campaign. Aspiring office holders, almost all of them wealthy and from prominent families, expressed allegiance to one or the other, either "the best men" (*optimates*) or "the people" (*populares*), and this allegiance functioned much the same as political parties – Republican versus Democratic in the United States, Conservative versus Labour in Great Britain – do today. Wealth also functioned much the same then as it does now in political campaigns.

The intense civil strife that bled the republic of its life force took root about sixty years before the birth of Virgil, when the Senate assassinated **Tiberius Gracchus**, a Tribune of the People, in 132 BCE. The issue was land reform: Tiberius had proposed confiscating the illegally obtained land of large landowners and distributing it to landless peasants. He considered this legislation so important, and the rules so prejudiced toward the Senate, that he violated traditional customs in the course of getting the legislation passed and attempting to get it enforced. Members of the Senate attacked and killed him and many supporters on the eve of an election day that might have seen him reelected to office. Nine years after Tiberius' assassination, his younger brother **Gaius Gracchus** won the tribuneship on an even more sweeping populist platform: not only redistribution of land, but also regulation of the price of grain, jury reform, limits on military service, and extension of the vote to some Italian allies. He got much of this passed, again by violating a few customs, but once he was out of office, the Senate, whose power he had greatly curbed, set about undoing what he had done. Gaius organized a protest on the Capitol that turned briefly violent when one of the consul's men provoked one of his. Seizing upon this brief episode of violence, the Senate gave the consul, Lucius Opimius, permission to do whatever he saw fit in order to save the state. Opimius then violently attacked the people with a mercenary army, killing a few hundred of them. Gaius either took his own life or was murdered, and the man who brought in his severed head was paid a handsome reward. Opimius proceeded to hunt down 3,000 alleged supporters of Gaius and murder them.

Tiberius and Gaius Gracchus were apparently genuinely committed to bettering the lot of the common people. Conservatives in the Senate, too, were genuinely committed to retaining what they considered to be "the best" government. Some of their actions, however, set disastrous precedents. The Gracchi brothers violated custom in their zeal to counteract the Senate's unequal balance of power, and the Senate, especially the consul Opimius, reacted with extraordinary violence in pursuit of their class interest. These two behaviors were many times repeated over the coming years by those who seem to have had fewer ideals: custom and law no longer set bounds to men's ambitions, and vengeful violence in pursuance of self interest escalated.

Marius, a greatly admired military commander whose base of power was the people and the army, was elected consul six times between 107 and 100 BCE, an unprecedented prolongation of supreme power. This repeated election was legal, for through fear of an approaching enemy, the Senate had in haste repealed the law that forbade back-to-back consulships. Ten years later, **Sulla**, a consul and soldier who looked to his fellow patricians as well as his own military legions for support, marched his legions against Rome when the Senate and the People's Assembly differed as to whether he or Marius should take command of the army. Since bringing an army into Rome was forbidden by law, a law that had never before been violated, Sulla easily conquered a surprised and unprepared Rome. He got the Senate to pass a death sentence on Marius, who fled into exile. While Sulla was away at war, Marius returned and, following Sulla's example, himself took Rome by force, thereafter killing and beheading about twelve of Sulla's patrician supporters. When Sulla returned in 83 BCE, again taking control of the city by force, the Senate declared him Dictator for an unlimited period of time. This declaration again set a new precedent: previously such absolute power had been granted to a single man only in emergencies, and then only for a maximum of six months. Sulla used his unlimited power to execute at least 1,500 of his opponents and confiscate their property. After taking this vengeance, which, perhaps not incidentally, made him wealthy, he instituted political reforms to enhance the power of the Senate and then resigned the dictatorship he had held for two years.

Patrician **Julius Caesar**, who at twenty years old had barely escaped being executed by Sulla, later became leader of the *populares*. Counting on the loyalty of his legions, he followed his predecessors' example in vengefulness, in marching on Rome during his quarrel with the Senate and Consul Pompey (49 BCE), in holding several consulships in a row, and finally, in being made Dictator for life (44 BCE), power that he, unlike Sulla, showed no intention ever of resigning. Although Caesar did not imitate Sulla in condemning Roman citizens and confiscating their property, he did murder and pillage for gain in the provinces he was sent to govern and subdue. After Caesar's assassination by a large group of senators in 44 BCE, **Marc Antony**, his most powerful supporter, and **Octavian**, his nephew and adopted heir, carried on the civil wars for thirteen more years, first against the senatorial assassins and then against each other.

Following Sulla's, Marius's, and Caesar's example, Octavian marched on Rome in 43 BCE, forcing the Senate to appoint him consul. Also like Sulla, Octavian and Antony in concert ordered as many as 2,300 condemnations and confiscations, many of which were done for the sake of revenue. Revenge motivated many atrocities. Antony, for example, took Cicero's hands and head to adorn the speaker's platform in the Forum in 43 BCE. Young Octavian acquired a reputation for acts of great cruelty, some committed in vengeance for attacks on himself, others committed in vengeance for his adoptive father's murder. According to the historian Suetonius, who is on the whole very positive about Octavian's career as ruler of Rome, these acts included summary executions, torture, ripping out a man's eyes with his own hands, and humiliating captured opponents before executing them, even going so far as to taunt one with denial of burial (*Life of Augustus* 27, 13). Suetonius saw written accounts of an even worse atrocity: after putting down a rebellion in the north-Italian city of Perusia in 41 BCE, Octavian was said to have had 300 Roman citizens sacrificed on an altar built in honor of Divine Julius (he had forced the Senate to proclaim Julius Caesar a god the previous year), and he burned their city to the ground.

In 42 BCE Octavian confiscated hundreds of farms in northern Italy to give to the veterans whose loyalty he had bought by promising them land. Virgil's small family farm in Mantua was among them, though story tells that he got the property back after intercession from two powerful literature-loving friends. In one of his early poems, the young poet (he was 28 at the time of the dispossession) voiced both the sadness felt by the dispossessed and the joy experienced at regaining the land. In *Eclogue* 1, a departing goatherd drives his "heretofore happy" herd away from well-known streams and verdant grottos, lamenting that "an impious soldier will have these well-tended meadows, a barbarian these fields. Behold where dissension has led wretched citizens!" (1.70–72, 74). A second shepherd, who has been allowed to stay on his land after traveling to Rome for an audience, praises the new young leader as the source of "liberty" and as a "god" to whom he will never cease to sacrifice (*Ecl.* 1.6–8, 27). This juxtaposition of the sad cost of Octavian's deeds with high praise for Octavian himself foreshadows the ambiguous vision Virgil will display in the *Aeneid*. Since many shepherds are harmed and only one is saved, and since rustic values are portrayed as antithetical to urban ones (the young god's realm is Rome), many readers finish the poem feeling that for all shepherds something irredeemable has been lost.

Virgil published this poem at the head of a collection of pastoral poems some years after the confiscations, probably between 37–35 BCE. Civil war continued to cause untold misery until 31 BCE, when Octavian defeated Marc Antony and Cleopatra in a naval battle at **Actium**. After Actium, Octavian became the supreme ruler of the Roman empire, exercising absolute control through the armies that were now more loyal to him than to the state. He acquired the name **Augustus** ("Revered One") in 27 BCE. He restored the republic in name, but the Senate and people did his will, first electing him consul from 31–23 BCE, and thereafter conferring on him continued command of the military and more than consular power. Our word emperor comes from the Latin *imperator*, "commander-in-chief," the first word of the title by which Augustus liked to be known from this point on: "*Imperator* Caesar son of a deity."

Rome's bloody history from 107–31 BCE lies behind Jupiter's promise near the beginning of the *Aeneid* that once Caesar (Augustus) returns victorious from the east, a golden age will begin. Hard times will soften and

> white-haired Faith and Vesta, Romulus with his brother Remus
> will give laws; the fearsome gates of war shall be closed shut
> with tight-fastened bars of iron; impious *furor* within,
> sitting on savage weapons and bound by a hundred knots
> of brass, shall roar, dreadful, with bloody mouth.
>
> (1.292–296)

Furor, fury, this passage implies, can be contained only by the strongest bonds; it is never extinguished, but remains within the human character like a chained lion, ready to devour trust and set brother against brother whenever passion takes control. Marius, Sulla, Julius Caesar, Marc Antony, and Octavian himself had all become *furor* incarnate at points in their careers, just as do characters in the epic: Juno, Turnus, Mezentius, and Aeneas himself. Did Augustus recognize part of himself in these characters when he finally got to read the *Aeneid* after Virgil's death? Perhaps not. Perhaps he was instead only pleased at Virgil's striking portrayal of the importance of control, the importance of the control that he, Augustus, had imposed on Roman citizens to give them freedom from civil war.

Perhaps when Augustus wrote his professional autobiography, the *Res gestae divi Augusti (Deeds of the Divine Augustus)*, he had forgotten that he had not actually "spared all citizens who asked for mercy" at Perusia.[2] No doubt he saw no contradiction between binding the *furor* of war and glorifying Mars the Avenger with a magnificent new temple. We may suspect, however, that his insistence that he had spared the defeated was in response to Virgil's compelling vision of what should distinguish a Roman from the rest of the world. This vision is enunciated by Anchises, father of the founding father: "Remember, Roman, (for these are *your* skills), to govern nations with authority and add law to peace, to spare the submissive and defeat the arrogant" (6.851–853).

Although other Roman philosophers had promoted the same moderate behavior in war, Virgil puts it at the heart of what swiftly became Rome's national poem. For Anchises, Roman devotion to law, mercy, and the eradication of arrogance is what justifies the national mission to rule the world. Although in Books 1 and 6 Virgil implies that Augustus has initiated a new golden age, and in Book 8 he lauds Augustus's victory at Actium in highly moral terms, in the pageant of Roman heroes in Book 6 he portrays Augustus mainly as a fearsome conqueror. He inserts the generic Roman of Anchises' exhortation immediately following a general who saved Rome by a strategy of *delaying* battle. Less than two years after Virgil's death, his friend Horace, taking the *Aeneid*'s version of the foundation myth for granted, points directly to Augustus, descendant of Anchises and Venus, as the ideal Roman who fights the arrogant and is lenient to the conquered (*Carmen saeculare* 49–55). Virgil's art had perhaps created a new reality, or a new illusion, depending on one's point of view.

Intellectual Currents and the *Aeneid*

Horace's song appears more convinced of Augustus's "Roman" character than does Virgil's epic, but this difference may be mostly a function of genre. Choral lyric has a focused celebratory and ritual purpose. Epic certainly celebrates a culture's heroes, but at its best it is comprehensive and explores hard cultural truths.

The *Aeneid* captures a world of political realities, one of which is the conflict between Roman history and Roman ideals. Philosophic theory, specifically that of the schools founded by Epicurus and Zeno in third-century Athens, complicates that relationship at the same time as it suggests some causes for the conflict. Virgil had studied Epicurean philosophy intensely, and although he is not reported to have studied under any Stoic masters, its influence on the *Aeneid* is strong. Stoicism, especially as formulated for a specifically Roman audience by the prominent orator and philosopher Cicero, was intellectually popular at Rome during the first half of the first century BCE, and it provides a key to the deeper issues that lie beneath the *Aeneid*'s adventure story and its relationship to Homer's epics.

For the Stoic, the soul's well-being depended on living in accord with reason, which was the same as living in accord with nature. The person who achieved this accord was "wise." One achieved this state of wisdom by conquering emotional "disturbances" such as grief, fear, desire (*cupido*), and anger (*ira*).

A person who succumbed to any of these emotions was considered to be ill, *insanus*. Although more militarily minded Roman Stoics compromised with anger, preferring Aristotles' view that righteous anger is acceptable as a spur to courage (*Nicomachean Ethics* 1125), for some thinkers, anger is the closest thing to insanity that there is. Cicero, for example, argues that nothing "resembles *insania* more than *ira*," and he cites in support a verse from the eminent Latin playwright and epic poet Ennius, which describes anger as the "beginning of *insania*" (*Tusculan Disputations* 4.23.52). Such a view would have profound implications for a Roman's interpretation of Homeric epic. Since the *Iliad* is about "wrath," both divine and human, a Stoic interpretation of its plot and heroes is necessarily going to be critical in ways unimagined by Homer and his archaic and classical Greek audiences.

In addition to rejecting strong emotion, both Epicurean and Stoic philosophies rejected the humanized gods of Greek and Roman myth. Epicurean gods live in bliss uncomplicated by human clashes. The Stoic God, on the other hand, is the totality of the world, the rational soul of the world, or Nature. Sun, moon, stars, rivers all are viewed as divine, but they are what they are; they do not take human form.

Epicurean and Stoic gods do not experience negative human passions, but exist supremely virtuous and happy in concord with Reason (the rational soul and guiding principle of the world). For the stoics another word for Reason is Fate, and the name Jupiter is merely a further way of designating it. Reason/Fate is beneficent, developing what is good for the world in all its parts, including especially human beings, who have been endowed with reason. Since every human being has a rational soul, everyone either is or has the potential to be a god, depending on how fixed they are on Virtue (that is, Reason). When death comes, it releases the rational soul to join the larger world soul, and the individual ceases to exist.

Educated Roman readers would have seen a disconnect between Virgil's intellectual beliefs and the wrath of Juno, the existence of Tartarus (Hell) in Book VI, and the personal deifications of Aeneas, Julius Caesar, and Augustus. They had all read Lucretius' epic poem *De Rerum Natura, On the Nature of Things* (55 BCE), which took the philosopher Epicurus and his ideas as hero and turned the unfounded fears caused by religion into the vanquished enemy. Such readers could accept the interfering gods of the *Aeneid* either as allegory (that is, Apollo is equivalent to rationality, truth), or as mere convention, a generic necessity for great epic. The deification of individual human beings, on the other hand, could be regarded as an extension of what happens to the virtuous soul when it is released from the body. Most educated readers, after all, would be acquainted also with Cicero's "Dream of Scipio" (51 BCE) written for the last book of his *On The Commonwealth* as a counterpart to the

"Dream of Er" in Plato's *Republic*. Combining traditional Roman mores with strands from various Hellenic philosophies, but principally Stoic and Platonic ones, Cicero here creates a compact Stoic doctrine designed to persuade the likes of Caesar and Pompey to use their monumental abilities to serve the public rather than to amass personal power.

Immortality of the soul and responsibility and reward are the keystones of this doctrine. In his dream vision, Scipio learns that human souls are sent to earth with a duty to be its guardians. This duty means specifically that they are to help preserve states (*civitates*), that is, associations of people bound by law. So much do the gods love states, that the men who save, increase, or in any way benefit their country (*patria*) are rewarded with eternal bliss in a special place among the stars (in the Milky Way, to be exact). Governors and saviors of states are singled out as being sent from and returning to the stars (*Republic* 6.13). Though the body is lost at death, the soul somehow retains the physical characteristics and memory of the living man. Cicero's "Dream of Scipio," then, offers a model for later Stoic compromise with Augustus' reach for personal divinity. When Jupiter tells Venus that she will receive Caesar into heaven (*Aeneid* 1.289–290) and when his household divinities promise Aeneas that they will "raise his progeny to the stars" (*Aeneid* 3.158), average Romans might take the promises literally, but Stoic readers would understand them as philosophic allegory.

What earns immortality among Cicero's Stoic stars is not military victory, but the virtues of justice and piety (*pietas*), which signifies dutiful and loving conduct toward parents, family, and, above all, toward the state (*Republic* 6.16). These are the very virtues Virgil chooses to characterize his own hero. Virgil deploys "*pius* Aeneas" as formulaically as the Homeric poems do "swift-footed Achilles" or "crafty Odysseus." When one of Aeneas' captains describes his leader as a man than whom "none other is more just in *pietas* nor greater in war" (*Aeneid* 1.544–45), the Stoic reader will understand that the former, not the latter, will earn him the promised place in heaven. Compare the list of people who merit reward in the *Aeneid*'s Realm of the Happy (epic's underworld counterpart to Cicero's Milky Way). Here Virgil places those who suffer wounds in fighting for the fatherland, chaste priests, pious poets, those who enhanced life by their discoveries, and those who have served others memorably (6.660–664). Virgil's emphasis is on risking one's life and enhancing the lives of others, not on killing great numbers of enemies.

Whether or not they believed it literally, Stoic readers would probably understand the public value of such a promised reward. As Cicero suggests earlier in *On The Commonwealth* and elsewhere in his writings, it is wise to promote the belief that men who serve the common good are not only godlike, but are actually gods (*Commonwealth* 2.4).[3] Eternal bliss in the afterlife should be a stronger goad than the human glory with which it is explicitly contrasted. Human glory cannot be eternal because human cities, which pass on great men's stories and vote them honors, cannot themselves be eternal. When Virgil's hero identifies himself as "*pius* Aeneas, savior of my household gods, known by fame above the heavens" (1.378–379), a Stoic reader would understand the difference between Aeneas' truly heavenly fame and Odysseus' metaphoric claim that his *kléos* for craftiness reaches the stars (*Od.* 9.20).

Homeric and Roman Epic

Homer's epics and the Epic cycle were known and loved in Italy from the eighth century BCE, not only in the Greek colonies but also in Etruria, just to the north of Rome. There we find the Troy story illustrated in wall paintings similar to ones we later find in Roman villas. Livius Andronicus translated the *Odyssey* sometime in the third century BCE, massively abridging it at the same time.[4] Early in the first century, two translators, Gnaeus Matius and Ninnius Crassus, produced Latin versions of the *Iliad* that have been entirely lost.

Well-educated Romans of the third to first centuries BCE had more than pictures and translations, however. They knew Greek as well as their native Latin, and their education included Greek rhetoricians, philosophers, and poets, which were often taught by Greeks. The father of Roman historiography, Quintus Fabius Pictor, wrote his account of early Rome and the first two Punic wars in Greek. Intellectually and culturally, Greece was the colonizer, Italy the colonized, until midway through the second century BCE.

However, just as Greece itself was incorporated into the political empire, so did Roman poets gradually appropriate and incorporate Greek literature into their own distinctively Latin body of literature. In the third century BCE, Roman writers began creating Roman versions of the great Greek literary genres. Livius Andronicus, the first, was soon followed by Gnaeus Naevius, who wrote many tragedies and comedies on Greek themes and also composed a history of the First Punic War in verse. Naevius's *Punic War*, like Andronicus' *Odyssey*, was composed in the native Italian Saturnian meter, a loosely trochaic meter that Horace later described as rough and impure (*Epistles* 2.1, 156–159). Naevius's attempt to create a uniquely Latin epic failed artistically, and like Livius' *Odyssey*, the poem has almost entirely disappeared.

The next attempt at specifically Latin epic was a much greater success, probably because the author, Quintus Ennius, adopted the Homeric epic meter. His subject, like Naevius's, was entirely Roman – a panegyric history of Rome from the beginnings to the present day – but the Muses he evoked in the opening line were Greek, as Greek as the marble Muses that his friend Fulvius had recently brought from abroad and installed in a temple on the Field of Mars. With utter confidence, Ennius proclaims that Homer's soul now resides in him, citing a dream in which Homer himself appeared to him to tell him so. Though judged "rough" by post-Virgilian sophisticates like Ovid (*Tristia* 2.259), the eighteen-book epic poem that resulted was a groundbreaking composite of Greek and Roman art, in which Latin versions of Homeric similes, formulae, and scenes give weight and stature to historical and contemporary Roman figures.

As the Roman empire grew, the relationship between Roman writers and Greek culture evolved from imitation and inclusion into one that involved active assertion of Roman superiority. Cicero's synthesis of Greek Stoic and Platonic philosophy was explicitly intended not to translate the originals, but to transform them into something better. Just as the Roman tragedian Accius (170–90 BCE) had improved on Homer's Achilles by putting a Stoic sentiment in his mouth, asserts Cicero, so his own work will improve Hellenic philosophy by making it congruent with Roman law and custom (*Tusculan Disputations* 1.1, 44.105). Rome had conquered Greece militarily and it was time to assert intellectual supremacy as well.

Poetic supremacy seems to have been on Octavian's mind after the battle of Actium. His eagerness for a great epic to immortalize his incomparable deeds seems to have put pressure on the best Roman poets, to judge from their many demurrals. The task seems to have been not just to write a good poem, but to write one as good as, if not better than, Homer's. When the word spread in 26 BCE that Virgil was writing an epic that would pair Caesar's deeds at Actium with Aeneas' legendary struggle to found a city in Italy, Propertius proclaimed that supremacy over Homer was about to be won: "yield, Roman writers, yield, Greek! Something greater than the *Iliad* is being born" (*Elegies* 2.34.61–66).

Virgil would probably have agreed. Although like Horace and Propertius, he himself had initially demurred in 30 BCE, unlike his friends he had not insisted that he was unequal to the task. If he lived long enough, he said, (and since he was only forty when he wrote this, it was quite likely he would), he would gird himself to sing Caesar's "blazing battles" once he had finished work on a poem about rural life for his patron Maecenas (*Georgics* 3.46). Confident in his ultimate ability to make the hexameter do his will, an ability he was obviously perfecting while writing the *Georgics*, Virgil promises that he will later return to a patriotic subject and be the first to bring the Muses from Helicon (thus implying he will achieve more than Ennius). He then constructs an elaborate metaphor, figuring himself as a conqueror wearing triumphal purple robes and an olive crown, his epic-to-be as a victory temple, and Caesar as the "god" to whom the temple is dedicated. The temple is adorned with images of Caesar's battles and conquered lands, and in it stand lifelike statues of Caesar's ancestors, including, prominently, the Trojan founder, Venus's son Aeneas. Also present are punishing images of the underworld, which on the one hand promote obedience to moral law and on the other foreshadow the inclusion of Odyssean heroics within his Iliadic epic (*Georgics* 3.1–48).

It is clear that Virgil began the *Aeneid* with the express purpose of making Rome the equal or superior of Greece in literature. It is equally clear after reading the *Aeneid*, that while Virgil does celebrate the achievements of Octavian (now Augustus) as promised, his focus is elsewhere. The sufferings, achievements, and failures of Aeneas, as well as the sufferings, achievements, and failures of those whose lives intertwine with his, invite the reader to interpret Augustus' deeds, Rome's deeds, from many angles. The ubiquitous shadow presence of the *Iliad* and *Odyssey* not only adds nuance to deeds and characters, but creates a contrast between Greek and Roman culture that at times seems to assert Roman superiority, at other times wipes out the distinction. The interplay of Roman legend and historical fact, Greek and Roman epic, pastoral and epic genres, and action and philosophy raises the *Aeneid* far above panegyric chronicle, far above patriotic myth. As in *Gilgamesh*, the *Iliad*, *Odyssey*, and the *Metamorphoses* that Ovid would soon write, in the *Aeneid* national culture holds a lens to the human condition.

The Poets

Publius Vergilius Maro lived from 70 to 19 BCE. Born on a Mantuan farm, he was educated in rhetoric and Greek literature in the cities of Milan and Rome, studied Epicurean philosophy in Naples, the city where he chose to be buried, and joined a literary circle of other highly educated poets and intellectuals in Rome. He and his fellow northern Italians became Roman citizens only in 49 BCE when he was twenty-one years old; some five years later, starting when he was not quite 26, he lived through the two years of terrible killings and appropriations that followed Caesar's assassination; then, as he approached forty, the final civil war between Octavian and Antony rocked the Roman world. Only in the last eleven years of his life did he experience real peace, and these years must have been freighted with uncertainty about a supreme leader who, though generous now, had shown such ferocity in his quest for power.

Virgil wrote the *Eclogues* and *Georgics* during the height of the civil wars. City politics occasionally disrupt these two beautiful excursions into country life, but in them on the whole Virgil follows the Epicurean directive to cultivate joy away from the moil of politics. The *Aeneid*, composed after the wars, is deeply engaged with politics throughout, reflecting a Stoicism concerned precisely with the role of the wise man as statesman. A statesman whose enemies are *furor*, grief, anger, and desire (for personal honor and for love), emotions that had plagued and finally destroyed the Roman Republic. A statesman who, in so far as Aeneas embodies him in the making, would much rather be anything – a loving husband, for example, or dead – than a statesman. Virgil's is a reluctant hero who undertakes his epic task not in order to gain immortality, honor or power, but to fulfill duty.

Virgil worked on his poem for several years until he died of a sudden fever at age fifty-two. Although he left the *Aeneid* unfinished, we need not think that we are missing its ending. According to an early biographer (Donatus), Virgil drafted the complete story in prose, divided it into 12 books, and turned it into verse (12,847 lines in all) as inspiration took him. His literary executors did a small amount of editing, but added nothing. Some passages, therefore, are less finished than others, some half-lines exist, and there are some contradictions. One could wish that Virgil had had time to do the final polishing, but even without it the *Aeneid* is a *tour de force* in which the Trojan War, Roman prehistory, history, and the present refract and blend in astonishing ways. Never has a poet more brilliantly orchestrated readers' emotions and harassed their intellects.

Publius Ovidius Naso lived from 43 BCE to 17 CE. He was born and reared in Sulmo, a town ninety miles northeast of Rome, one year after the assassination of Julius Caesar. Despite the ongoing civil wars, he and his older brother received a normal upper-middle-class education in

Rome. His brother from an early age displayed talent at oratory, but Ovid preferred poetry. When his father advised him to follow a more practical career, arguing that even Homer died poor, Ovid tried to heed his father's advice, but, he says, every time he tried to write prose, it came out as poetry. When his brother died at age twenty, Ovid tried for a time to follow the political career his parents wanted, but after holding a minor office he decided to opt out of politics, drop the quest for senatorial rank, and devote himself entirely to poetry. He describes his choice as between "anxiety-ridden ambition" and "safe leisure" (*Tristia* 4.10.38–40). He did not, however, write "safe" poetry.

Virgil died when Ovid was twenty-four. Ovid saw him but never heard him read his poetry as he did many other poets: Propertius's elegies, Bassus's iambics, Ponticus's Theban epic, Horace's intricate lyric. Ovid himself was a valued member of poetic circles, for he published his first book of elegiac love poems, the *Amores*, when he was under twenty. His poetic output was steady: four more books of *Amores*, then the *Heroides* (fifteen love letters from abandoned heroines like Dido), *Cosmetics for Women*, the *Art of Love* (a handbook on seduction and intrigue), and the *Cure for Love*. All of these erotic poems are in elegiac rhythm, which is a six-foot dactylic hexameter followed by a five-foot pentameter. Just as his prose turned into verse as a teenager, so, according to the first book of the *Amores*, his intended epic became elegy: "I was preparing to write of arms and violent war, with meter proper to the subject, the second verse equal to the first, but Cupid laughed, took away one foot," and subsequently shot him with an arrow, thus transforming him into an erotic poet. After writing witty and irreverent poems about love for twenty-five years, he returned to epic. He did not, however, give up being witty and irreverent.

From approximately 2 CE to 8 CE, Ovid worked on two poems, the *Fasti* ("Religious Calendar") in elegiacs and the fifteen-book *Metamorphoses* ("Transformations") in dactylic hexameters. Since the *Metamorphoses* flouts all the rules of epic, which prescribe unity at least of hero and preferably also of time and place, one might well ask why Ovid nonetheless chose to write it in dactylic hexameter, which together with the mythological subject matter insists that the reader think of it as epic. Perhaps he did it purely for the delight of changing an old form into something dazzlingly new. It is possible, too, that its form invites the reader to seek a serious political message lurking behind the poem's wit and humor: rely on no leader, believe no doctrine, accept no hierarchy as natural. All, including imperial propaganda, is fiction.

The *Metamorphoses* was essentially complete by 8 CE when disaster struck. In that year Augustus, who had instituted a program to regenerate Roman morality, banished his granddaughter, Julia, for adultery and then turned on Ovid for having written an offensive poem, which seems most likely to be the *Art of Love*. Ovid writes only that a *carmen* incurred the emperor's wrath (*Tristia* 2. 207)[5] and that in addition he committed an unspecified "error." The result was exile in Tomis, a bleak locale on the Black Sea. From exile he wrote a few revisions of the *Fasti* and wrote quantities of verse epistles unsuccessfully begging the emperor to let him return. It is from these poems, the *Tristia* ("Sorrows") and "Letters from Pontus," that we know what we do about his life. He died in exile in 17 CE, three years after Augustus.

Further Reading

Legendary Origins of Rome

Tim Cornell's masterful *The Beginnings of Rome: Italy from the Bronze Age to the Punic Wars* (London and New York, 2001) discusses origin myths on pp. 48–73. Andrew Erskine's *Troy Between Greece and Rome: Local Tradition and Imperial Power* (Oxford, 2001) focuses on how Greeks first developed myths of Trojan city-founding and then on how the Julian family shaped the story of Aeneas. Erich S. Gruen's *Culture and National Identity in Republican Rome* (Ithaca, NY, 1992) discusses origin myths on pp. 6–52, and in the rest of the book gives an excellent discussion on art and its interplay with changing Roman values. N. Horsfall carefully analyzes "The Aeneas-Legend from Homer to Virgil" in J. N. Bremmer and N. Horsfall, *Roman Myth and Mythography* (London, 1987), 12–24. This essay is also available on the Web at http://theol.eldoc.ub.rug.nl Files/root/BremmerJN/1987/117/aeneas.pdf.

Roman Epic before Virgil

Joseph Farrell gives a good overview of the problem of precursors to Roman epicist Livius Andronicus and what Greek literature contributed in "The Origins and Essence of Roman Epic" in John Miles Foley, ed., *A Companion to Ancient Epic* (Oxford and Malden, MA, 2005), 417–428. Sander Goldberg introduces Andronicus, Naevius, and Ennius and other of Virgil's predecessors in "Early Republican Epic" in Foley 2005, 229–239. For several excellent essays on Ennius, see a special edition of *Arethusa* edited by B. W. Breed and A. Rossi, *Ennius and the Invention of Roman Epic. Arethusa* 39, 3 (Fall 2006).

Ancient Sources on History and Philosophy in Modern Translations

Appian, *The Civil Wars*, translated by John Carter (New York and London, 1996).

Cicero, Marcus Tullius, *On the Commonwealth and On the Laws*, translated by J. E. G. Zetzel (Cambridge, 1999).

Lucretius, *On the Nature of Things*, translated by Martin Ferguson (Indianapolis, IN, 2001).

Suetonius, *Lives of the Caesars*, translated by Catharine Edwards (Oxford, 2001).

Notes

1 For two examples of vase paintings dated to 520–500 BCE see Susan Woodford's *The Trojan War in Ancient Art* (Ithaca, 1993), 114. Both examples are Attic, but there exist twenty-one similar Etruscan vase paintings from the area to the north of Rome.

2 See *Res Gestae* 3. I should note that Appian, an historian writing a little later than Suetonius, follows Augustus' version, relating that Octavian pardoned everyone and that Perusia burned down by accident (*The Civil Wars* 5.48–49). Suetonius, who was head librarian and archivist in Rome, lived c. 70–130 CE. Appian, who lived mostly in Alexandria but also for a while in Rome, wrote his history before 162 CE.

3 See Spencer Cole's "Cicero, Ennius, and the Concept of Apotheosis at Rome" (*Arethusa* 39.3 [2006], 531–548) for a thorough discussion of deification in Cicero's writings.

4 Sander Goldberg ("Early Republican Epic," 432) says that it filled only one book roll. For purposes of comparison, Naevius' contemporary epic on the Second Punic War filled seven.

5 B. R. Nagle believes that the poem in question was the *Metamorphoses*, which revealed "the working of myth in Augustan propaganda" and "disguised the introduction of a new form of monarchy" (*Ovid's Fasti*, Bloomington, IN, 1995).

7

The *Aeneid* of Virgil

I sing of arms and a man, he who, fugitive by fate,
first came from Troy to Italy and the shores of
Lavinium – buffeted greatly over land and sea by the force of
celestial gods on account of ferocious Juno's remembering wrath,
suffering greatly in war until he could found a city
and bring his gods into Latium; whence the race of Latins
and Alban fathers and walls of high Rome.
Muse, remind me of the cause. For what wound to her godhead,
what grief, did the queen of gods force a man outstanding for
pietas to undergo so much misfortune, meet so much hardship?
Does such wrath exist in the hearts of gods?

(Aeneid 1.1–11)

The poet sings of war, as does the *Iliad*, and of a man, as does the *Odyssey*. Like Odysseus, the *Aeneid*'s hero will suffer as he wanders the sea; like Achilles, he will suffer and then triumph in war. Unlike either Achilles or Odysseus, however, his goal is not self-fulfillment. He struggles for neither *timé* (honor) nor *nóstos* (return home), but to find a new home in a foreign land. He does not circle back to a city he loves, but goes forth, because he must, to found a new one. Like Gilgamesh, part of his immortality will come from a city, but that city, Rome, will be built not by him, but by distant descendants. As Roman readers of the *Aeneid* would know, without waiting for Jupiter to specify it (1.265–277), a minimum of 350 years separates the fall of Troy from the founding of their capital city.

Virgil starts his story in Carthage, but by making Aeneas a dinner-table raconteur like Odysseus, he is also able to include the fall of Troy (Book 2) and some wanderings (Book 3) that raise thematic questions similar to those we found in the *Odyssey*, that is, which "wife" should the hero choose? What locale must he choose as home? Like Odysseus, Aeneas is persecuted by a vengeful god, and like him also Aeneas will have to travel to the world of the dead for information about his journey. Unlike Odysseus, however, Aeneas needs information not about *how* to reach his goal, but *why*. Once in Italy, he will, like Odysseus, have to fight a rival to win a wife and kingdom. This fight for a wife also moves the epic into Iliadic territory, for the battle is between two armies and Aeneas' rival is termed "another Achilles" (6.89). In this battle, Aeneas defeats "Achilles." This symbolic reversal of the Greek victory at Troy produces an ending that is happy like the *Odyssey*'s but feels tragically more like the *Iliad*'s.

The reader's complex response to this ending is the product of how Virgil has portrayed Aeneas' journey toward it, a journey that is both physical and psychological and steeped in a morality created largely by interplay with the Homeric texts. Virgil appropriates these texts not only to lend breadth and stature to his epic, but also to define what is Roman by comparison to what is Greek. Readers familiar with the earlier epics will be looking for patterns and themes, and when they find them will be both reassured by their familiarity and arrested by their sudden strangeness.

Virgil's hero brings his family's household gods, elsewhere called the Penates (1.68), from Troy to Italy. He is, as we hear often, "outstanding for *pietas*" (variously translated as "goodness," "devotion," "justice," *Aeneid* 1.10), a quality that is his defining characteristic, just as "resourcefulness" and "divine wrath" define Odysseus and Achilles, respectively. *Pietas* is the Latin word behind the English word "piety," but it has a larger meaning: it means devotion not only to the gods, but also to one's parents and, as Cicero emphasized, to one's state (or city). Aeneas' traditional devotion to his father and to the gods is the foundation of his *pietas* in the *Aeneid*, but Virgil makes devotion to the state, that is, Rome, part of Aeneas' heroic task. Attaining this kind of *pietas* is difficult, because it requires wrenching personal sacrifice and, when the poem opens, Aeneas has no clear idea where or what his new city will be.

The opening verses of the *Aeneid* identify two competing agents as responsible for Aeneas' unhappy predicament: "Fate" has made him a fugitive (1.1) and "ferocious Juno's remembering wrath" buffets him (1.4). Fate in the *Aeneid* is a more loaded term than it is in Homer. Fate represents not just what happens to a person or city – in the Homeric texts usually death, destruction – but also the grand march of history. It is the Stoic force for good, and it will later in Book 1 be embodied in the calm Jupiter. Passionate Juno, on the other hand, embodies Homeric *mênis*, parallel to the *Odyssey*'s Poseidon. As the phrase "remembering wrath" indicates, Juno looks to the Greek past, while Jupiter and fate look to the Roman future (1.257–296). Juno and Jupiter are the "celestial gods" of verse three of the proem, and the first third of Book 1 will be devoted to delineating the opposition between them.

When the proem shifts from the laboring hero to Juno's wrath, Virgil finally invokes the Muse that had opened the Homeric poems and Ennius' *Annales*, asking her for help in understanding why a god would persecute an innocent man. The Muse's belated appearance makes a statement about poetics that both links Virgil to and separates him from Homer's poetics. Virgil asserts his tight control over his verse with "I sing" (*cano*) in the first line, and he turns to the Muse for help only when he wants to probe an Iliadic emotion. The implication is that the poet's rational human understanding cannot comprehend "such wrath" existing in "the hearts of gods."[1] It is appropriate to evoke her now also because what Juno refuses to forget are the events of the Trojan War, those events recounted so memorably by Homer and the Epic Cycle.

The Divine Apparatus

In the verses that follow, the poet probes the source of Juno's anger. She cherishes the newly founded city of Carthage, which she would make the ruling power of the world if she could. Fate, however, has decreed that a new race descended from Trojans shall one day destroy Carthage (1.12–22). Fear of what Aeneas' descendants will do is thus part of Juno's motivation. The other part is anger over what she sees as personal dishonor: Trojan Paris had spurned her beauty, Jupiter had carried off the beautiful Ganymede to live in Olympos, and she hates the Trojan race, which as everyone knew was descended from a liaison between her husband and a rival consort (see *Aeneid* 8.133–137). "Aflame" over all these things, she blocks the Trojan ships from reaching Italy while Fate simultaneously drives them forward (1.25–32).

Although the hero of the *Odyssey* had little choice, he did personally trigger Poseidon's Iliadic revenge by doing physical harm to the god's son. Aeneas, guilty only by association, is even more innocent of wrongdoing than Odysseus. His innocence casts into sharp relief the irrationality of Juno's anger, an irrationality that is exacerbated for the Stoic reader by wound imagery (1.8, 36) and repeated use of the adjective *saevus*, "ferocious," which connect her anger to the unhealthy and the bestial.

Juno's unhealthy inhuman anger stems from a fixed focus on her own desire and prerogatives as queen of the gods. Like the Iliadic Hera, whose savage hate prolonged the Trojan War to its bitter end, Virgil's Juno interprets any check to her power as a lessening of honor (1.46–49), a trait shared by many Homeric heroes. Invested in the heroic code of the Homeric Greeks and famous as a partisan of the Greeks, Juno's opposition to Fate becomes symbolically an opposition between Greece and Rome.

Juno's first act in the *Aeneid* is to create a tempest to sink and scatter Aeneas' ships as they are nearing Sicily. The imagery used to describe this act is significant: Aeolia, land of storms, has a male ruler and is called by the normal word for nation, "fatherland," but at base it is feminine, a cave "pregnant" with "raging" winds. Like unruly human beings, the winds struggle, moan indignantly, and need to be bound in prison where their passions are soothed and angers calmed with the (male-held) scepter. Were they not so bound, they might confound the universe itself, which is why the "all-powerful father" (that is, Jupiter) has appointed a king to tighten and loosen their reins (1.50–63).

Juno subverts male control of the winds by bribing Aeolus to break his "fixed compact" (1.62) with Jupiter. Her offer of marriage with a beautiful nymph succeeds in switching Aeolus' allegiance from the "all-powerful father" to herself. Unleashed by personal desire, which is here intimately associated with sexuality and the feminine, a monstrous storm ensues, sinking one ship and scattering the others.

The storm is ended by Neptune, who raises his "calm" head above the seething waters and, recognizing the "tricks and anger" of Juno at work, immediately "calms the swollen sea, banishes the clouds and brings back the sun" (1.127–143). Neptune's act calls forth the first simile of the epic, which compares his calming of the seas to a statesman's calming a rebellious crowd:

> Just as often happens when discord breaks out in a large crowd, the rabble's passions rage and now rocks and firebrands fly (fury provides arms) – if then they chance to see a man respected for *pietas* and service, they fall silent and stand still with attentive ears; and he with words controls their passions and soothes their breasts. So the crashing of the sea subsided as soon as the Father, looking out over the sea, [rode in his chariot through the open air.] (*Aeneid* 1.148–155)

This simile presents an elitist view of human nature, with the mass of the people needing a great leader to keep them from doing violence to each other. The enemies of civil accord are the passion and fury (*furor*) that are the norm, which only the calm statesman can subdue. Note that while the weapons of the people are physical, those of the statesman are intellectual. Note too that the power of the statesman is grounded not in martial glory but in service and *pietas*, the defining virtue of the *Aeneid*'s hero. Finally, the statesman of the simile is parallel to a god (Neptune) while the people and their passions are parallel to natural forces (the chaotic winds). This statesman is, of course, the ideal to which Aeneas (and Augustus?) must aspire.

By the end of the Neptune scene, a polarity of ideas and images has begun to take shape. On one side are Juno (mother), passion (wrathful and sexual), nature, discord, the masses, and Greece. On the other are Neptune (father), Fate, civilization, order, the statesman, and Rome. This opposition will hold and grow for almost the whole of the epic, as Juno creates both physical and mental trials for Aeneas, blasting him with literal storms and erratic enemies and tempting him to un-Roman passions of his own.

After Aeneas and his ship make it to land and set up camp in Libya, Virgil again brings divinity to the fore, this time as a way to inscribe the destiny of the Roman Empire. Virgil introduces Venus as a tearful mother concerned for her son and for the rule over "all lands and sea" that had been promised to his Roman descendants (1. 228–237). Jupiter, who is given a breadth of vision as wide as Juno's is narrow, and who has a "calming" function like Neptune, first assures Venus that Aeneas' fate is secure. Then he goes on to describe something much larger than Aeneas and the power per se of his descendants (1.254–296).

The image of Jupiter's "unrolling the secrets of Fate" suggests that human destiny is not something chaotic, but something orderly, something that can be understood progressively like a history book (unlike prophetic tea leaves or animal entrails). Jupiter gives an orderly succession of numbers: Aeneas will reign for three years; Ascanius will found Alba Longa thirty years after Aeneas' death; and Romulus, founder of Rome and the Roman people, will be born three hundred years after that. Then, in a verse that fuses him with Fate, Jupiter declares that he "has granted" these Romans "power without end" (*imperium sine fine*), a sentiment bound to have had, in the words of R. D. Williams, "a profound patriotic impact on Virgil's readers."[2]

Jupiter's vision of the mission of Rome includes several important steps. First, Juno will amend her thinking and cherish the Romans as he does; then Trojan descendants will reverse the defeat at Troy by conquering the homeland of Achilles, Agamemnon, and Diomedes; and finally, a Caesar will be born (possibly Julius, but probably Augustus) who will be welcomed to heaven and worshiped as a god (1.279–290). The capstone of this prophecy is the vision of Romulus and Remus giving laws while "fury" sits bound within the closed gates of war (1.293–296), an image that vividly evokes the civil wars even as it purports to end them.

Despite the personification, Jupiter here in Book 1 corresponds to the Stoic idea of the rational principle that guides the universe. He contributes to the dichotomy earlier created by the opposition between passionate Juno and calm Neptune, cementing the association between masculine gender and public order. Juno, the Greeks, and irrational fury must all be conquered before Rome can reach its full promise of manly calm and order.

Dido and the Problem of Femininity

Women are not identical with the female principle represented by Juno, but their gender does seem to make them somewhat more susceptible to passion than men. Juno incites women weary of wandering to burn the ships in Book 5 while the men are involved in orderly athletic contests (5.604–663). While her husband Latinus remains calm, Queen Amata burns with "feminine anxiety and anger" and becomes the first victim of the fury Allecto, whom Juno unlooses to stir Latin people to war (7.343–353). Even love for a son can make a woman dangerous: the one mother who makes it to Italy laments so loudly when her son is killed that she unmans the Trojans for battle and must be removed (9.499–502). Camilla, the great warrior maiden who seems immune to love, nonetheless dies because she is distracted by what Virgil calls "a feminine love (*amor*) for plunder" (11.781–782). These women, and Dido too, are part of a pattern of imagery meant to reinforce the ideal, the manly ideal, of suppressing personal desire for the sake of public good, of controlling passion through reason.

Masculinity, represented at its peak by Jupiter, is, naturally, superior to femininity, which is represented by Juno. In so far as men succumb to uncontrolled passions – and they do – they too must be associated with the feminine, not necessarily by the other characters but by the reader who can see the larger pattern. When Virgil has two characters bring up the issue in what we may call a standard Homeric way, it highlights the issue of who may genuinely lay claim to masculinity in the *Aeneid*'s world. Iarbas, Dido's rejected African suitor, and Turnus, Aeneas' Italian rival for Lavinia, insult Aeneas and the Trojans by calling them women or "half-men" with curled and perfumed hair (4.215–216, 9.617, 12.99–100). Iarbas, who utters the insult in a prayer to Jupiter, may be half right, not on the basis of coiffure, of course, but because Aeneas has temporarily abandoned his Roman mission to linger with the queen of Carthage. Turnus's insult, which comes after Aeneas and his men are back on mission, creates a discrepancy, which focuses the reader's attention on what really matters, inward state of mind, not outward appearance. Turnus, externally the manliest of men, is the devotee and tool of Juno and is suffering from two debilitating passions, love and anger. These facts put him squarely in the camp of the feminine, and the resulting irony draws attention to the new kind of masculinity Virgil's epic is promoting.

Despite their increased vulnerability, women, like men, can control their passions. Or at least they can when they are out of their bodies. The ghost of Creusa, Aeneas' Trojan wife who appears retrospectively in Aeneas' description of the fall of Troy, sets an important example. When Aeneas exits Troy, he carries his father on his back and leads his son by the hand, while Creusa is left to follow behind. When he gets his father and son to safety and discovers she is lost, Aeneas once more heads back into the burning city, risking all to find her. He does not give up until her ghost appears to him, asks him to stop indulging his "unhealthy (*insanus*) grief," and tells him that he is fated to be happy with a new royal wife in Hesperia (2.776–784). Creusa is the ideal self-sacrificing wife: she exhibits no jealousy, no anger at being forgotten, only support for whatever needs to be done to promote the future Roman state, even at the cost of her own life. At the same time, she provides her husband important information, including naming Hesperia (Italy) as his destination. When readers later come across repeated scenes of Aeneas' wondering where he is to go, they can only conclude that he was too distraught with grief to take in what his wife said.

Readers are never in any doubt about why Dido, who also hears Creusa's words, does not understand what they mean. As she listens enthralled to Aeneas' story about Troy's last night, she is already "poisoned" by love (1.686), the unconscious victim of Venus, Aeneas' overprotective mother. Juno, in an attempt to thwart fate and keep Aeneas from reaching Italy, subsequently colludes with Venus, creating another storm in which both Dido's *pudor* (sense of shame) and Aeneas' *pietas* come to wreck. Aeneas, with the help of Jupiter, recovers. Not so Dido, who has been betrayed by her own patron goddess of Carthage. Transfixed by admiration, pity, and horror, readers witness passionate love transform this magnificent epic hero into a tragic heroine. Gender is very much an issue in this transformation, because Dido is forced to choose between her ability to rule and her natural feminine desires for husband and children.

Dido had become an exemplary leader only after becoming a widow. According to Venus, she was at first "sick with love," but after her murdered husband's ghost appeared to her in a dream to tell her what she must do, she had immediately assumed responsibility. She got her people and treasure away on ships, cleverly bought sufficient land for a new city in Libya, and started building a thriving sophisticated city (1.360–368, 498–504). In this role as leader she is compared to the goddess Diana: beautiful, stately, full of joy, and implicitly virgin (1.498–504). Still wedded to Sychaeus in her mind and therefore not a sexually active wife, she has internalized the masculine qualities a leader needs.

Dido's early trajectory from unhealthy passion to action finds a parallel in Aeneas' reaction to Creusa in Book 2. Dido and Aeneas are thus positioned as equals, but with two major differences. First, Aeneas will, Creusa promises, become a happy husband in the future, while Dido has taken and reaffirms a vow of fidelity to her first husband (4.15–17, 26–29). We may note that for Roman widows, though not widowers, such a commitment was the ideal. Second, after losing his wife, Aeneas has a father and son to guide his actions (even after Anchises dies, he admonishes Aeneas in dreams [4.351–3]), while Dido has only a sister. Once Dido has been invaded by Venus's fire, her sister Anna will "inflame" rather than curb her natural yearnings for children and sex. Third, female Juno, not masculine Jupiter, will manipulate her behavior after she is attacked by Venus. Venus, Juno, and Anna, a powerful female trio, deflect Dido's life from healthy balance into one of all-consuming passion. Dido in turn deflects Aeneas, who ignores his dead father's repeated dream visitations until Jupiter intervenes.

Although Dido is guilty of breaking her vow to Sychaeus, Virgil does not press the issue. There is a lesson about yielding to passion in her tragic fall from dignified joyful city builder to frantic bacchante raging through its streets, but she evokes pity more than blame. Virgil calls Dido "unlucky" (1.712, 4.68, 450) and chooses medical vocabulary rather than moral language to describe her destructive passion. In addition to causing "ill health" (4.8), her love is twice termed a living wound (4.1–2, 67), and a touching simile compares her to a fatally wounded deer whose only fault is to be incautious around an armed shepherd (4.69–73). Dido's metaphorical wound becomes literal when, like the sympathetic tragic hero of Sophokles' *Ajax*, she kills herself with Aeneas' sword at the end of Book 4 (689).[3]

At the same time as her wound becomes literal, so too does the fire imagery that Virgil has also used to image her love. In addition to the funeral pyre that signals her death to Aeneas as he sails toward Sicily (4.661, 5.3–7), a simile describes the lamentation of Dido's people as identical to what would happen "if all Carthage . . . fell to invading enemies, and furious fire rolled through the rooftops of homes and temples" (4.669–671). The fire in the simile is all the more vivid because we have just seen through Aeneas' eyes this exact thing happen to Troy, just as it had been foretold in the simile that followed Hektor's death in the *Iliad* (22.410–411). Like the simile in the *Iliad*, this simile too foretells the future of the heroine's city, which will be burned to the ground by a Roman army in 146 BCE.

Carthage's future destruction is the direct result of Dido's raging passion, which, when Aeneas leaves, turns from love to despair to hate and provokes a deathbed prayer for unending enmity between Carthage and Aeneas' future nation. She prophesies an avenger (usually interpreted as foretelling Hannibal) who will pursue Aeneas' descendants with fire and sword, and she prays that for all time the two peoples will fight on sea and on land (4.621–629). As Roman readers knew, Dido's vengeful curse on Rome came back to curse her own people.

Dido regains her dignity before she dies, partly through her curse and partly through her proud summary of her accomplishments. These accomplishments include having revenged her husband's murder, which aligns her with the Greek (both epic and tragic) imperative for vengeance. It also, of course, aligns her with passionately vengeful Juno who, like her, suffers from an "eternal wound" (1.36). This latter alignment must make readers rationally critical of Dido's final moments even as they emotionally sympathize with her. Her suicide, while noble, exemplifies not how a leader should act but what "a raging woman is capable of" (5.6). Love and anger, that most *insanus* of passions according to Cicero, are linked with each other and associated with the feminine and the Greek as Virgil portrays the corrupting effect of passion on the leader of a well-ordered state.

It is important to recognize that Virgil chose not to portray Dido as another Helen, the "loathsome Fury" of Book 2 (573–574), or as a

Cleopatra, *femme fatale* and "*monstrum fatale*" (Horace 1.37.21), who in Roman propaganda had corrupted Antony and stirred up war between him and Octavian. Instead, Virgil portrays her as an admirable woman worthy of Aeneas' love. As such, she embodies both a genuine temptation for Aeneas and a tragic lesson about consequences when those with public responsibilities give rein to personal desires. She foreshadows Turnus, the designated Italian "Achilles," who in the second half of the poem will again tempt Aeneas to a corrupting emotion fomented by Juno: wrath.

Aeneas as Odysseus

In Books 1–6, Aeneas is the hero of an "Odyssey" that is primarily a psychological journey away from his investment in the personal heroics of Homeric epic to a firm commitment to Roman public *pietas*.[4] Odysseus' actions in the *Odyssey* shadow Aeneas' actions, adding resonance but also creating irony. As we will see, they function as a foil both to Aeneas' "Roman" qualities and to some frustrated Iliadic ones.

When we first meet Aeneas, he is caught in Juno's furious storm and, like Odysseus caught in Poseidon's storm, is terrified and wishes he were dead. More precisely, they both wish they had died at Troy, Odysseus so that he could have won *kléos* (*Od.* 5.306–312), Aeneas so that he could have died at home under his father's eyes (*Aeneid* 1.94–101). Their two wishes share some language and the desire to die in war, but we can see an immediate difference between dying for personal glory and dying for family. In addition, while Odysseus' wish specifies an event from the Trojan Cycle, Aeneas' wish pinpoints three specific days in the *Iliad*: the day he would have been killed by Tydeus had he not been rescued by his mother and Apollo (*Il.* 5), the day Patroklos killed Sarpedon (*Il.* 16), and the day of Achilles' rampage (*Il.* 20–22). By this specificity, Virgil identifies Aeneas' death wish with Iliadic values at the same time as he draws a distinction between Aeneas' motivation and Odysseus'.

When Aeneas tells the story of Troy's death throes, he portrays himself as doing his best to die heroically with his city. Ignoring Hektor's instructions to take Troy's gods and leave (2.293–297), Aeneas madly seizes his weapons and, driven by fury and anger, thinks only of "beautiful" death in battle; he exhorts some comrades to die with him in arms (2.314–317, 353). He swears that if it had been his fate, his deeds had earned him the right to die (2.433). Virgil makes it clear that Aeneas wanted to be an Iliadic hero, that is, gloriously dead in battle after taking as much revenge as he could.

What stops him is an image of his father, and then of his wife and son, which comes into his head when he sees the raging son of Achilles slaughter Priam and his son Polites. After a detour in which, with "inflamed" and "furious mind," he almost takes revenge on Helen, a deed deflected by Venus, his desire to die is replaced by a desire to save his family. Anchises, too, however, seems to prefer death to leaving, and it takes a portent of flame playing harmlessly around his grandson Iulus's head to convince him that such is Jupiter's will. Aeneas takes the family to safety on Mount Ida, but only after the subsequent scene with the ghost of Creusa does he completely give up martial heroics and take on his fated role as leader of Troy's survivors.

We can sum up the lesson of Book 2 by revisiting Creusa's first words to Aeneas in this scene: "What help is it to indulge so greatly your unhealthy grief?" Grief may be said to be the prime mover of the *Iliad*'s action, for Achilles' wrath is a response to his grief first at Agamemnon's insult and then at Patroklos' death. Anger caused by sharp grief fuels all warriors' ability to kill enemy soldiers. It is not, however, productive for Aeneas to indulge grief or any other emotion in the *Aeneid*. Passion now connotes sickness, insanity. When weeping Aeneas at last yields to his dead wife's words and to the needs of the band of refugees waiting for him, he gives up the role of Achilles and reluctantly assumes the role of Odysseus the survivor.

In the *Aeneid*, survival is psychically far more difficult than dying, and at times Aeneas does not seem up to the task. In comparison with his exciting Homeric counterpart, whose adventures are ever present in the background of Books 1–6, decent, responsible Aeneas often seems to come up short. He is weary, sad, frequently close to despair, and lacks Odysseus' cleverness and energy. While Odysseus established happy and helpful relationships with female characters, Aeneas drives Dido to suicide and provokes a deadly curse not only on himself, but also his descendants. Despite his shortcomings, however, Aeneas is not an anti-hero. His failures in comparison with Odysseus emphasize two things: first, that in the ideology of the *Aeneid*, personal success is relatively unimportant, and second, that mental fortitude and self-control do not come easily even to the best of men. Odysseus demonstrates endurance and resourcefulness that are at the same heroic level from beginning to end, while Aeneas only gradually enlarges his *pietas* to include commitment to the idea of Rome.

Aeneas' *pietas* towards his father plays a crucial role in his learning process. Anchises was Aeneas' steadfast guide and support in Book 3, and once he is dead, Aeneas is obviously not strong enough to carry on alone – witness his disastrous conduct in Carthage. It will take a trip to the underworld at his father's behest to give him the mental strength he needs to complete the project of founding a city in Italy. He does not go because he must, as Odysseus does, nor does he weep and thrash about as Odysseus does when Circe gives him the bad news. Aeneas goes eagerly to meet his father, comparing himself to Orpheus and Pollux, who both sought beloved companions in Hades (6.119–121). He needs something different than Odysseus did. Heroic endurance enables Odysseus to learn from Teiresias how to get home, while heroic *pietas* enables Aeneas to discover not *how* to found his fated city, but *why* he should.

Aeneas' many encounters in Hades include several that are parallel to Odysseus' encounters, but two parts of the *Aeneid*'s underworld are entirely different. In Homer's Hades only three great mythic sinners are punished; all others mingle aimlessly, equally unhappy at being dead. Virgil's Hades contains Tartarus and the Realm of the Happy, regions of punishment and reward. Among the groans of the punished, a lesson is audible: "Learn justice and not to slight the gods" (6.620).

Father Anchises is among the Happy, surveying the souls of his Roman descendants. When Aeneas is first given to understand that the souls he sees here are eager to be reborn, his response is astonishment: "Poor wretches, why this dreadful desire (*dira cupido*) for the light?" (6.721). His lack of enthusiasm for life is striking when compared to Achilles lecturing Odysseus about how he would rather be the living slave of a serf than king of the dead (*Od.* 11.488–491).

Anchises' explanation of why souls long to be reborn involves an elaborate fusion of Stoic and Platonic cosmologies. Human beings combine a heavenly spirit with an earthly body that pollutes the spirit with fear, desire, grief, and joy. After death these passions must be purged with "punishments," and then the souls get sent to Elysium. A very few souls (presumably those less polluted by passion) get to stay in the Realm of the Happy until as pure fiery spirit they return to the ether from which they came. Most, however, stay only for 1,000 years before going through another cycle of embodiment and purification. This cosmological digression confuses Virgil's underworld, for it negates almost everything that has come before, but it offers to more intellectual readers a more "scientific" motivation for purging passion. More importantly, it makes possible the pageant of Italian and Roman heroes that follows.

As Anchises points out seminal figures in the grand march of Roman history, Virgil acknowledges some sad costs, but emphasizes glorious achievement. At the pageant's unchronological center is Augustus, who will institute a new "golden age" (6.792); preceding him are Aeneas' mythic descendants, plus Julius Caesar, and after him come historical figures who had great impact on Rome's development. At this point Anchises sums up what it means to be a Roman: other peoples (understand "Greeks") may be better at the fine arts and physical sciences, but Romans will excel in the arts of government. A Roman must remember "to govern with authority and add law to peace; to spare the submissive and conquer the arrogant" (851–853).

Once you have power, Anchises seems to say, govern according to law and not according to personal emotions. Living up to this precept is what it means to be devoted to Rome. Now, finally, *pius* Aeneas knows what he must commit to. Trojan *pietas* involved commitment to gods, parents, birthplace, friends, and immediate family as they already existed. Roman *pietas* adds to the above commitments an overriding commitment to live for the future, to live as part of history. To have Roman *pietas* means that one's heart is fired not with love or hatred of individual persons but, as Anchises finally fires Aeneas', with "love of coming fame" (889), that is, a history of deeds that will eventually fulfill this vision of civilized government.

This then is the reward for Aeneas' excruciating sacrifice of past loyalties, present self-fulfillment, and all personal desire: the character of a humane governor who fights to establish the rule of law and stops short of vengeance when his opponent submits. We have been shown the cost, we have been shown the reward. The cost is abiding; but is the reward? We shall get our answer in the "Iliadic half" of the *Aeneid*, when Aeneas is forced back into the role of martial hero by the "Achilles" who awaits him in Italy.

In Books 1–6, Aeneas plays the role of Odyssean survivor, but the only trait he has in common with Odysseus is endurance. Will the same dissimilarity hold true in the Iliadic books? In Book 8, as he is preparing to lead Greek and Etruscan allies into battle against the Latins and their allies, he receives from his mother a shield made by Vulcan. The making and delivery of the shield, modeled on the making and delivery of Achilles' shield in *Iliad* 18, creates a likeness in stature, while maintaining an utter contrast in character. This contrast can be felt both in the scenes depicted on the shields and in the heroes' reactions to their mothers' wondrous gifts.

The heroes' reactions to their shields correspond to the emotion most characteristic of each: wrath and *pietas*. Aeneas and Achilles both feel joy and admiration (*Il.* 19.18–22, *Aeneid* 8. 617, 730). Achilles' very first reaction, however, is to grow more angry: "his anger increased, and his eyes shone terribly like firelight beneath his brows" (*Il.* 19. 16–17). After admiring the divine workmanship, he says, "Now indeed will I arm" (*Il.* 19.23). Aeneas finishes admiring his shield (with the reader looking over *his* shoulder, not Vulcan's) and "ignorant of the events, rejoices in their image as he lifts to his shoulders the fame and fates of his descendants" (8.730–731). Aeneas' shouldering the burden of unknown history marks him as a very different kind of hero from the angrily arming Achilles.

Achilles' shield contained scenes of generic human life in all its myriad changes. Presenting no insistent morality, these scenes depicted life in an eternal present. Aeneas' shield, on the other hand, presents the "history of Italy and Roman triumphs" (*Aeneid* 8.626). They specify events and names of the future. They depict progress from Romulus' rough and uncivilized kidnapping of the Sabine women to the controlled strength of Augustus subduing the champions (Marc Antony and Cleopatra) of Eastern monster gods and accepting an organized triumph (635–641, 675–706; 714–728). They preach morality: the traitors Mettus and Catiline are punished; the virtuous Roman matrons and Cato are rewarded (642–645, 667–669; 665–666, 670). In short, these scenes comprise a condensed and more strictly moral version of what Aeneas saw in the Underworld. The heroes' shields are thus paradigmatic of their differing concerns: Achilles, who had to wrestle with the complex implications of being human, carried generic life on his shield, while Aeneas, who must wrestle with responsibility to history, carries Rome.

Readers are prepared thereby for Aeneas to become an Achilles without taking on the negative characteristics of Achilles that have been evoked in the *Aeneid*. With the Trojan War pictures on the gates of Juno's temple in Carthage (*Aeneid* 1.458–486), Hektor's appearance in Aeneas' dream (*Aeneid* 2.270–279), Neptune's reminiscence of the day he saved Aeneas (5.804–808), and eleven other more minor evocations of Achilles in Books 1–6, Virgil has portrayed Achilles as an invincible serial killer, ferocious enemy and pitiless conqueror of Trojans. To this portrait will be added another vehement passion, that of love, when Turnus, the "other Achilles" predicted by Sibyl (*Aeneid* 6.89), comes on the scene.

Turnus and the Problem of Achilles

When Aeneas sails into the Tiber river, in Italy at last, Virgil creates a second proem complete with invocation of a muse to introduce the new theme of war: "Come now, Erato, I will recount who were the kings, what was the sequence of events, what the situation in Latium when a foreign army beached its ships on Italian shores. You goddess, you warn your poet. I shall speak of horrible war" (*Aeneid* 7.37–41). It may seem odd that Virgil evokes Erato, the muse of erotic poetry. Apollonios had invoked her at the opening of the second half of the *Argonautika*, which was about how Medea's love for Jason helped him complete his quest, but what has she to do with war? Everything, as it turns out. Just as Dido's rejected love had earlier turned to furious anger and a promise of war, so too will Italy be suffused with *furor* through love: a mother's love for her daughter, a bridegroom's for his bride, and the people's love for their land.

Aeneas' fated wife Lavinia, only child of King Latinus, had once been promised to Turnus, a handsome young prince much beloved by her mother, Amata. Omens, however, have decreed that Lavinia must marry a foreigner, and when Aeneas shows up, her father quickly betroths her to him. Amata, "boiling with feminine anger" over this decision (*Aeneid* 7.345), is ripe for Juno's intervention.

Juno feels "sharp grief" when she notices the Trojans building homes by the Tiber (*Aeneid* 7.291). As she sees it, Aeneas, with his "contrary fate," has "conquered" her (*Aeneid* 7.293, 310), and though she acknowledges she cannot stop the wedding, she vows to take payment in blood from both sides. Bellona, goddess of war, shall be Lavinia's matron of honor, and Aeneas, like Paris, will torch his rebuilt Troy (*Aeneid* 7.318–322). Since she cannot bend Olympian gods to her will, she seeks aid from infernal ones, calling forth the fury Allecto, who joys in "sad war, anger, treachery and crime" (*Aeneid* 7.325–326). Anger is here linked with every societal ill.

Allecto first attacks Amata, whose feminine anger makes her easy prey. When Latinus stands firm on the marriage, Allecto's venom causes Amata to erupt into frenzy, race wildly out of her home and through the city streets, much as Dido had, calling all matrons who believe in "a mother's rights" to join her in Bacchic rites in the mountain forests, where she hides her daughter. The Latin mothers, "breasts aflame with *furor*" follow her from their homes, shrieking and casting off the accouterments of civilization as they race to the woods (*Aeneid* 7.324–405). With the royal house and domestic space throughout the city successfully cast into confusion, Allecto now turns to a male victim.

Before Allecto hurls her firebrand into Turnus's breast, he appears quite rational and not at all upset by Aeneas' appearance in Latium. When, disguised as a priestess of Juno, she urges him to take up arms against the interloper, he laughs at her concerns and, echoing Hektor to Andromakhe, asks her to attend to her temple and leave matters of war and peace to men (*Aeneid* 7.721–744). After she returns to her real form and hurls the firebrand, war-madness and anger rage ferociously (*saevit*) in him, and he announces himself ready to fight both Trojans and Latins (*Aeneid* 7.460–462). Thus turned into an "Achilles" by Allecto, he calls his Rutulians to arms, while Allecto turns to infect with *furor* the good people of the Italian countryside.

Fire imagery, rage, extreme violence, and self identification in Books 9–12[5] reaffirm that Turnus is the "other Achilles" predicted by the Sybil in Book 6. There is, however, a major difference in the two heroes' relationship to the anger that makes them such effective killers on the battlefield. Divine wrath, *mênis*, emanates from within the *Iliad*'s super hero, but in the *Aeneid*'s universe, divine wrath turns a normal man into an Achillean, that is, a destructive martial hero. Divine wrath is incarnated in all men forced by Juno to take up arms. This conception of traditional martial heroism as something originating in the feminine (Juno, Allecto) and associated with lovesick female frenzy (Dido, Amata) must weaken its claim to be a manly Roman ideal.

Juno and Achilles, linked as Greek, as destroyers of Troy and Trojans, and as founts of murderous fury, represent the uncontrolled passion that it is the special mission of Romans to curb. Readers are set up to believe that Turnus, who in Book 9 reenacts some Iliadic deeds of Hektor (raging invincible during Aeneas' absence and setting his opponent's ships on fire), will reincarnate the outmoded character of Achilles but will reenact the career of conquered Trojan heroes. Aeneas, on the other hand, is expected to incarnate the new character of self-controlled Roman and enact the role of a perfected Achilles, that is, one who conquers with firm but limited violence.

Aeneas *alius* Achilles

Aeneas returns from his trip to Arcadia to find Trojans and Rutulians fighting fiercely. To give hope to his men, he arms and stands in the bow of his ship like Octavian at Actium (compare 8.680 and 10.261). Flames pour from his helmet as they did from Octavian's and as they also did from Diomedes' and Achilles' heads in the *Iliad* (5.4, 18.206–214). These flames portend heroic valor and victory. Then Virgil compares Aeneas' appearance to comets glowing "mournfully and blood-red" against the night sky, and to the Dog Star, which "brings drought and sickness to suffering mortals, and glooms the sky with ill-omened light" (10. 273–275). The Dog Star recalls a striking simile from *Iliad*, when Priam saw Achilles racing across the plain toward Troy and Hektor, "shining like a star, which rises in the autumn, its rays shining conspicuous among many stars at the edge of night, the star named Orion's Dog; the star that is brightest but is made a sign of evil and brings high fever to wretched mortals" (*Il.* 22.26–31). Brilliance coexists with harmfulness in Homer's image. Virgil's image subdues the brilliance and focuses on the harmful effect. Aeneas' star not only brings specific evils, as did Achilles', but it affects the whole atmosphere. The phrase "glooms the sky with ill-omened light" prepares for a less than happy result of conjoining Achillean prowess with Aeneas' *pietas*.

Aeneas lands and quickly kills six Latins. After some generalized fighting, Virgil focuses on young Pallas, beloved only son of Aeneas' new ally, the aged Arcadian king Evander. Virgil has made his audience care about Pallas by means of his father's emotional farewell, and his age has been emphasized by his relationship to Aeneas, who was asked to be his role model in warfare and who, on shipboard, was portrayed as his teacher (8.515–517, 10.160–162). Virgil will emphasize his youth again after Turnus kills him, when he comments that this is Pallas's first and last day in battle (10.508). Pallas's *aristeía* establishes his martial worth, and his fight with Turnus creates sympathy for his courage in the face of far superior strength and ability. Turnus alienates sympathy by his arrogance and his exultation in the spoils (a sword belt) he rips from Pallas's body. As with Hektor's despoilment of Patroklos in the *Iliad*, this alienation of sympathy makes the audience emotionally ready for the vengeance to be taken by the main hero.

As if to recall Anchises' dictum about what it means to be a Roman, Aeneas sets out after "arrogant" Turnus (10.514). On his way to "conquer the arrogant," however, he detours to take eight sacrificial victims, reject a suppliant, immolate a fallen priest of Apollo whose armor he takes as a trophy for Mars, joke cruelly to two brothers as he kills them, and kick a decapitated corpse over which he vaunts. The vaunting is a combination of Odysseus' threat that Sokos's body will be eaten by birds and Achilles' that Lukaon's will be eaten by fishes (*Aen.* 10.557–560, *Il.* 11.452, 21.122–127). All this unexpected behavior is modeled on Homeric heroics and Achilles' rampage in particular, but Virgil infuses it with imagery that in the context of Aeneas' hard-won Roman *pietas* makes it seem more troubling than mere backsliding.

Two episodes are particularly significant. The first is when Aeneas takes eight men for sacrifice on Pallas's funeral pyre (*Aeneid* 10.517–520). We say loosely that Achilles "sacrificed" twelve Trojan youths on Patroklos' pyre, but the Greek words for his action do not connote anything religious. The youths are taken as "blood price" and Achilles "slays" them on the pyre, a verb used for killing enemies, never for ceremonial sacrifice. Virgil, on the other hand, uses religious terminology: "sacrifical offerings to the dead" (*inferias*) and "immolate" (*immolare*). Given the Achillean context, and knowing that human sacrifice was a most un-Roman practice (see Livy 22.57.6), Aeneas' action must be judged harshly as one more emanation of *furor*, a *furor* that in this case perverts the religious mission that is at the very heart of Aeneas' fated enterprise. Hektor had commanded Aeneas to take "Troy's sacred rites" as well as his family gods (2.293), and in Book 12 Aeneas will insist that his mission is to contribute "sacred rites and deities" to the new state (189–193). Jupiter will confirm later in Book 12 that "custom and manner of sacred rites" will indeed be Aeneas' *only* contribution (aside from his genes) to the new nation that will surpass all others in *pietas*. The perversion of this religious mission in Book 10, a perversion that is repeated in Book 11 (81–2), and again at the end of Book 12 (949), is deeply disturbing.

The perversion of sacral *pietas* that is produced by this fusion of Achilles and Aeneas may have had historical resonance for Roman readers who would have remembered stories of Octavian's sacrifice of 300 Perusians to his deified father in 41 BCE, a perversion of both religious and familial *pietas*. Some may also have remembered an earlier perversion of sacred ritual by Julius Caesar who, as both *pontifex maximus* (chief high priest) and *dictator*, is alleged to have used the combined power of these two supreme offices to order a human sacrifice to Mars in 46 BCE. As Cassius Dio, a second-century CE historian, tells the story,

Caesar grew angry at some rioting soldiers, killed one, and took two others, who were subsequently sacrificed by priests (*Roman History* 43.24.4).[6] Virgil may be recalling either or both of these men who justified (to themselves, perhaps, as well as to others) ruthless deeds with claims of *pietas*.

Aeneas' second Achillean action is to reject the pleas of Magus, a scene based on Achilles' rejection of Lukaon at *Iliad* 21.68–105. Lukaon begs for his life on the basis of Achilles' previous mercy and is rejected because Patroklos' death has taken away Achilles' inclination to be merciful to those he captures. Magus appeals on the basis of the father–son relationship that has been the motivating force of Aeneas' *pietas*. Evoking Anchises' shade and young Iulus to induce Aeneas to spare "my life for my son and my father," Magus offers ransom and adds, "Not on me does the victory of the Teucrians turn"(10.524–529). No longer fighting for victory, but for personal vengeance, Aeneas rejects Magus's plea with the following words: "save your silver and gold for your sons, such commerce in war Turnus has already taken away, before when Pallas was killed. This is the judgment of Anchises' shade, this the judgment of Iulus" (10.531–534). Achilles' rejection focuses on his own reaction to Patroklos' death. Aeneas reaches outside of himself for justification of what he is doing, answering Magus's appeal in the name of father and son with the "judgment" of that father and son – that very father who instructed Aeneas to "spare the submissive." This misuse of his father's name pollutes the familial as well as the public aspects of Roman *pietas* as Aeneas plunges his sword full length into the suppliant's body.

Virgil infuses every part of Aeneas' *aristeía* with the same careful transformations of the Homeric models. Again and again he shows the dreadful perversion of *pietas* that Achillean fury produces in Aeneas, until the pernicious light of his Homeric heroics "glooms the sky" all the way to Olympos. Jupiter, who has before been the symbol of wisdom and the impartial working of fate, does not send Mercury to get Aeneas back on track; instead he baits his unhappy wife with what he approvingly calls Aeneas' "right hand energetic for war and fierce spirit unyielding in danger" (10.609–610) and then allows Juno to go to earth to get Turnus out of danger. For the sake of making his wife happy, that is, Jupiter is willing to postpone confrontation between Aeneas and Turnus and thus to prolong the war.

In an epic world where the sovereignty of principle is supposed to be the reward for sacrificing personal desire, the descent of Jupiter to the level of the Homeric Zeus confuses the epic's worldview. Jupiter's trajectory is the opposite of Zeus's, who in the final book of the *Iliad* ascends to the role of equitable mediator and makes it possible for Achilles and Priam to set things right. Jupiter will play a decisive role in the denouement of the *Aeneid*, but Virgil leaves it open as to whether it sets things right.

Virgil does not limit Aeneas to acting out only the negative aspects of Achilles' character. Once Juno lures Turnus off the field, Virgil brings on an enemy who unequivocally merits the adjective arrogant. Mezentius, whose hideous deeds were recounted in Book 8 (481–488), crushes and cuts through men like a rock in the sea, a charging boar, a lion tearing its bloody prey, a whirlwind (10.689–768). This "despiser of the gods" (7.648) hurls his spear at Aeneas and misses; "pious" Aeneas drives his spear straight through seven layers of shield into the groin and moves in for the kill. Suddenly, Virgil interposes Lausus, the son earlier described as meriting a better father (7.653–654) and who now groans and weeps with filial love. Virgil steps outside his role as narrator as he, like Homer, does occasionally at moments of affection and foreboding, to promise the youth not to leave his noble deed unsung. This song turns out to be a difficult but instructive one, for Lausus's intervention complicates Aeneas' straightforward action, pushing him into another scornful attack on *pietas*, but then into strongly reaffirming its value. As Lausus holds him off, allowing his wounded father to retreat to safety, Aeneas chides him for allowing his *pietas* to deceive him (10.812), and then in "ferocious anger" buries his sword in Lausus's body. His anger spent, "Anchises' son" sees in the dying youth an image of his own filial *pietas* and immediately reverts to his pious self. Like Achilles in *Iliad* 24, he feels pity, and also like Achilles, he himself lifts the body of his victim to return it to his people (10.821–831).

Achilles, whose fury took him away from his humanity, was returned to that humanity as he grieved with Priam. Aeneas, whose fury perverted his *pietas*, reconstitutes that *pietas* in his sorrowful praise of Lausus. When he returns to battle, he is once again a good Roman: he kills Mezentius, to end both battle and book. The power of *pietas* is also shown in a surprising change in the character of Mezentius. His love for his son and grief over his death teaches him shame for his previous crimes, and he declares he owes his country a debt as he prepares to take vengeance on Aeneas and die.

Aeneas' return to good Roman *pietas* does not end his story as Achilles' return to humanity ended his. In Book 11 Aeneas performs proper Roman ritual – offering as a trophy to Mars the arms of Mezentius rather than those of Apollo's priest – grants a truce for burying the dead, and proposes peace to Latin envoys. In the midst of this, Virgil has Aeneas bind the hands of the eight captives and send them with Pallas's body to sprinkle his pyre with sacrificial blood (81–82). This action shows that his fury in Book 10 was not just a momentary aberration; the personal violence of the old heroic world is still a part of Aeneas waiting to be released by the events of war. In Arcadia, the grieving Evander insists that Aeneas "owes Turnus to father and son" (11.177–179), reaffirming the Homeric imperative to vengeance. Aeneas is going to have to choose between fathers. When the time comes, the choice between the competing claims of *pietas* and vengeance is going to prove even more difficult than his previous choice between *pietas* and love. Evander's words ensure that, for the reader, the choice to approve or condemn Aeneas' final action will also prove difficult.

Book 12

The beginning of Book 12 returns to the original premise that "Achilles," in the person of Turnus, is an external enemy to the Roman cause. When Turnus feels the Latins' desire that he decide the war by single combat, Virgil compares his increased ardor and heightened courage to that of a Carthaginian lion who "when gravely wounded in the breast by hunters then at last enters battle and rejoices as he shakes his muscled mane. Unafraid, he breaks off the brigand's implanted weapon and roars with bloody mouth" (12.4–8). This simile with its personification ("enters battle") and the detail that the lion waited to attack until after being wounded, recalls the striking simile that introduced Achilles' entry into battle at *Iliad* 20.164–173. It thus renews awareness that Turnus is the "other Achilles" predicted by the Sybil. The simile and the following scene are, in addition, rich with nuance that prejudices the reader's conception of what Achilles will represent in this final book.

The lion has previously been established as a beast that serves Aeneas. A lion's skin cushions Anchises on Aeneas' shoulders when he leaves Troy (2.722); he sits on a lion's skin in Arcadia (8.177); the horse Evander gives him is decked in a lion's skin (8.522); his ship has lions on its prow (10.156–157); and when he begins to fight in Book

10, he invokes Cybele "who is fond of yoked lions" (252). The skin of the lion and yoked lions are equivalent to nature tamed and made useful by culture. The simile presages, therefore, that Turnus and the Achillean heroism he embodies ought to and will be tamed by Aeneas,[7] just as Augustus will bind *furor* "roaring with bloody mouth" (1.294–296).

Previous lion similes for Turnus (9.792–796, 10.454–456), Nisus (9.341), and Mezentius (10.723–729), the only other lion similes in the *Aeneid*, have associated lions with joy in battle and with either lack of foresight or ultimate defeat and death. The first quality cannot be derived from the Iliadic Achilles, whose raging fury comes not from joy but from grief. But ultimate death does pertain to Achilles: a lion simile describes the beginning of the revenge that he knows will make his own death inevitable (20.164–173); another describes his state of mind as he kills Hektor and thus seals his own doom (22.262). When the combined associations from previous lion similes and from the *Iliad* are added to the tamed or skinned lions associated with Aeneas, they charge Turnus's lion simile in Book 12 with foreboding. Thus charged, the simile portrays Turnus/Achilles as embodying a fury that, mindless as an animal, exults in its own destructive strength because it fails to comprehend the dreadful cost of war. It also implies that Aeneas will not only tame Turnus, he will kill him.

Turnus's violence grows "sicker" through the "healing" attempted by Latinus (12.45–46), thus firmly linking the lion's wound and Turnus's dangerously unhealthy state of mind. Dido, whom the adjective "Carthaginian" may invoke, was also wounded by love, first metaphorically and then fatally by Aeneas' sword. In Book 12, Virgil locates Turnus's violence specifically in erotic love for Lavinia (12.70–71), which strengthens the parallel with Dido. In the very last scene of the epic, when Turnus is compared to a stag hemmed in by hunters nets' and pursued by a lunging biting dog (12.750–754), readers are likely to recall Dido's doe struck by a shepherd's unaimed arrow (4.69–73) as well as Silvia's pet stag, who was wounded by Iulus in Book 7. The effect is both sympathy and a renewed association with the feminine. Turnus, who has hung bloody heads from his chariot (12.511–512), cannot easily be viewed as innocent, but like Dido he is the noble but luckless victim of a god and the Roman enterprise. Like the sacred wild olive tree that "the Trojans had cut down so that they might fight in an open field" (12.766–771), he represents nature forced to yield to the impersonal force of higher civilization.

In the first half of Book 12, while Turnus is flashing sparks from his eyes (101–102) and rampaging like Mars and Achilles (331–340), Virgil depicts Aeneas as calm and rational. Although he is "fierce" in his arms as he prepares to duel Turnus, he comforts his comrades with knowledge of "fate" (107–111). He sets eminently fair terms for the duel, asking for no personal power. After the truce is broken and both sides rush at each other "in love with battle" (282), he tries to restrain their anger and call them back. It takes being wounded by an arrow to make him eager to enter the fray. Even then when, healed by Venus, he heads back onto the battlefield "like a tempest" (450–457), he still restrains himself from killing anyone as he seeks for Turnus. However, when he sees that Turnus, whose chariot is being driven by his goddess-sister Juturna, will not meet him, he "loosens the reins" of wrath and commences a ferocious and indiscriminate slaughter (498–499).

The poet cries out to Jupiter, asking if it was really through his will that peoples destined to live in peace had so clashed (503–504), and then details the horrors committed by both Aeneas and Turnus, alternating from one wrathful hero to the other for fifty verses until Aeneas, inspired by Venus, decides to burn down Latinus' city. This horrifying repetition of what the Greeks had done to Troy puts the final events in motion. Conflicted with shame, insane misery, furious love, and valor (666–668), Turnus faces up to what he must do and returns to duel Aeneas.

A shift to Olympos just before the heroes' final confrontation achieves two things. First the divine civil war ends as Juno yields, extracting the obliteration of Trojan name, mode of dress, language, and customs as she does so. Second a new image of Jupiter emerges to shrink the polarity between him and Juno. Is the Fury Juno unloosed from Tartarus in Book 7 very different from the ones Jupiter has by his throne, ready to terrify mortals when he is "ferocious" (845–852)? When Jupiter sends one to signal Juturna to abandon her brother, it changes into a small owl beating against Turnus's face and shield, shrieking and creating a mood of pure terror. Although terror of Jupiter would have been seen as a normal part of Roman religion, as Lucretius' Epicurean fulminations testify, Jupiter's terror is just as irrational an emotion as Venus's love or Juno's hate. Despite the fact that Jupiter acts in the service of Fate, and therefore justly, his Fury creates sympathy for Turnus.

Turnus attempts to throw a boulder at Aeneas, as Aeneas had at Achilles in the *Iliad* (20.285–287), but his strength is sapped by the Fury. Like Hektor facing Achilles, he is compared to a man in a nightmare

(*Il.* 22.199–200, *Aeneid* 12.908–912). He hesitates in fear. Then Aeneas hurls his spear, which like a black whirlwind or the thunderbolt of Jove, flies straight into Turnus's body.

Virgil could have made it easy for his readers. He could have had Aeneas' spear kill Turnus on the spot. The poem would then have ended on a tragic but morally clear note as the life of Fate's doomed opponent, like that of Camilla, fled indignant to the shades. Instead, Aeneas' spear enters Turnus's thigh, causing him to sink to one knee and allowing time for Turnus to declare Aeneas the victor, yield him Lavinia, and make a request similar to but slightly modified from that of the mortally wounded Hektor to Achilles: "if you respect a parent's pain – for you had a father, Anchises – pity the old-age of Daunus and return either me or my lifeless body. Carry hatred no further" (*Aeneid* 12.932–939; compare *Il.* 22.338–342). "Return me or my body" is a clear request for mercy, and the stage is set for Aeneas to follow his father's precept to spare the submissive.

Achilles viciously rejected the dying Hektor's plea, but readers expect Aeneas to be merciful. Three verses that describe him holding back, hesitating, encourage this expectation. Suddenly, however, Aeneas notices young Pallas's sword belt, "memorial of ferocious grief," on Turnus's shoulders. "Fired with *furor* and terrible in anger," he buries his sword in Turnus's breast, crying, "with this blow, Pallas sacrifices you, Pallas, takes punishment from your criminal blood" (948–950).

What are we to make of this ending? Some readers interpret Aeneas' act as choosing duty to Evander over his own desire to spare Turnus, in which case it is the act of a statesman in conformity with *pietas*. Some see impetuous and uncontrolled Turnus as so inimical to Rome that killing him is a necessary evil – as necessary, perhaps, as clearing the land. Aeneas' "ferocious grief," which appears to align him with Juno (1.25, etc.), actually aligns him with the "ferocious" Jupiter who sends the Fury, and his action is therefore an instance of the righteous wrath that is sometimes fully appropriate. "Sacrifice" is an appropriate verb. This is no doubt how Augustus interpreted the ending.

Virgil has made it impossible, however, to feel happy about Aeneas' choice. Aeneas has chosen Pallas's Greek father over his own "Roman" father. He ends the poem aflame with the *furor* that has been presented as the enemy of the Roman mission in the figures of Juno, Dido, and Turnus, all of whom have failed those who depend on them. With this ending Virgil raises profound questions about Rome's recent past and national character, leaving his readers to find their own answers. What follows is my own tentative response.

The *Iliad* is the subtext Virgil uses to establish most clearly that the war he depicts is a civil war. As he battles the new Italian Achilles, who is infected with the divine wrath of Juno, Aeneas himself becomes Achilles with all the passion and cruelty of that warrior at his worst, alternating this role with that of Hektor and Roman statesman. In the final battles of Book 12, the two opponents are united in representing Homeric heroism in general. Then in the end, role finally fixes character as Aeneas becomes solidly identified with Achilles, supreme symbol of Homeric heroism in victory, and Turnus becomes identified with Hektor, supreme symbol of that heroism in defeat.

Achillean heroism destroys the self as well as others. This is at least partly what the closing scene suggests. In Aeneas' case this destruction involves the perversion of principles to destructive ends. Just as Juno wins at last the obliteration of her old enemy Troy except for the "custom and manner of sacred rites" (12.836), so Homeric passion obliterates all of its new enemy, Roman *pietas*, except for that component which manifests itself in ritual sacrifice. When Aeneas kills Turnus and says that Pallas "sacrifices" him, it is possible to see not an enthusiastic Roman *pietas*, but a sanctimonious Roman fury. The worst of two epic worlds fuse in an act of personal vengeance conceived as religious duty.

Further Reading

What follows is a small selection of the vast literature available.

Translations and Texts

John Dryden's 1697 translation into heroic couplets is still a classic in its own right (Penguin, 1997).

Three new translations by Frederick Ahl (Oxford, 2007), Robert Fagles (New York, 2006); and Stanley Lombardo (Indianapolis, IN, 2005) each contain maps, glossaries and excellent introductions by Elaine Fantham, Bernard Knox, and W. R. Johnson, respectively. Ahl's version has the benefit of following the Latin line by line, while Fagles' and Lombardo's use a shorter line that is smoother and easier to read. The somewhat older translation by Alan Mandelbaum (New York, 1961) remains a worthy alternative.

For those who prefer reading prose, David West has produced a much-admired translation (London and New York, 1991).

The second volume of the Loeb Classical Library two-volume edition, which gives facing Latin and English versions in a 1916 translation by H. R. Fairclough, has been revised by G. P. Gould (Cambridge, MA, 2001).

The Latin text on which I have based my translations is that edited by R. D. Williams, *The Aeneid of Virgil*, 2 vols. (London, 1972–1973; reprinted London, 1999).

Interpretation and Commentary

Fine short book length introductions to the *Aeneid* and its world are available by: K. W. Gransden and S. J. Harrison, *Virgil: The Aeneid*, second edition, (Cambridge, 2003); Jasper Griffen, *Virgil* (Oxford, 1986). Somewhat older but still worth reading are W. A. Camps' *An Introduction to Virgil's Aeneid*, (Oxford, 1969), which contains a very interesting discussion (in "Echoes of History" and Appendix 5) of allusions to and subconscious associations with historical events; and Viktor Pöschl's *The Art of the Aeneid*, translated by G. Seligson (Ann Arbor, 1962).

Servius's Commentary on Book Four of the Aeneid, edited and translated by C. M. Mc Donough, R. E. Prior, and M. Stansbury (Wauconda, IL, 2004) offers facing Latin text and English translation, with Servius' comments on the bottom half of page and Virgil's text on the top half; Servius, a fourth-century scholar, presents fascinating observations about interpretations of words, how one passage resonates with another, or the relevance of a text that Virgil might have read but that we have now lost.

More Advanced Studies of Virgil

The book-length studies that have most influenced my own work are W. R. Johnson's *Darkness Visible* (Berkeley, 1976), which gives a brilliant reading of the ethics and anxieties of the epic; Brooks Otis's classic, *Virgil a Study in Civilized Poetry* (Oxford, 1963; reprinted Norman, OK, 1995), which is especially valuable for its third chapter, "The Subjective Style" (pp. 41–96). Michael C. J. Putnam's *The Poetry of the Aeneid* (Cambridge, 1965; reprinted Ithaca, 1988), *Virgil's Aeneid: Interpretation and Influence* (Chapel Hill, NC, 1995) and the essay "Virgil's *Aeneid*" in John Miles Foley, ed., *A Companion to Ancient Epic* (Oxford and Malden, MA, 2005), 452–475, which offers a brilliant exposition of Anchises' words to Aeneas about what it means to be Roman; Kenneth Quinn's *Virgil's Aeneid: A Critical Description*. (Ann Arbor, 1969; reprinted Exeter, 2006), which gives close readings of the Latin and shows the mastery with which Virgil turned Homer's verse to his own purposes.

Other influential book-length studies are G. B. Conte's *The Rhetoric of Imitation: Genre and Poetic Memory in Virgil and Other Latin Poets* (Ithaca, NY, 1986); S. Farron, *Vergil's Aeneid: A Poem of Grief and Love* (Leiden, 1993); Philip Hardie's *Virgil's Aeneid: Cosmos and Imperium* (Oxford, 1986). J. D. Reed's *Virgil's Gaze: Nation and Poetry in Aeneid* (Princeton, 2007) talks about beautiful death(s) and the forging of a multivalent Roman national identity, narrative techniques and intertextuality; Susan F. Wiltshire's *Public and Private in Vergil's Aeneid* (Amherst, 1989) brings a feminist perspective.

Essays that have most influenced my thinking are: W. S. Anderson's "Vergil's Second *Iliad*," *Transactions of the American Philological Association* 88 (1957), 17–30; W. Clausen's "An Interpretation of the *Aeneid*," *Harvard Studies in Classical Philology* 68 (1964), 139–147; B. M. W. Knox, "The Serpent and the Flame: The Imagery of the Second Book of the *Aeneid*," *American Journal of Philology* 71 (1950), 379–400; L. A. MacKay "Achilles as the Model for Aeneas," *Transactions of the American Philological Association* 88 (1957) 11–16. A. Parry, "The Two Voices of Virgil's *Aeneid*," *Arion* 2.4 (1963), 66–80. All of the above are reprinted in Hardie below. Also in Hardie is K. Galinsky's forceful essay "The Anger of Aeneas," *American Journal of Philology* 109 (1988), 321–48, which argues for an unambiguously positive reading of the *Aeneid*'s final passage.

Collections of Essays: Philip Hardie's *Critical Assessments of Classical Authors: Virgil* vols III and IV (NJ, 1999), which reprints many seminal articles on the *Aeneid*, should be available in libraries. S. J. Harrison's *Oxford Readings in Virgil's Aeneid* also reprints important articles and contains an excellent survey of Virgil criticism since 1900. Charles Martindale's *The Cambridge Companion to Virgil* (Cambridge, 1997) contains scholarly essays on reception, genre, historical context, poetics, and gender.

Philip Hardie's *Virgil* (Oxford, 1998) gives a brilliant account of how a multitude of scholars have approached Virgil's texts, along with bibliographical references.

Afterlife

Domenico Comparetti's *Virgil in the Middle Ages,* first published in 1872 but recently reprinted (Princeton, 1996), tells the story of Virgil's importance in medieval Europe, including many fascinating legends about Virgil's life. Christopher Baswell's *Virgil in Medieval England* (Cambridge, 1995, reprinted 2006) examines manuscript marginalia to demonstrate three approaches to Virgil's text (allegorical, romantic, pedagogical) that illuminate popular English rewritings like Chaucer's. Marilyn Desmond's *Reading Dido: Gender, Textuality and the Medieval Aeneid* (University of Minnesota Press, 1994) discusses the many medieval texts that focus on Dido as the central plot of the *Aeneid* and also outside the *Aeneid,* the so-called historical Dido. Craig Kallendorf's *In Praise of Aeneas* (Hanover and London, 1989) and Theodore Ziolkowski's *Virgil and the Moderns* (Princeton, 1993) discuss reception in the early Italian renaissance and in the modernist American and European period, respectively.

Stephanie Quinn and Michael C. J. Putnam, eds., *Why Virgil? A Collection of Interpretations* (Wauconda, IL, 2000) offers a variety of interpretations from important scholars and poets.

Richard Waswo's *The Founding Legend of Western Civilization. From Virgil to Vietnam* (Hanover, NH, 1997) reads the *Aeneid* as a story of perpetual colonization and examines its influence in texts, intellectual currents, and political rhetoric.

Fiction: Christopher Marlowe's *The Tragedy of Dido, Queene of Carthage* (1594); Hermann Broch *The Death of Vergil,* translated by J. S. Untermeyer (New York, 1945), explores Virgil's desire to destroy his masterpiece through a stunning death-bed monologue. Ursula K. Le Guin's *Lavinia* (2008) intelligently explores issues raised by the *Aeneid* through the voice of the hitherto silent title character.

Notes

1 Compare Theokritos: "Muses are divine, and therefore sing of divinities, but since we are human, let us sing of men" (*Idyll* 16.3–4).

2 R. D. Williams, ed., *The Aeneid of Virgil Books 1–6* (London, 1972), 181, note to 1.278–279.

3 In the underworld, Dido behaves just as Ajax does in the Odyssey's underworld. Although Aeneas addresses her most tenderly, she refuses to speak to him. So too Ajax, also a suicide, keeps his hatred for Odysseus even after death and turns away without speaking (compare *Od.* 11.541–567 and *Aeneid* 6.467–476). The parallel places Dido firmly within the heroic world.

4 For a detailed demonstration of Aeneas' development toward embracing Roman *pietas*, see Brooks Otis, "The Originality of the *Aeneid*" in *Virgil*, ed., D. R. Dudley (London, 1964), 27–66.

5 Fire imagery: 9.59–76; self-identification: 9.742. In addition, see 7.470, 9.136–139, 12.49.

6 For more on Octavian as the historical model for Aeneas' human sacrifice, see W. A. Camps, *An Introduction to Virgil's Aeneid* (Oxford, 1969), 142–143. For more on Julius Caesar's human sacrifice and on Virgil's use of Achilles, see K. C. King, "Foil and Fusion: Homer's Achilles in Vergil's *Aeneid*," *Materiali e discussioni per l'analisi dei testi classici* 7 (1983), 31–57.

7 So discussed by W. R. Nethercut, "The Imagery of the *Aeneid*," *Classical Journal* 67 (1971–1972), 128.

8

The *Metamorphoses* of Ovid

In nova fert animus mutatas dicere formas/corpora; di, coeptis (nam vos mutastis et illa) /adspirate meis primasque ab origine mundi/ad mea perpetuum deducite tempora carmen.

> My spirit moves me to speak of forms changed to new
> bodies; Gods, breathe life into my beginnings (for you
> changed those too), and fine-spin my unceasing song
> from the first origin of the world to my times.
>
> (*Metamorphoses* 1–4)

These introductory verses contain jokes aimed at the literarily sophisti-cated Roman reader, jokes impossible to translate into English. The first word of the *Metamorphoses* is a preposition indicating movement "into" or "toward," the second one looks like a noun, "new things," but actu-ally turns out to be an adjective modifying "bodies" at the beginning of the second verse. This surprising grammatical switch from noun to adjective, which exemplifies the "changed forms" that are the poem's announced subject matter, creates the first of the poem's many broken expectations and double meanings. Another surprise for the literary sophisticates of Ovid's day comes in the fourth line, where "unceasing song" (*perpetuum carmen*), the Alexandrian-Roman code for "big bad epic," is juxtaposed with "fine-spin" (*deducite*), code for the refined short poems loved by the Alexandrian poets and their Roman followers. *My* Muses, this verse declares, can make these allegedly opposed forms work together; come along and see how I do it.

Quite unlike the wrath of Achilles, the versatile endurance of Odys-seus, the exuberant adventure of the Argonauts, or the foundational *pietas* of Aeneas, the subject of Ovid's epic is Change, or the life of the cosmos itself. There is an apparent movement from the Chaos that opens the poem to the predicted deification of Augustus that closes it, but the two hundred and fifty short stories that intervene diffuse any idea of progress. Thematic patterns start and stop; no unifying design emerges. No hero – not Ennius' Rome, nor Virgil's Augustus, nor even an Apollonian collection of Roman ancestors – ties these stories together. What ties them together, in addition to the ingenious transitions, is only the constancy of change itself: changes in form (that is, "metamorphoses") within the plots of the stories, and shifts in narrative voice, in tone and in generic models.

Starting as it does with the chaos that preceded the formation of the world, the poem appears at first to be a creation epic crossed with philosophical epic. Instead of presenting the sequential births of primal gods, as does Hesiod's *Theogony*, the *Metamorphoses* separates and orders Chaos's warring elements as in Lucretius' *On the Nature of Things*. Characteristically, Ovid refuses to choose between theology and science: both Hesiodic "god" and Lucretian "supple nature" (1.21) are invoked initially as directing the separation, followed by "some god or other" (1.32), who creates earth, and a "craftsman" (*fabricator*, 1.57), who apportions the atmosphere to winds and clouds. The stars appear of their own volition, fish appear in the sea, birds in the sky, and animals on land. And now "humankind was born," either "made of divine seed by the artisan who made everything else" or made of "earth that still retained celestial seed" (1.78–81).

This constant offering of choices, which denies the existence of one Truth, is one of the ways epic seriousness is undercut throughout the *Metamorphoses*. In addition to creating ambiguity about how the world came into being, Ovid offers no fewer than three creation myths to explain the origins of humankind. The first creation from the above-mentioned celestial seed accounts for human intelligence and the erect stature that allows human beings to look toward the heavens while animals must look downward toward earth (82–86). The second creation of humankind comes after a retelling of Hesiod's Four Ages, which explains the presence of evil in human life by showing a slow degeneration from a Golden Age of endless summer and ease through a Silver Age of seasonal work and technology, then a hot-tempered Bronze Age, and finally to the Iron Age, where greed, war and injustice hold sway. At this point the Giants attack Olympos, are felled by Jupiter's thunderbolt, and Earth, drenched by their blood, creates new human stock from their gore. This second origin accounts for human impiety, violence, and bloodlust (1.157–162). The third creation of humankind is from stones cast by Deucalion and Pyrrha, sole survivors of the great Flood. From this third origin we are "unyielding and able to endure a life of work" (1.414). These three creations are sequential but also cumulative. Despite the destructions that occur between them, human beings retain characteristics from all three origins: they are intelligent, violent, and enduring.

Let us backtrack to before the flood. In a scene that satirizes Olympian gatherings in the *Iliad* and *Aeneid*, Jupiter calls all the gods to a council in his palace on the Milky Way. The plebian gods live elsewhere, the poet comments; only the noble gods put homes here on heaven's Palatine (1.168–176). Using contemporary Roman place names and sociopolitical categories to describe heaven is amusing enough, but there is a further joke in the Latin: the word I have translated as "homes" is actually *penates*, the standard word for the guardian gods worshiped in the form of statues in the inner recesses of a house. They are the household gods Aeneas carries from Troy to Italy in the *Aeneid*. The word's meaning was often extended to signify the home as a whole, but to do so with reference to a god's home creates a humorous incongruity; the thought of a god's possessing statues of guardian gods carries the anthropomorphism of Roman myth and religion to its absurd extreme.

Ovid carries his satire further in a passage that many have interpreted as flattery of Augustus. When Jupiter announces that he has been attacked by the savage Lycaon, all the gods tremble "just as the human race was struck with terror of immediate ruin, and the whole world shuddered" when Julius Caesar was murdered (1.199–203). Exaggeration draws attention to itself as artifice, and the silliness of gods fearing a human attack on Jupiter undermines the flattery of the comparison between Jupiter and Caesar, and then between Jupiter and Augustus (1.204–205). Furthermore, the supposed flattery backfires when Jupiter sends the obliterating Flood, whose horror makes the king of the gods no model for a human ruler.

The flood is magnificently described, and the visual pictures of dolphins frolicking in the branches of trees is delightful. Less delightful is the picture of boar and stag powerless against the waves and wandering birds falling into the sea on tired wings after failing to find a place to rest (1.302–308). Even worse is the end: "most were taken by the waves; those the waves spared, long hunger conquered through lack of food" (1.311–112). Behind the humor that sustains the *Metamorphoses* from beginning to end lies a painful universe ultimately as sad as the *Aeneid*'s. Sometimes pain comes from divine or human folly, sometimes from pure accident. In this particular episode, it comes from deliberate divine intent and may be an oblique comment on the misuse of absolute power.

Sadness soon dissolves into a "happy ending": the story of Deucalion and Pyrrha, who are allowed to live and restart the human species because of their goodness. Ovid then quickly moves on to another humorous story that well illustrates the way he undercuts epic "truth" by plucking themes, characters, or similes from their tragically serious contexts and employing them in ridiculous situations. The hero of this story is Apollo, who begins as a monster-slaying hero and ends as a frustrated lover.

After using his golden bow to slay the giant serpent, Python, and after establishing the Pythian Games at Delphi to commemorate the event, Apollo sees Cupid drawing his own small bow. Naturally, the great Python-slayer scorns the boy archer, and, naturally, Cupid pays him back by shooting him. The power of love conquers the warrior, who suddenly becomes a stock character in Roman love elegy, burning with passion and trying to catch his beloved as she flees from him. We may see this change from warrior to lover as parallel to Ovid's turning from epic poet to amatory poet after being shot by Cupid's arrow in *Amores* 1.[1] The difference is that here Ovid imports the subject of amatory poetry into the epic frame, choosing to transform the genre rather than choosing between genres.

Daphne, the object of Apollo's sudden love, has been shot with an antilove arrow and thus runs from him as fast as she can in order to preserve her virginity. Ovid sprinkles the chase that follows with both amatory and epic imagery. While Apollo pursues he imagines how Daphne's loosely streaming hair would look done up, imagines the beauty under her clothes from the beauty of her bare arms and legs, worries about her scratching her legs on brambles. He tries to persuade her that they are not in an epic chase to the death: he is not an Iliadic wolf to her lamb, a lion to her deer, an eagle to her dove; he will slow down if she does (1.490–524). As the issue proves, Cupid has turned the god of truth into a liar: the lustful lover is indeed the predatory animal of epic simile. Daphne runs faster, but since flight only enhances her beauty, Apollo increases his own speed. At the moment when Apollo is about to catch her, Ovid employs a simile that evokes the desperate flight of Turnus from Aeneas: Daphne is like a hare fleeing for its life, and Apollo is like a hound trying to bite it, always almost able to get his teeth into it, but always failing as at the last minute it escapes the closing jaws (*Metamorphoses* 1.533–588; compare *Aeneid* 12.754–756 and *Il.* 22.159–161). The incongruous excess of the epic simile in comparison to his earlier amatory caricature makes Apollo look ridiculous, but at the same time, the simile makes the reader feel the intensity of Daphne's desperation and the inequality of this contest, just as similar ones did with Turnus and Hektor before her.[2]

Ovid's episode ends differently from Homer's or Virgil's, of course. In martial epic the victim dies not too long after a simile like this, but in amatory epic metamorphosis takes its place. Daphne's father saves her from a fate worse than death by turning her into a laurel tree, which is what *dáphnē* means in Greek. We note, however, that she does not escape Apollo entirely. Although she shrinks from his kiss on her bark, she must yield her leaves to make crowns of victory for Roman generals. The same happens in the later episode of Pan and Syrinx, which is a shorter but parallel story. After her metamorphosis into reeds, Syrinx, like Daphne, is appropriated by Pan, who makes a musical instrument of the "complaining" reeds and calls it a "syrinx" ("pan-pipe") after her (1.710–712). Both amatory epic heroes achieve a victory of sorts.

A series of divine love affairs follows this introductory one. Cupid is not needed for these, since they involve Jupiter, famous since early epic for his many sexual liaisons (see, for example, *Iliad* 14.312–324). These episodes employ the same incongruity between majestic status and comic depiction of the god that we see with Apollo's pursuit of Daphne, but there is a grimmer tone with regard to the fate of the young women victims.

The ambiguity the reader may feel about the fate of Daphne is voiced within the poem by the rivers and streams who do not know "whether to congratulate or console" her father, the river Peneus (1.578). Transition to the story of Jupiter's rape of Io is made through Io's own grieving father: Inachus, the only river who does not come to the gathering of rivers, remains hidden deep in the earth, weeping for his missing daughter. The story that follows explains what has happened to her, and despite many humorous elements, it is not pretty.

Jupiter's attempted seduction of Io includes offering her "protection" in the dangerous countryside, an offer that is in itself humorous since he himself is the danger. As Apollo did with Daphne, Jupiter attempts to impress Io with his rank, identifying himself as not "a plebeian god" but one of highest status, the wielder of thunderbolts. Unimpressed, she flees before he is even finished speaking (1.593–537). Since in this episode Ovid is more interested in the aftermath, the chase only lasts for two lines before she is caught. Enter Juno, who swoops down to find out what that big dark cloud she sees below might be hiding. Although Jupiter quickly changes Io into a beautiful white heifer, Hera is suspicious. Ovid makes her ask for the heifer as a gift, which sets up a situation in which Jupiter can be amusingly portrayed as a weak-willed husband, the thunderer afraid of his wife's anger. Like Apollonios' Medea (*Argonautika* 3.345–355), Jupiter is torn between *pudor* and *amor*, shame and erotic desire, but, unlike Medea, he yields to shame, and turns his beloved over to his wife (*Metamorphoses* 1.617–621).

The comedy of what follows is very dark comedy indeed: Io is still Io inside the cow's body, but her diet is now grass, leaves, and muddy water. She moos when she tries to speak, is terrified at the sound of her own voice, and is horrified when she sees her horns and huge bovine mouth mirrored in her father's waters. She manages to tell her father who she is by pawing an I and O in the dirt (1.632–650). It is hard not to laugh when her father laments that he will have to find her a husband (*vir*, "man") among the herd and expect cattle as grandsons (660), but in the end the father's and daughter's tears are more powerful than the laughter.

Jupiter only makes things worse for Io when he sends Mercury to kill Argos, the hundred–eyed guardian appointed by Juno to keep Io isolated. After first taking time to transfer Argos's eyes to her peacock, Juno flames into the wrathful goddess of the *Iliad* and *Aeneid*, sending a Fury, not merely a gadfly as in Aeschylus' version of the story (*Prometheus Bound* 565–585), to drive Io throughout the world (*Metamorphoses* 1.724–727). Juno's wrathful persona, which persists through Jupiter's next love affair, is itself a literary joke, for the divine wife's wrath is caused by her two-timing husband's lies rather than by the earthshaking conflict of wills in the Homeric and Virgilian epic worlds. In Io's case, the wrath ends suddenly: all it takes to get Juno to give over her anger is Jupiter's confession and promise to have nothing more to do with the young woman (1.734–748). The ease of this reconciliation after the long persecution compels readers to wonder why Jupiter did not make this promise sooner, even though they know, or at least some of them do, that, since Io became a goddess in Egypt, the story cannot let Juno yield until Io gets there. Such are the constraints of aetiological, or origin, epic, constraints that Ovid lays bare by inviting his readers to question the logic of Jupiter's behavior.

The next divine love affair is still more grim, though it starts off with the same comic incongruity that we found before. Again the king of the gods is portrayed as a philandering husband, well-skilled in appraising female beauty (1.423–424, 410–413). The unfortunate object of

Jupiter's gaze this time is a virgin attendant of the goddess Diana. To catch her, Jupiter changes himself into his opposite, from lusty male into virgin female, impersonating Diana herself so as to get close. The rape accomplished despite her fierce struggles, he returns to Olympos, leaving Callisto (for that is her name, as we know from other sources) with the crime marked on her body. Callisto's response to the rape provides an excellent example of how the narrator adopts the point of view of characters even when he is theoretically telling the story objectively. It is hard for Callisto not to show "guilt" (*crimen*) in her face (1.452); her blushes would reveal her "fault" (*culpa*) if Diana were less naive (447); her pregnant body finally reveals her "guilt" (*crimen*, 462).

This remarkable portrayal of guilty female response to rape, which is later repeated in the aftermath of Philomela's rape by her sister's husband, Tereus (6.541, 605–09), shows Ovid to be a shrewd observer of his culture. The sympathy he arouses for the rape victim here would tempt one to call him a protofeminist, were it not for the strong countervailing factor of Diana's and Juno's behaviors. Diana rejects her pregnant nymph, and when she gives birth to a baby boy, Callisto is hideously punished by "ferocious" Juno, who blames *her* for Jupiter's misconduct. Reviling her as "concubine" and "adulteress," Juno takes away "the beauty with which you pleased my husband" and turns Callisto into a bear (1.466–481). In this shape she suffers like Io for fifteen years. When Jupiter finally intervenes to turn both Callisto and her son, a hunter who was about to spear her, into constellations (1.497–507), Juno again attempts to punish her. Juno expresses no anger toward her husband in this episode, but she turns on his victim as vehemently as Virgil's Juno persecutes the Trojans (compare *Metamorphoses* 1.518–522 with *Aeneid* 1.48–49). No female solidarity here. When Ovid does portray female solidarity, as with Procne and Philomela in Book 6, he depicts the women's revenge as spiraling out of control, savage beyond what even that most horrible story of rape and infanticide anticipates.

Both male and female gods take terrible revenges, as they do in the Greek myths on which most of Ovid's stories are based. Greek versions tend not to give all the gruesome details, however, while Ovid sometimes seems to revel in them. Apollo, for example, punishes Marsyas by flaying him alive, which Ovid describes in seven lines of excruciating detail (6.385–391). Ovid's wit – for example, Marsyas' cry "why do you remove me from myself?" – only makes one's stomach churn the more. Does this kind of description reflect the vulnerability people felt in the Rome of Ovid's day? Torture was a regular practice, and though it was theoretically not used on Roman citizens, there were apparently exceptions in the early years of Augustus' power.

One scene that it is tempting to correlate with Ovid's own experience is that of Actaeon. For the act of accidentally seeing her nude while bathing, Diana punishes Actaeon by turning him into a stag who is torn apart by his own 35 dogs. Ovid stresses Actaeon's innocence in his introduction to the story, ascribing whatever fault there was not to the young man, but to fortune, and asking: "for what criminality (*scelus*) does error (*error*) contain?" (3.141–142). In addition, Ovid adds a coda to the end of the story: "public opinion was divided; to some the goddess seemed more violent than necessary, others approved and called it worthy of her strict virginity; each side found grounds for argument" (3.253–255). In one of his verse epistles from Tomis, Ovid compares himself to Actaeon, referring to the fact that Actaeon was horribly punished despite his having no malicious intent. He adds, "Clearly, among the gods, even ill-fortune must be atoned for, nor is mischance an excuse when a deity is wronged" (*Tristia* 2. 103–108). Since in the *Tristia* he often refers to Augustus as an angry god, and since he also often insists (for example, at *Tristia* 3.4.25–26) that what he did was an error (*error*), not a crime (*scelus*), it is tempting to think that he added the introduction to the Actaeon episode while in exile. If not, there is great irony in his writing these verses in the years before he was sent to a place that felt like torture to him.

Another story that has relevance to an artist's being punished for daring to challenge the status quo is that of Arachne, the weaver. Arachne's story ought to be a classic one of hubris, that is, of a mortal's forgetting that all human talents and prosperity come from the gods. Most such stories begin with someone boasting that he or she surpasses a god in some way and end with the god punishing them appropriately. The story of Niobe, who boasts that she has more children than Leto is a classic example: Leto's two children Apollo and Diana kill all fourteen of Niobe's children, and Niobe is (literally) petrified in grief (6.170–312). In the case of a challenge to the god, the god should win the contest and then punish the challenger. Such is the case with Apollo and Marsyas and also with the daughters of Pierus, who are changed to magpies by the Muses (5.302–678) just before the story of Arachne begins. When we read that Arachne refuses to worship Minerva but instead challenges the goddess of weaving to a contest (6.23–42), we expect that Arachne will lose the contest before she is punished by being turned into a spider (as educated Roman readers would know, *arákhnē* means "spider" in Greek).

Minerva accepts Arachne's challenge and weaves a tapestry with all twelve Olympian gods in the middle, ten of them watching Minerva and Poseidon compete over who can give the most valuable gift to Athens. In each corner the goddess weaves an exemplary scene of hubris punished, and she creates a border of "peaceful olive," symbol of usefulness and stability (6.70–102). Minerva's tapestry is orderly and moral: the gods are powerful and beneficent to mortals except when mortals are bad. Arachne's tapestry, on the other hand, shows Jupiter, Poseidon, Apollo, Bacchus, and Saturn changed to various animal and other shapes (twenty in all) in order to seduce and rape women; she weaves a border of flowers and Bacchic ivy, symbols of transient beauty and anarchy (6.103–128). Her tapestry takes away the gods' moral superiority and thus their moral right to punish hubris, and its design is free-flowing rather than orderly. Its design and content are, of course, like the *Metamorphoses* itself.

If Ovid were writing in a classic mode, Arachne would lose the contest. Instead, Ovid's Minerva can find no flaw in the tapestry that depicts "celestial wrongdoing." Enraged, she therefore destroys the tapestry – what else can one do with a brilliantly executed piece of subversive art? – and, in a totally undignified manner, repeatedly strikes its creator's head with her shuttle, thus driving Arachne to attempt suicide by hanging. When Minerva changes Arachne into an eternally weaving spider, the goddess calls her "impious" (*improba*, 6.136). Two lines earlier, however, the narrator has termed Arachne "courageous" (*animosa*, 6.134).[3] The poet takes the human artist's side against the powers that be, asserting the freedom to create art without regard for its effect on public morality.

Although Ovid gives them Roman detail, the stories in Books 1–11 of the *Metamorphoses* are taken from the world of Greek mythology. Starting in Book 12, however, he begins to describe what the Romans would call *translatio imperii*, the transference of power from Greece to Rome. In Book 14, he shifts to describing the overt transference of culture from Greece to Rome, which the Romans would call *translatio studii*. These are not mere transferences, of course. They are transformations of Roman culture by Greek (and vice versa), metamorphoses in their own right.

The first step in the transference of power is the Trojan War, which, in the story made famous by Virgil, resulted in defeated Trojans migrating to Italy. *Metamorphoses* 12 launches a sustained retelling of events from the Epic Cycle, *Iliad*, *Odyssey*, and *Aeneid*. In this retelling, Ovid generally avoids or condenses events found in the Homeric epics and the *Aeneid*, elaborating instead stories and legends that his great predecessors chose not to use. Remarkably, he almost entirely omits the battle scenes that for many readers form the core of Greek and Roman epic. Instead, Ovid makes good use of Nestor's propensity for long-winded storytelling to devote 350 verses to the story of the Brawl between Thessalians (a.k.a. the Lapiths) and drunken Centaurs at a wedding banquet (12.171–535), which, aside from Achilles' initial single combat with Neptune's son, Cygnus, offers the only prolonged combat in either the Trojan War or Aeneas' later war against Turnus in Italy. Ovid slights even Hektor's deeds: three verses note that he killed Protesilaus when the Greek ships landed and that during the initial battles Hektor became known to the Greeks for his martial prowess; another two verses mention his being slain by Achilles, but only after the fact at the time of Achilles' own death (12.591, 607).

The neglect of martial activity may be due in the first place to the necessity to tie every episode to metamorphoses, which are absent from Homeric and cyclic Trojan War epic. Ovid frames the brawl between the Lapiths and Centaurs, a very early story that may have been attached to the Theseus cycle, with the story of the Lapith Caenis/Caeneus, a woman who was transformed into a man as compensation for being raped by Neptune. Her/his story appears to be very early and is reported in Hesiod's "Catalogue of Women,"[4] but the *Iliad*'s Nestor says only that "he" was one of the great heroes he had fought with in his youth (*Il.* 1.263–270). Achilles' battle with Cygnus occurs in the Epic Cycle, but Cygnus's metamorphosis into a swan appears to have been added by Ovid, who was enabled to do so by Cygnus's name, which means "swan" in Greek (*kúknos*). The relative dearth of battlefield scenes may in the second place be due to a fundamental lack of interest in men killing each other with spears and swords. Ovid's genre-shaking epic is much more focused on a broad spectrum of change in human motivation, reaction, desire, and competition than it is on the relatively simple change from life to death or from inglorious to glorious.

The *Metamorphoses* gives us our first extant detailed account of the Judgment of Arms, the famous pitting of brain against brawn by which Ulixes (the Latin spelling of Greek Odysseus) and Ajax contend for the title of most valuable player and the arms of the dead Achilles

(13.1–398). Both contenders adduce famous episodes from the *Iliad* to back up their claims: Ajax describing his felling of Hektor with a stone in *Iliad* 14 (402–420), the duel in Book 7, and his single-handed defense of the ships in Book 15 (674–746), as well as Ulixes' cowardice in Book 8 (93–98) and his needing to be rescued in Book 11 (459–486). Ulixes cites his calming of the men in *Iliad* 2 and his night raid with Diomedes in Book 10; the rest of his deeds come from the Epic Cycle: persuading Achilles to join the army, persuading Agamemnon to sacrifice his daughter, his upcoming persuasion of Philoktetes to rejoin the army after ten years' abandonment on Lemnos, the theft of the statue of Pallas from Troy, and the capture of the seer Hellenus. Achilles' shield figures importantly in both men's claims: Ajax asserts that he needs a new one because his shield, unlike Ulixes', is riddled with holes from being used so much (*Metamorphoses* 13.117–119); Ulixes, on the other hand, contends that the shield's complex artwork would be wasted on a rough and ignorant soldier like Ajax (*Metamorphoses* 13.287–295). Ulixes' delight in the power of words is evident, as is the poet's.

The contest of words over, the poet's interest in the war is over too. After describing Ajax's suicide and the requisite metamorphosis of his blood on the ground into a purple flower with markings that look like A's and I's,[5] Ovid sums up the final stages of the war in six verses (omitting even a mention of the Trojan Horse) and moves on to its more emotionally interesting aftermath. The tragedy of Hekabe, whose daughter Polyxena is sacrificed on Achilles' tomb and whose son Polydoros is killed by the family friend to whom he had been sent for safety, plays out basically as presented by Euripides in his *Hekabe*, with Hekabe's metamorphosis into a dog framing the episode and justifying its inclusion (13.404–406, 565–571). A final metamorphosis, the creation of fighting birds out of the ashes of Memnon's funeral pyre, concludes the Trojan War stories. We may note that Memnon here is not granted immortality as he is in the Epic Cycle; Ovid is apparently reserving it for Aeneas and his descendants.

The next section of the *Metamorphoses* (13.623 to 14.448) follows Aeneas' journey to Italy, giving only five lines to his sojourn in Carthage (14.77–81) and seventeen to his trip to the Underworld (14.105–121), but devoting over 300 to love stories that are elsewhere treated in elegiac poetry: Polyphemos' unrequited love for Galatea, Glaukos' for Skylla, and Circe's for Glaukos (13.733–14.71). Most interestingly, the latter two stories put a sympathetic character into the *Odyssey*'s purely monstrous Skylla. All three tales of tragic passion and transformation are tied to Odyssean episodes in the *Aeneid* (Book 3). Ovid also manages to summarize Books 9–10 of the *Odyssey* in the form of a tale told by one Macareus, a companion of Ulixes who had decided to jump ship in Italy rather than face the dangers Circe had foretold for the journey to Ithaka. Macareus adds to the Homeric story about Circe a purely Italian story about how the goddess turned Picus, father of Faunus and grandfather of Latinus, into a bird. This story, to which Virgil does not allude when he mentions Picus at *Aeneid* 7.48, initiates a shift in the *Metamorphoses* from Greek to Italian myth.

The next 160 verses describe Aeneas' triumph over Turnus and his deification through the ministrations of Venus. Again, the fighting proper to epic is given short shrift in favor of stories involving metamorphoses, for example, the tale of Diomedes' return home from the war and the metamorphosis of the ships to nymphs. After the ships turn into nymphs, the narrator comments that there was hope that Turnus would cease fighting in fear of the omen, but he did not. Ovid then sums up *Aeneid* Books 10–12 as follows: "War continues; both sides have gods, and both have what is as good as gods: spirit (*animos*); now they seek neither royal dowry nor the scepter of a father-in-law, nor you, virgin Lavinia, but they seek to conquer, and they wage war for shame of stopping" (14.568–572). This brief summary, which is not untrue to the last half of *Aeneid* 12, presents not a glorious battle for a divinely sanctioned Roman future, but war waged for its own sake and for public opinion.

When Aeneas is deified, he does not become a star, but instead a local god, Indiges, who is invoked by the Roman people (14.607–608). He is transformed; that is, not only from human to deity, but from foreigner to native. Romulus, who is native born, is carried off to the stars by Mars, but like Aeneas changes names when he is deified, becoming Quirinus. His wife Hersilia, is deified along with her husband, becoming Quirinus's consort Hora, goddess of the passage of time. This cluster of deifications, or metamorphoses from human to divine, which now seem to be *de rigueur* for the truly exceptional man just as they were for the heroes of the Hesiodic and Epic Cycle corpus, prepare for the deifications of the Caesars in Book 15.

Before we get to those deifications at the end of Book 15, Ovid has a lot more to say about immortality, permanence, and transference of culture. The beginning of Book 15 portrays Numa, the early king thought of as the Roman spiritual guide, listening to the Greek philosopher

Pythagoras expound his theory of metempsychosis, the movement of souls from one (dead) body to a new one as if from one house to another. Protagoras claims that he himself once was a Trojan, and now he has been reborn as a Greek. "All things change" he preaches, "nothing dies" (165).

Pythagoras' metaphor of warm wax, which can take any shape but still remains the same bit of wax (15.169–172), may remind the reader of Daphne, Io, Callisto, Actaeon, and indeed all the wondrous metamorphoses that Ovid has described. Pythagoras' shape-shifting, like Ovid's, involves passing from human to beast, from beast to human (166–168). Pythagoras includes more than humans and animals in his schema, however. Every element in the cosmos is in flux: days, months, years, the elements, and human bodies throughout the life span (176–258). Most important for what Ovid is saying in Book 15, there is no immortality for cities. Some cities are engulfed by natural processes (water, for example), others by political processes. Troy, Sparta, Mycenae, Thebes, Athens have all fallen (anachronistically true from the perspective of Ovid's time); now also, predicts Pythagoras from the per- spective of 500 BCE, Rome is coming to birth and "will be head of the world" (431–435). This list of fallen cities followed by "Rome also . . ." undercuts the promise made by Virgil's Jupiter (*Aeneid* 1.278) that Rome's imperium would last forever.

Scholars are divided on how seriously Ovid means his readers to take Pythagoras's doctrine. There is no doubt that in some of the metempsy- chotic arguments for vegetarianism there is much mocking humor, which many Romans, who appear to have disliked vegetarian diets as much as the Greeks did, would have appreciated. The theme of constant change, however, fits perfectly with the themes of the *Metamorphoses* as a whole, and humor is a way to undercut what needs to be undercut – the "truth" of an eternal Augustan Rome – while still appearing to praise the Augustan achievement.

Immediately following Pythagoras's speech, Numa returns home to lead warlike Romans to the arts of peace (15.483–484). Then Ovid tells the story of how the Greek god, Aisklepios, voluntarily moved from his temple in Greece to a new home in Rome. Aisklepios's move is a clear example of the transfer of culture. Ovid uses the coming of the Greek god to Rome as a (somewhat arbitrary) point of transition to the subject of Julius Caesar becoming a god. In Book 1, we may recall, gods descended to mate with humans; now at the conclusion of the epic,

Ovid devotes more than one hundred lines to two humans ascending to the realm of gods, one in recent time and one in future time.

Why does Julius Caesar become a god? Did his great achievements, most of which Ovid lists, win him this honor? No. More important than all his achievements is his son: his progeny is responsible for his becoming a star (15.749). What exactly does this mean? Ovid explains: begetting such a great and beneficial leader as Augustus is the greatest achievement possible (758–759), and "lest Augustus be created from mortal seed, it was necessary to make Caesar a god" (760–761). Since we know that Augustus (as Octavian) demanded that the Senate declare Caesar a god in 42 BCE, and since we also know that Caesar "created" his son by adoption, not begetting, the circular reasoning here is wonderfully witty. Augustus makes Caesar a god and Caesar's divinity makes Augustus a god. These deifications, unlike the mythologically straightforward ones of the semidivine Aeneas and Romulus, are human acts. As such, of course, they also cast doubt on the previous ones. In a very modern way, Ovid is pointing out the political nature of myth. As we might put it today, deity is socially constructed, not natural.

This sly joke at the beginning of the story of the assassination and deification of Julius Caesar allows Ovid to end his poem with fulsome praise of Caesar and Augustus without losing his self respect. He does not actually end with this praise, however. He adds an epilogue, something entirely new to epic, that claims for poetry and poets the only true immortal status. The very last word of the poem is *vivam* "I will live."

With its constant metamorphoses of humans into animal or vegetable form, and its relentless shifting of attention and gods from one culture to another, the *Metamorphoses* denies immortality to any individual human or national identity. But as the descendant of Homer, Hesiod, Apollonios, Lucretius, Virgil, and all the poets – epic, tragic, and lyric – whose masterful art of storytelling continued to enthrall people in Ovid's time as it does in ours, Ovid can say truthfully that the poet will live in the form of his poem when his body dies. My poem, Ovid proclaims, will survive authority's wrath and the civic ruin that time will make inevitable. "As long as Rome has power, I will live."

Ovid's prediction has proved true. Although Rome is no longer the political capital of an empire, cultures throughout the world continue to delight in its literary masterpieces. Celebrating not heroes, but the seemingly endless inventiveness of the poet, the *Metamorphoses* proves that Rome's truly eternal power, like that of Greece and Babylon before it, comes not from its armies but its art.

Further Reading

Text and Translations

Several good verse translations are available. Horace Gregory's (New York, 1958), Rolfe Humphries' (Bloomington, 1955), and Allen Mandelbaum's (New York, 1993) are mellifluous but have no notes; Charles Martin's (London, 2004) and A. D. Melville's (Oxford, 1986, 1998) are highly readable and also have introductions and notes; David Raeburn's (London, 2004), which also has notes, is in hexameters.

For those who prefer prose, there is Michael Simpson's highly recommended translation (Amherst and Boston, 2003) with extended commentary.

Arthur Golding's 1567 creative translation of the *Metamorphoses*, which is newly edited and introduced by Madeleine Forey (Baltimore, 2002), is what Shakespeare and many English writers read and loved.

The Latin text on which I have based my translation is P. Ovidi Nasoni *Metamorphoses*, ed., R. J. Tarrant (Oxford, 2004).

Interpretation and Commentary

W. S. Anderson's excellent commentaries to Books 1–5 (Norman, OK, 1998) and 6–10 (Norman, OK, 2000) are available in paperback. I am especially indebted to Anderson's commentary on the Arachne episode in Book 6.

Carole Newland's "Ovid" in John Miles Foley, ed., *A Companion to Ancient Epic* (Oxford and Malden, MA, 2005) 476–491 offers an accessible, scholarly and concise introduction. Elaine Fantham's *Ovid's Metamorphoses*, Oxford Approaches to Classical Literature (Oxford and New York, 2004) is an excellent introduction, written in her customarily lively style.

There are three fine collections of essays that contain useful material on the *Metamorphoses*: Philip Hardie, Alessandro Barchiesi, and Steven Hinds, eds., *Ovidian Transformations* (Cambridge, 1999); Philip Hardie (ed.) *The Cambridge Companion to Ovid* (Cambridge, 2002); and B. Boyd, ed., *Brill's Companion to Ovid* (Leiden, 2002).

The more advanced reader will find the following studies worthwhile: Philip Hardie's *Ovid's Poetics of Illusion* (Cambridge, 2002) uses modern theoretical approaches to analyze Ovid as conjurer of illusion both for his characters and his readers. Steven Hinds' *Allusion and Intertext* (Cambridge, 1998) discusses the poetics of appropriation in Roman poetry including Ovid's *Metamorphoses*. James J. O'Hara *Inconsistency in Roman Epic* (Cambridge 2007) which analyzes contradictory passages within epic, has excellent chapters on both Virgil and Ovid. Sophie Papoiannou, *Epic Succession and Dissension* (Berlin, 2005) analyzes "the little Aeneid" in *Metamorphoses* 13.623–14.582 and finds competitive emulation and sophisticated design. Patricia B. Salzman's *Web of Fantasies: Gaze, Image and Gender in Ovid's Metamorphoses* (Columbus, OH, 2005) offers a feminist study of the epic. Joseph Solodow *The World of Ovid's Metamorphoses* (Chapel Hill and London, 1988) analyzes narrative techniques.

Steven M. Wheeler's *A Discourse of Wonders: Audience and Performance in Ovid's Metamorphoses* (U. Penn Press, 1999) uses close readings to demonstrate the trickiness of Ovid's unfolding verses.

Modern Adaptations and Transformations

Sarah A. Brown's *The Metamorphosis of Ovid from Chaucer to Ted Hughes* (New York, 1999) discusses the pervasive influence of Ovid's epic on English literature. Charles Martindale, ed., *Ovid Renewed* (1988), surveys Ovid's influence on artists, playwrights, and poets from the twelfth century through the twentieth.

Poetry: Michael Hoffman and J. Lasdun, eds., *After Ovid: New Metamorphoses* (New York, 1996), present 42 poets' responses to the *Metamorphoses* by major poets from English speaking countries around the world. Ted Hughes' *Tales From Ovid* (New York, 1997) translates twenty-four passages into his own distinctive poetry.

Drama: Mary Zimmerman's *Metamorphoses* (Northwester U.P, 2002) has received critical acclaim nationwide in the United States. George Bernard Shaw's *Pygmalion* (1916) was made into a classic film in 1938, into the still-popular Broadway musical *My Fair Lady* in 1956, and then into a film of *My Fair Lady* in 1964.

Novel: Christoph Ransmayr's award-winning *The Last World*, translated by J. Woods (New York, 1990), is set in Tomi, Ovid's place of exile. David Malouf *An Imaginary Life* (Vintage 1996) also sets his novel in Tomi, and like Ransmayr uses Ovid's work to inform the plot.

Notes

1   See above, chapter 6, p. 140.

2   See J. Solodow (reference in Further Reading: Interpretation and Commentary) pp. 171–172, for a nice discussion of point of view in this episode.

3   To be precise, it is Arachne's neck that is termed "courageous." The adjective *animosus* may also be translated as "proud," but when so used it normally designated a justified pride, not hubris.

4   Hesiod, *The Shield, Catalogue of Women, Other Fragments*, ed. and translated by Glenn W. Most (Cambridge, MA, 2007). Most believes that the *Catalogue of Women* was composed in the first half of the sixth century BCE (p. lv).

5   This is the same flower produced by the blood of Hyacinthos in *Metamorphoses* 10.214–216. Cygnus's being turned into a swan is also a duplication of an earlier transformation, that of Phaethon's identically named friend (2.367). In both cases, Ovid calls attention to the duplication, thus once again undermining any idea of a singular truth.

Appendix: Chart of Olympian Gods and their Akkadian Counterparts

---

Greek (and Roman) Olympian Gods and their Akkadian Counterparts:

Zeus (Jupiter), the sky god, rules the other gods. He uses the thunderbolt to subdue rebellious gods, incinerate evildoing humans, and signal his intentions. As god of hospitality and suppliants, he oversees what we might today call international law.

    Anu (An) is Zeus's Babylonian (Sumerian) counterpart as supreme sky god and impartial ruler. **Enlil** is Zeus's Babylonian counterpart as punitive storm god.

Poseidon (Neptune), lord of the sea, wields the trident. When angered he can cause earthquakes and turbulent waters; and when propitiated properly he can prevent or calm the same. He is associated with horses and bulls. He protects both Greeks and Trojans.

    Ea (Enki) is Poseidon's Babylonian (Sumerian) counterpart. Ea, however, is lord of all waters, both salt and sweet, that come from deep below the earth's surface. Ea's wisdom and devotion to human well-being are more characteristic of Athena than Poseidon.

Hades (Pluto), lord of the dead, drew as his lot the dark realms beneath the earth. His queen is **Persephone (Proserpine)**, daughter of Demeter.

    Ereshkigal is Persephone's Sumerian/Babylonian counterpart as Queen of the dead and ruler of the netherworld. She is the sister of Ishtar.

Hera (Juno), queen of the gods, is the goddess of marriage and legitimate rulers. Ironically, her own marriage is far from perfect, and she is often angry at Zeus's infidelities. She aids the Greeks in their war against the Trojans partly because she is offended by the Judgment of Paris (see Chapter Two) and partly because Paris adulterated the marriage of a Greek king.

Demeter (Ceres) is the goddess of agriculture. She is an extremely important goddess in Greek and Roman culture, but she does not play a large role in the epics of Homer and Virgil.

Aphrodite (Venus) is the daughter of Zeus and Dione in the *Iliad*, which prefers not to evoke the divine succession myth. Elsewhere Aphrodite is born from the severed genitals of Uranos which fall into the sea after Kronos castrates his father and takes his place. She is the goddess of sexual attraction and generation in all living creatures. Aphrodite is also the goddess of beauty. She protects the Trojans both as patron of Paris and mother of Aeneas.

    Ishtar (Inanna) is Aphrodite's Babylonian (Sumerian) counterpart. As goddess of both fertility (human, animal and plant) and warfare, she is the highest ranking Babylonian goddess.

Athena (Minerva), daughter of Zeus (and Metis), is normally the executor of Zeus's will. She is goddess of wisdom, victorious war, strategy, and the craft of weaving. Zeus swallowed Metis, whose name means Craftiness or Counsel, while she was pregnant with Athena; a few months later Zeus had a dreadful headache, and Athena sprang out in full armor. She protects the Greeks partly because she is offended by the Judgment of Paris (see Chapter-Two) and partly because Zeus is offended at Paris's abuse of Menelaos' hospitality. She carries Zeus's *aegis*, a goat-skin shield with Gorgon head meant to terrify mortals with whom Zeus is angry.

Hephaistos (Vulcan), son of Zeus and Hera, or of Hera alone. He is the god of fire and of the forge, patron of metalworkers. In the *Iliad* he is married to Charis, whose name means Grace, but elsewhere he is married to Aphrodite/Venus; both wives apparently represent the beauty that graces his creations. The forge-work that creates a beautiful iron spear, bronze shield, or decorated silver bowl is itself hard and dirty, and perhaps for this reason Hephaistos himself is considered ugly. He is lame either from a birth defect or from being thrown from Olympos. One story has him thrown by Hera who wanted to hide her lame newborn from the other gods (*Il.* 18.395–397); another has him thrown by his father when Hephaistos tried to help his mother avoid Zeus's punishment (*Il.* 1.590–594). As god of the male metalworking crafts, he is often allied with Athena, goddess of the female cloth-working crafts.

Ares (Mars), son of Zeus and Hera, is god of war. He delights in battle, in hacking with swords, piercing with spears, trampling with chariots, burning with fire. He is not associated with victory or with stratagem, but merely with war per se. In Rome, he is a much more important god, second only to Jupiter, and he has agricultural as well as military associations.

Apollo is the son of Zeus and the goddess Leto. He is the god of the sun and patron of civilized arts associated with light: truth, prophecy, poetry, and the lyre (that is, what today we would call classical music). He is the god of healing and, if angered, of sickness. In classical Greece and Rome he becomes associated with hierarchy and the aristocracy.

   Shamash (Utu), his counterpart in Babylonian (Sumerian) culture, represents light, truth, and justice.

Artemis (Diana) is the twin sister of Apollo and goddess of the moon. As patron both of wild animals and the hunt, she is a nature goddess, operating almost exclusively outside the city. Her only function within the city is as goddess of childbirth, which the Greeks associated entirely with nature.

Hermes (Mercury) is the son of Zeus and the minor goddess Maia. He is the boundary crosser, bringing messages from the gods to humans and escorting the souls of the dead to Hades. He is the patron god of heralds, travelers, and the lucky finders of buried treasure.

Dionysos (Bacchus, Liber) is the son of Zeus and the princess Semele. He is god of wine, of night, of transformations, and of the passionate music of flute and drum. A god of the people, he becomes associated with equality as opposed to hierarchy. Like Artemis, he is associated more with nature than with the city.

Hestia (Vesta), goddess of the hearth and third sister of Zeus, is not an active player in divine or human affairs. One story says that she yielded her place as one of the twelve great Olympians to the deified Herakles.

Glossary of Greek and Latin terms

aidṓs (Greek): respect for the good opinion of family, community or gods

aítion (Greek): the cause or origin of something

aristeía (Greek): an extended period of superiority in battle

dáktulos (Greek): finger; a dactyl = a metrical unit composed of three segments, one long and two shorts, similar to the human finger

dactylic hexameter: a verse containing six dactyls

dólos (Greek): guile, trickery

géras (Greek): a gift of honor awarded by the community in recognition of a person's value

furor (Latin): extreme passion

insanus (Latin): unhealthy

kléos (Greek): a story in epic song about admirable achievement

mênis (Greek): absolute, divine wrath that sweeps away the innocent along with the guilty

nóstos (Greek): return home. Plural: *nóstoi* = the Returns of the Greek Heroes from Troy

pietas (Latin): devotion to family, city, and gods

pudor (Latin): shame, modesty (equivalent to Greek aidos)

saevus (Latin): savage, ferocious

timḗ (Greek): honor in the form of material benefits and prerogatives

xeínia (Greek): hospitality, proper treatment of strangers

xeínos (Greek): host, guest, or stranger; a person bound by ties of hospitality to another

Index